SHIPPING, MARITIME TRADE, AND THE ECONOMIC DEVELOPMENT OF COLONIAL NORTH AMERICA

SHIPPING, MARITIME TRADE, AND THE ECONOMIC DEVELOPMENT OF COLONIAL NORTH AMERICA

by

JAMES F. SHEPHERD

and

GARY M. WALTON

CAMBRIDGE

AT THE UNIVERSITY PRESS

1972

Published by the Syndics of the Cambridge University Press
Bentley House, 200 Euston Road, London NW1 2DB
American Branch: 32 East 57th Street, New York, N.Y.10022

© Cambridge University Press 1972

Library of Congress Catalogue Card Number: 76–176256

ISBN: 0 521 08409 1

Typeset in Great Britain by Staples Printers, Kettering
Printed in the United States of America

CONTENTS

PREFACE AND ACKNOWLEDGEMENTS

The period from the time of the first English settlement at Jamestown to the Revolution encompasses a span of American history nearly equal to that from Independence to the present. Yet, with certain notable exceptions,[1] there has been relatively little attention paid to the economic development of the British North American colonies by economic historians. As Douglass North said several years ago at a meeting of the American Economic Association:

> the colonial period of American history, lasting for almost two hundred years, is nearly a void as far as any economic analysis is concerned. This period has been the exclusive province of the historian, and therefore it is not surprising that the treatment of economic issues leaves much to be desired. There have been no studies of the performance of the colonial economy, particularly in the crucial years 1763–75, although historians have drawn broad inferences from scraps of evidence. The relationship between the money supply, price levels, specie flows, and the balance of payments has not been adequately treated. There are no analytical studies of the major industries.[2]

For these and other reasons, we ventured into this statistical 'dark age' of American economic history, beginning with our dissertations: 'A Quantitative Study of American Colonial Shipping' (Walton) and 'A Balance of Payments for the Thirteen Colonies, 1768–72' (Shepherd) (both completed at the University of Washington in 1966). Considerable further research since this initial groundwork has permitted us to widen our scope, enlarge our accumulation of necessary data, and refine our analysis.

This study represents our attempt to view certain important aspects of the external economic relations of the British North American

---

[1] The contributions of such scholars as Bezanson, Bidwell and Falconer, Cole, Gray, Harper, and Nettels, as well as other literature on the merchants and trade of particular colonies or regions, should be stressed. See the bibliography for specific citations.

[2] Douglass C. North, 'The state of economic history,' *American Economic Review*, LV, 2 (May 1965), p. 88.

vii

colonies as they can be pieced together from the voluminous evidence that has survived. The central focus is upon the critical role that overseas trade and improvements in transportation played in the economic development of colonial North America.

Because the questions raised in this study are of both a quantitative and a theoretical nature, we have based our research explicitly upon the relevant quantitative evidence and economic theory, whenever possible. The theoretical issues and framework are made explicit in the early chapters. In this sense our study is in the spirit of the 'new economic history'. We are obviously indebted, however, to many of the older works which provided an important basis for our own study, especially in furnishing much factual information and many insights into the operation of the colonial economy.

We have by no means intended to provide a general economic history of the colonial period, or even an exhaustive analysis of all aspects of the maritime trade and shipping of the colonies. Undoubtedly, further research will provide refinements and additions to our efforts. We believe, however, that our research is sufficiently complete and our conclusions adequately supported, that they can and should be subjected to the scrutiny of other scholars. Our immodest hope is that this study will contribute significantly to an understanding of early American development and growth.

Aside from the dissertation period (and even at that time we mutually benefited from discussions and collaboration), this project has been a joint effort. Nevertheless, there have been some gains from the division of labor. The research on shipping has come primarily from Walton's efforts, and that on trade from Shepherd's. Even this distinction is somewhat inadequate, however, and over a lengthy period of collaboration such as ours, it is almost impossible to recall which ideas, suggestions, and the like were due to whom. We share equally in the responsibility for all parts of the study and its findings.

The academic debts we have accumulated throughout the period of research are many. To our teachers of economic history, Douglass C. North and Morris David Morris, we are deeply indebted for the initial guidance, stimulation, and continuing encouragement which they have provided. Professor North has also read the entire manuscript and suggested many improvements. Lawrence A. Harper has generously shared his extensive collection of data and knowledge of the colonial economy with us over the entire course of our research. Many others, too numerous to mention or attempt to recall at this point, including several anonymous readers, have contributed various suggestions and criticisms along the way. Not all these suggestions and criticisms were accepted, but many have resulted in improvements. Valuable assistance was furnished by several persons in numerous archives and libraries which we visited over the course of our research. To all these persons, named and unnamed, we are most grateful.

Financial assistance for our research has come from several sources. Support for the dissertations was provided by the Social Science Research Council (for Shepherd) and the Ford Foundation (for Walton). The primary financial assistance which enabled us to extend our research and produce this joint study was provided by the National Science Foundation under grant number GS–2116. Additional assistance was provided by the Purdue Research Foundation and by Ohio State University. Without this financial assistance, the research required would have been impossible.

In addition, we are grateful to the *Economic History Review*, the *Journal of Economic History*, and *Explorations in Economic History* for their permission to reprint portions of our research that have already appeared in article form.

Finally, may we express our thanks to our wives, Catharine Shepherd and Susan Walton, for their help many times during the past several years; and to them and to our children for their support and forbearance over the term of this research.

J. F. S.
G. M. W.

CHAPTER I

INTRODUCTION

The main objective of the economic historian is to describe and explain the course of economic change in the past. Keeping this objective as our own, we offer here a new approach to the study of the economic development of the British North American colonies.[1] Ours is a quantitative study, and we explicitly rely on and use economic theory in the analysis. The time period covered by the study is from the middle of the seventeenth century to the beginning of the American Revolution, with emphasis upon the eighteenth century and the later colonial period.

The main focus is on the maritime trade of the colonies with overseas areas, and on shipping and other costs of distribution; but the analysis does touch upon a wide variety of issues regarding the development of a market economy in the colonies. Whatever material improvements occurred in the colonies stemmed, we believe, primarily from improvements within the market sector; and so an analysis of overseas trade greatly improves our knowledge of colonial development.[2] The analysis also improves our understanding of the process of international migration, and of the patterns of settlement, resource allocation, and regional specialization that occurred in the colonies.

The explicit use of a theoretical framework to describe the process of colonial development is one of the characteristics of this study that differentiates it from previous studies of the colonial economy. This

[1] At the time of the Revolution, these colonies included Newfoundland, Nova Scotia, Quebec, the thirteen colonies which revolted, and East and West Florida.

[2] While production for overseas markets did not form the major share of colonial economic activity, it almost certainly was a significant part of total output. Furthermore, the importance of production for overseas markets and trade did not lie solely in its magnitude. Its most important contribution was probably that of playing a leading role in the further development of domestic markets for products and factors and in improving the monetary system, in furthering knowledge and skills of labor force participants (which is necessary if they are to perform more specialized roles in the economy), in developing the institutional arrangements and other elements of a viable market system, and, in general, developing the framework for future growth. Thus, our interest in overseas trade is due partly to the fact that trade within markets (in which overseas trade was initially an important part) came to occupy a central rather than a peripheral position during the economic development of those areas which later became the United States and Canada.

framework is presented in Chapter 2, and we urge its serious consideration by all. The use of theory in explanation cannot be avoided, and
we believe that one of the most common deficiencies of past literature
is the failure to specify explicitly the theoretical framework of the study.
One consequence of the use of implicit hypotheses and theories is that
it is difficult for the reader to determine which events or economic
forces were of major significance. The mere choice of which events are
important, and which should be described and which excluded, is
based on theoretical propositions. Clearly when issues of causality or
relationships among events are stated (or implied), theory is being
used. Here, we attempt to provide an explicit theoretical framework
in which the development of the American colonies is examined in
conjunction with the relevant quantitative evidence. This framework
allows one to include and examine all important general aspects of the
long-run growth and development of the colonies. Hopefully, it also
leads us to examine and emphasize those particular aspects of colonial
economic life which led to improvements in productivity and to higher
standards of living.

As the new American areas were gradually populated and the
resources found there brought into production, the initial problems of
mere survival and of establishing a foothold in the new world were
overcome. Means to improve standards of living were sought, and these
largely took the form of learning what products could be most profitably
produced and what the demands were for such products, especially in
overseas markets. Such products tended to be primary products which
exploited the abundance of natural resources found in the colonies.
Some of them became so important (relative to total output or trade)
as to be labeled 'staples' by contemporaries – a practice which has been
followed by historians.[1] Staples such as codfish were produced even
before the first permanent English settlements were established. Others,
including tobacco, were produced in the very early years of English
settlement, and still others, such as rice in the lower south and wheat
and flour in the middle colonies and the upper south, were established
later. As production developed in these new areas and they became a
part of the North Atlantic economy, new patterns of output and regional
specialization were determined and flows of various mobile resources
(usually classified as labor and capital) influenced.

Product and resource flows and the coincident patterns of economic

---

[1] The term 'staple' is usually taken to mean the 'principal industrial product of a country,
town, or district' (*The Oxford Universal Dictionary*, 3rd ed. (Oxford: The Clarendon Press,
1955), pp. 2001–2). In some of the recent literature however, and, especially in Canadian
economic history, the term has taken on the additional meaning of 'a product with a large
natural resource content' (Richard E. Caves and Richard H. Holton, *The Canadian
Economy: Prospect and Retrospect* (Cambridge, Mass.: Harvard University Press, 1959), p.
31). See the discussion of the 'staple theory' in Chapter 2.

activity and regional specialization provide the central focus of this study. In Chapter 3 an overview of these flows and patterns is examined in the light of population growth and scattered (and conjectural) evidence about colonial output. The evidence suggests that trade with overseas areas was substantially greater relative to total output than has heretofore been realized. Although it varied from region to region, economic activity became increasingly oriented towards production for markets, and by the end of the colonial period exports to overseas areas alone (including services) accounted for about 15 per cent of total output.

Besides the production of commodity staples, colonists provided many important commercial services associated with trade. Although the production of shipping services by New England and the middle colonies has been recognized, these services generally have not been accorded the attention merited by their value relative to commodity staples. An important feature of this study is our emphasis on the distributional aspects of trade and our argument that improvements in shipping and distribution were a major impetus to colonial development.

In Chapter 4 we examine shipping activity in the colonies in the eighteenth century and attempt to measure changing total costs of distribution in various trades over time. Costs of transporting and distributing commodities from producer to consumer were large relative to the initial costs of production. This means that improvements in distribution could have raised overall productivity significantly (even with no improvements in production). Because freight costs were a large proportion of total distribution costs, our examination is focused on improvements in shipping. The evidence on productivity change in shipping is striking; it clearly indicates that substantial improvements occurred. This evidence removes any doubt about whether economic growth was occurring in the colonies – it was, however slow it may have been.

In Chapter 5, the cost determinants of shipping are analyzed in order to learn the sources of productivity advance. We conclude that improvements in economic organization, stemming from the reduction of piracy, privateering, and similar hazards, explain a substantial portion of the observed improvement. The elimination of these obstacles to technical diffusion eventually permitted the adoption of specialized cargo-carrying techniques similar to those of the Dutch flyboat, which had appeared as early as 1595. On the other hand, technological change appears to have played only a very minor role, and economies of scale were similarly unimportant.

In Chapter 5 we also examine reductions in other types of distribution costs, such as insurance, inventorying, packaging, information and other transaction costs, and analyze the sources of their reduction. Because the evidence is fragmentary and incomplete it is not possible to give precise quantitative measures of these types of cost reductions. The evidence clearly suggests, however, that these costs were declining, and that the sources of these improvements were similar to those in shipping.

For the five-year period 1768–72, for which more complete data exist, it is possible to place the values of both goods and services in a balance-of-payments framework (or more specifically, the current account of the balance of payments). Direct evidence is available to estimate the value of commodity exports and imports (Chapter 6), the value of 'invisible' earnings (most importantly the sale of shipping services) in Chapter 7, and other factors which affected the colonial balance of payments, such as immigration and British civil and defense expenditures (Chapter 8). Little direct evidence concerning facts about capital and monetary flows during the colonial period exists; therefore, statements about these flows are based mainly upon the residual balances estimated for the current account.

An important product of this balance-of-payments study for 1768–72 are estimates of the magnitudes of trade with each of the five important areas of overseas trade, which were Great Britain, Ireland, southern Europe and the Wine Islands (the Canaries, Madeira, and the Azores), the West Indies and Africa. The relative importance of trade with each of these overseas areas is indicated, and these findings will enable historians to place each trade in proper perspective. The colonies by no means formed an integrated economy, and so these estimates are broken down by region, each region being composed of colonies with roughly similar natural resource endowments. While each region was not composed of colonies completely alike in every respect, the character of the more important types of economic activity within each region was not as widely diverse as that of all the colonies, and the emerging patterns of trade reflected this fact. The composition of each major colonial region's trade with each of the major overseas trading areas is also formed in the process of estimating these aggregative balances on current account, and the relative importance of the various goods and services entering into each of these trades is indicated. The importance of 'invisible' earnings, especially shipping earnings, to the New England and middle colonies is apparent from the estimates and discussion in Chapter 7. All this information should enhance future efforts to describe and explain the economic growth of the colonies.

Much of the quantitative information given in this study supports past descriptions and interpretations of colonial economic life. Nevertheless, our findings and interpretations do depart at times from the traditional view[1] of colonial economic history. We summarize these differences in Chapter 9.

This study is not a complete treatise on all aspects of the colonial economy, and many important issues have been neglected. We have assumed that the reader is generally familiar with the political and legal framework imposed on the colonies. The course of development occurred within a free enterprise type of economy, but it must be remembered that this was a mercantilist world, and that there were certain bounds to the freedom of enterprise within such a world. Some of the regulations, e.g. those regarding ocean shipping contained in the Navigation Acts, or the enumeration of certain colonial exports imposed on the colonies by English mercantilism, undoubtedly did affect the lines that colonial trade and development took. It is hoped that the estimates made in this study will better enable historians to make more meaningful assessments of the effects of these regulations on colonial development.[2] It is also hoped that these estimates will shed some light on the effects of the series of revenue measures imposed by England on the colonies after 1763. The economic effect of British policy on colonial welfare has been long debated among historians. It will be remembered that these revenue measures provoked various reactions on the part of the colonies which eventually culminated in the Revolution. Among these reactions were the non-importation agreements which drastically reduced imports from Great Britain in 1769 and 1770, and which are reflected in our estimates of imports from Great Britain for these years.

For the purpose of exposition, we have placed the methods of estimation and much of the basic statistical work in appendices. This has not reduced the level of critical inquiry of our findings, we trust, and we urge the interested scholar to examine our estimates carefully. No measures should ever be accepted on faith. Unless explicitly stated otherwise, all estimates, values, and prices are expressed in English sterling.

[1] Clearly there is no single view or interpretation of colonial development and there is disagreement among scholars on a variety of issues. The lack of reliable data has contributed to this disagreement. Nevertheless there appears to be a considerable amount of agreement, as is reflected in the colonial sections of textbooks on American economic history. We use the term 'traditional view' to refer to those interpretations which repeatedly appear in the literature.

[2] The importance of this study and its findings is not limited to the above descriptions and discussions of issues in colonial history. Our quantitative evidence and estimates have already been used in other research; for example, papers by Klingaman and McClelland show how basic trade data can be applied to important development and historical issues. In particular, the study by McClelland concerning the burdens of British imperial policy shows a rather novel way in which these data can further improve our understanding of the colonial economy. Hopefully, this study will be useful in still further research on various aspects of colonial economic development and the growth process in general. See David Klingaman, 'The significance of grain in the development of the tobacco colonies,' *J. Econ. Hist.*, XXIX, 2 (June 1969), pp. 268–78, and Peter D. McClelland, 'The cost to America of British imperial policy,' *American Economic Review*, LIX, 2 (May 1969), pp. 370–81.

CHAPTER 2

COLONIAL ECONOMIC DEVELOPMENT: A SUGGESTED FRAMEWORK

Economic growth in the colonies was strongly affected by the development of trade and a market sector, especially with regard to overseas trade and markets. Therefore, we focus closely on overseas trade and its primary mode of transport, ocean shipping. Preceding an analysis of the empirical evidence, we provide in this chapter a specific framework within which to view colonial economic development and the influences of overseas trade on this development. We begin with a general discussion of the sources of growth and the importance of trade, and then present a specific analytical framework that relates to the course of economic change in the colonies.

SOURCES OF GROWTH

The issues related to development perhaps can be seen best by using the conventional procedure of dividing the sources of growth between changes in the stock of resources ('inputs') and changes in productivity ('output per unit of input'), and then looking specifically at the sources of growth themselves. Growth of total output may result from increases in inputs (that is, increases in labor, capital, or natural resources), from increases in productivity, or from some combination of the two. Growth of per capita output may stem from the same two general categories of sources – from increases in inputs *if* they increase relative to population,[1] and from increases in productivity. It is this latter source which has been thought responsible for the largest part of more recent U.S.

---

[1] If population increases at the same rate as total output, there will be no increase in output per capita, but if population increases, say, at around 2 per cent per year and total output grows at $3\frac{1}{2}$ per cent per year, then output per capita will increase at approximately $1\frac{1}{2}$ per cent per year. This roughly has been the long-run experience of the United States from 1840 to 1960; see Simon Kuznets, *Economic Growth and Structure* (New York: W. W. Norton and Company, 1965), p. 305. Note that increases in labor inputs must not stem from proportionate increases in population. If the increased labor is due to increased population, then output will increase, but so will the denominator – population – and increases in per capita output will not occur. Increased per capita labor inputs may result from such events as increased participation rates in the labor force due to a changing age composition of the population (which in turn may be due to changes in birth or death rates or migration), or from people working longer hours.

growth.[1] In the following chapters, we shall adopt the convention of defining economic growth as increased output per capita; growth of total output will be specifically labeled as such.

It is useful to distinguish three general sources of productivity change: (1) technological change, (2) improved skills and abilities of the labor force (what is now popularly called increases in 'human capital') and (3) what can be called improvements in the economic organization of society.[2] Technological change is defined as a shift in the production function due to advances in knowledge. An important aspect of this source of productivity advance is the process of technical diffusion, or the process of replacing older, less productive techniques over time with newer, more efficient ones. It must be remembered, however, that the use of different techniques in different places may not always mean that one place is using more advanced techniques than another. These differences may be due to differences in the relative prices of resources between the areas. Granted that some substitution of inputs in the production processes is possible, there will be an incentive to use more of the relatively cheaper inputs and less of the relatively expensive ones to produce some given level of output. For example, in the colonies, land was relatively cheaper and labor relatively more expensive than in England. Colonists often farmed around tree stumps, did less to retard depletion of their land (by such things as fertilization), and followed other practices that used relatively less labor than did farmers in England. This did not reflect different technologies of farming, but rather differences in the relative prices of labor and land. There is little doubt that technological change has played a major role in advances in productivity in the last two hundred years. The application of new forms of energy and the incorporation of better techniques into a growing capital stock has led to radical changes in levels of production. The very rapid advances in technology, however, have been a fairly recent phenomenon. Energy sources and methods of production showed little change over the colonial period. Indeed, a

[1] See, for example, Edward F. Denison, *The Sources of Economic Growth in the United States and the Alternatives Before Us* (New York: Committee for Economic Development, 1962); Moses Abramovitz, 'Resource and output trends in the U.S. since 1870,' *American Economic Review*, XLVI, 2 (May 1956), pp. 5–23; or Robert M. Solow, 'Technical change and the aggregate production function,' *Review of Economics and Statistics*, XXXIX, 3 (August 1957), pp. 312–20. Dale W. Jorgenson and Zvi Griliches ('The explanation of productivity change,' *Review of Economic Studies*, XXXIV, 3 (July 1967), pp. 249–82) apparently would not agree, at least for the period 1945–65, but the differences revolve around the proper definition and measure of an input. See following note.

[2] See Douglass C. North, *Growth and Welfare in the American Past* (Englewood Cliffs, N.J.: Prentice-Hall, Inc., 1966), pp. 3–11. Note that the problem of classification here (whether something should be called an increase in inputs or an increase in productivity) is partly a matter of definition of an input. If capital is broadly defined to include not only physical capital but increased skills embodied in the labor force as a result of investment in education or training, as Denison does (*op. cit.*), then this will be classified as an increase in inputs.

colonist probably would have felt more familiar with the economy of the late medieval period than with the present-day American economy. Consequently, we suspect that technological change played a far less important role in improving per capita output during the colonial period than it has in the past two centuries.

The degree of skills and abilities embodied in the labor force may be determined by such things as the amount of formal education each member of the labor force has acquired, the skills acquired from experience, on-the-job training, levels of nutrition and health, and so forth. These investments in human capital contribute to the special skills needed to adapt and modify techniques, the quality of labor required for their widespread use, and the many professional and other skills demanded in a more sophisticated society. Such investments are thought by many to have played an important role in U.S. growth, and they are an essential complement both to technological advance and to investments in physical capital – especially those investments embodying new and improved techniques. It would seem that formal education did not play a vital role in the process of colonial life. Learning from experience and apprenticeship programs (often in the form of indentured servitude) and on-the-job training were most probably the main forms of investment in human capital. It seems quite likely that the accumulation of practical experience over time did mean an increase in such investments during the colonial period.

Improvements in economic organization that bring increased productivity in a market or free enterprise economy represent a category in which a number of other factors may be considered. In general, these include improvements resulting from the development of more perfect resource and product markets, and from increased specialization. Such improvements from increased specialization may occur within firms, industries or regions. An important aspect of colonial economic development was the increasing regional specialization that was made possible through greater exchange and trade, especially for overseas markets. This may have involved a greater division of labor of the sort envisaged by Adam Smith, but probably a better description of this increased regional specialization was that, as time passed, more people simply turned their activities toward producing certain commodities or services for markets. These types of production were ones in which the colonists held a comparative advantage and thus received a greater remuneration.[1]

[1] Smith's division of labor meant a reduction in the number of activities or functions that a worker performed in a production process. Productivity increase stemmed from the fact that the worker learned how to perform these fewer functions better and thus became more efficient at them; that he wasted less time in moving from one function to another; and that by separating out these functions in the production process, it became more apparent how machines could be adapted and used in performing these functions. Smith's division

The American economy has always been organized around a market system in which individuals have been able to follow their own self-interest in making decisions about production and their participation in the market economy. The opportunity for gain has provided the motivation to produce those goods and services in demand, and the search for the highest wages or returns has tended to bring about an allocation of resources toward those types of production that provided such returns. An important characteristic of the American people from the period of first settlement has been their motivation and respon-siveness to economic opportunities.[1] This has resulted not only in a greater degree of labor and capital mobility than existed in Europe, but also a willingness to accept other changes in economic organiza-tion, provided such changes brought the possibility of reaping greater benefits, to society or to some group, than the costs of such changes.[2]

The evidence provided here suggests that improvements in economic organization were the main determinants of colonial growth. The development of product and factor markets, a monetary system, and the other trappings of a market economy was a lengthy and gradual process; but self-sufficiency was never complete, and our evidence suggests a gradual and early shift out of subsistence activities and towards production for markets. For example, the periods of rapid settlement generally followed, rather than preceded, the development of markets for colonial goods (such as rice) or the discovery of new goods that could be produced for the market (such as tobacco). The market sector was always a main force in determining what, where, and how goods were produced.

THE IMPORTANCE OF TRADE

Our assertion about the importance of trade and the market to colonial development is not a new one. Historians of the colonial period have

---

of labor probably was one aspect of the increasing regional specialization in the colonies; but another, and probably more important aspect, was one that did not necessarily involve the division of labor. A shift of resources into the production of goods (such as tobacco, rice, and grains and grain products) and services (such as shipping and mercantile services) where the returns were higher would have resulted in increased average productivity and thus increased per capita output.

[1] This motivation also probably hastened the development and application of new techniques which achieved lower costs in the production and the distribution of products. Note that this may include not only the techniques of producing goods and services, but also the techniques of administering business firms and carrying out activities associated with shipping, merchandising, and other aspects of distributing goods.

[2] For an elaboration of this problem of changing institutions and organizations, see John C. H. Fei and Gustav Ranis, 'Economic development in historical perspective,' *American Economic Review*, LIX, 2 (May 1969), pp. 393–4; and Douglass C. North and Robert P. Thomas, 'An economic theory of the growth of the Western world,' *Economic History Review*, 2nd series, XXIII, 1 (April 1970), pp. 1–17.

frequently stated or implied that overseas trade played a significant role in the development of British North America.[1] The exact way in which overseas trade furthered colonial development has not usually been spelled out explicitly, but its general importance has been frequently emphasized by economic historians. For example, Douglass North states:

> There are few exceptions to the essential initiating role of a successful export sector in the early stages of accelerated growth of market economies. The reason is that the domestic market has been small and scattered. These economies have been predominantly rural, with a high degree of individual self-sufficiency. Reflecting this aspect of the market, specialization and division of labor have been limited and rudimentary. An expanding external market has provided the means for an increase in the size of the domestic market, growth in money income, and the spread of specialization and division of labor.[2]

In addition Bruchey argues that 'it is also probable that the pull of expanding foreign markets on subsistence agriculture, by reducing unemployed or underemployed resources, also contributed to growth.'[3]

Other influences of trade on growth in the colonies undoubtedly existed. Factors such as an increasing stock of capital, technological advance, and increasing levels of skill and education of members of the labor force were not directly dependent upon the extent of trade, but certain relationships surely existed. For example, through trade, capital goods were provided more cheaply than the colonies themselves could produce them, and many colonial imports – such as the tools and other items of hardware acquired from Great Britain – were of a capital nature. Also important is the fact that trade served as a vehicle for the dissemination of technical knowledge, of skills and know-how, of managerial talents, and entrepreneurship.[4] The growth of trade and increasing specialization probably encouraged a more intensive search for new techniques and brought forth greater effort to acquire the skills and knowledge necessary to make production in those areas of

---

[1] See, for example, Curtis P. Nettels, *The Roots of American Civilization: A History of American Colonial Life* (2nd ed.; New York: Appleton-Century-Crofts, 1963), pp. 251–2; and Stuart Bruchey, *The Roots of American Economic Growth, 1607–1861: An Essay in Social Causation* (London: Hutchinson & Co. Ltd, 1965), p. 32.

[2] Douglass C. North, *The Economic Growth of the United States, 1790–1860* (Englewood Cliffs, N.J.: Prentice-Hall, Inc., 1961), p. 2.

[3] Bruchey, p. 32.

[4] For a discussion of the relationship between trade and growth, see Gottfried Haberler, 'International trade and economic development,' reprinted in Theodore Morgan, George W. Betz and N. K. Choudhry, *Readings in Economic Development* (Belmont, Cal.: Wadsworth Publishing Co., 1963), pp. 240–9.

increasing specialization more efficient. The rewards for such effort are greater when economic activity is more specialized than when the larger part of the economy is engaged in self-sufficient production. It is possible that trade not only had these effects on the level of skills of the existing population, but also encouraged immigration of skilled people to the developing areas. Commercial contact served to increase the knowledge of potential immigrants about opportunities in the colonies, and trade tended to increase these opportunities for the more highly skilled. Finally, trade served as a vehicle for transferring capital (in the balance-of-payments sense of indebtedness incurred) and this was at least a small benefit to the colonies. It is true that profitable opportunities, or favorable expectations of profits, must first exist if persons from other areas are going to invest in ventures in new areas or make loans to others who wish to do so. But the larger the volume of trade, the more easily the transfer of interest and repayments of principal can be effected.[1]

Given the dominance of agriculture in the colonial economy, it becomes especially important to consider what impact trade may have had on agricultural productivity. Fei and Ranis, in discussing the economic growth of the western world in long-run historical perspective, designate the period from approximately 1500 to 1750 as the epoch of mercantile agrarianism.[2] In this period the major form of economic production continued to be agriculture, but the authors stress the impact of mercantile activities on the economy: 'it is the penetration of this agrarian system by mercantile activities dedicated to interregional trade that gradually transforms the latter – ridding it of the local self-sufficiency attributes and substituting in its place an integrated economic system covering a larger space, ultimately the entire national economy'.[3] They go on to state 'that it was mainly through the expansion of trade that agricultural productivity was raised and the tendency to stagnation reversed'.[4] The various mechanisms by which agricultural productivity was stimulated include the Smithian division of labor; changes in the method of organization;[5] the transmission of better agricultural techniques through growing contacts brought about by growing trade; and the emergence of a national economy which lowered local trade barriers and allowed such developments as national transport and communications systems, a national currency, and

[1] *Ibid.*, p. 248.
[2] Fei and Ranis, pp. 386–400.
[3] *Ibid.*, p. 390.
[4] *Ibid.*, p. 392.
[5] Changes in the method of organization are concerned with changing economic institutions, and deal 'with matters of incentive, coordination, authority, and information. With the emergence of mercantile agrarianism the very right to organize and control the economic affairs of the nation comes to rest increasingly in the hands of those who own and control the commercial capital stock rather than those of the landed aristocracy.' *Ibid.*, pp. 393–4.

national financial institutions. These insights offered by Fei and Ranis help clarify many of the issues and points raised earlier.

With regard to the specific character of the development of the colonial economy, the abundance of the natural resources found in the colonies was of special importance. As Bruchey argued in the quotation above, increasing exports may mean the employment of resources (specifically natural resources or labor) that would otherwise be unemployed, or underemployed. If the argument regards the employment of natural resources, then at least one author, Richard Caves, would say it has been expounded under the guise of the 'staple theory'.[1] Caves argues that as 'bundles' or 'deposits' of natural resources in a newly settled region begin to be exploited, this new region begins to export goods which 'require for their fabrication capital, labor, and substantial quantities of natural resources';[2] and import 'manufactured goods...using inputs of labor and capital'[3] from the older, mature region. The discovery of these new 'bundles' of natural resources thus creates a situation of disequilibrium between these two regions. The process of bringing these newly 'discovered' resources into use in production represents the beginning of an adjustment process which brings the allocation of resources back into equilibrium. This new equilibrium is the one described in conventional microeconomic theory where resources are allocated to those uses where they achieve the highest marginal productivity. Not only does this reallocation of resources bring about changes in the location of production and trade between the two regions; but it also involves the migration of factors of production to the new region. It should be noted that the 'surplus', 'unemployed', or 'underemployed' natural resources of the new region are not surplus or unemployed in the sense of there being inadequate aggregate demand, but rather in the sense that they have no economic value until they are 'discovered' and are brought into use in production. Caves' argument, then, is concerned with the increasing specialization of production and the growth of trade of a region; it is a specific application of the theory of comparative advantage to newly-settled

---

[1] See Richard E. Caves, '"Vent for surplus" models of trade and growth,' in Robert E. Baldwin *et al., Trade, Growth and the Balance of Payments* (Chicago: Rand McNally & Company, 1965), pp. 97–104. If the 'staple theory' is to be equated with the earlier writings of Harold A. Innis, as commonly is, then other interpreters of the 'theory' would say it is concerned with more than simply the bringing of 'surplus' or 'unemployed' natural resources into production via a neoclassical re-allocation of resources. See Melville H. Watkins, 'A staple theory of economic growth,' *Canadian Journal of Economics and Political Science*, XXIX, 2 (May 1963), pp. 141–58.

[2] Caves, p. 97.

[3] *Ibid.*, p. 98. Caves states: 'Staples may also enter into the production functions of manufactures as raw-material inputs, but we suppose their importance to be small enough that no variation actually experienced in the price of any rth staple will directly cause any perceptible variation in the equilibrium price of any rth manufacture employing it as an input' (p. 98).

regions. In the following section, these ideas are developed in detail from the point of view of the colonies.

AN ANALYSIS OF PRODUCTION COSTS

The growth of colonial exports can be viewed analytically by the use of supply and demand analysis. Changes in the values of exports came either from a change in demand or a change in supply, or both. As shown in Figure 2.1, these changes would be from points *a* to *b*, *a* to *c*, or *a* to *d*, respectively. The growth of demand (outward shifts of the demand curve, such as D_1 to D_2) in Great Britain, in southern Europe, and in the West Indies for colonial goods was determined by an expanding population in these areas, growing incomes, relative price increases (decreases) of substitutes (complements) for colonial goods, and possibly (perhaps as in the case of tobacco) changes in tastes. Outward shifts of the supply curve (S_1 to S_2) of colonial exports resulted from reductions in two general types of costs: production costs, and transaction or distribution costs.

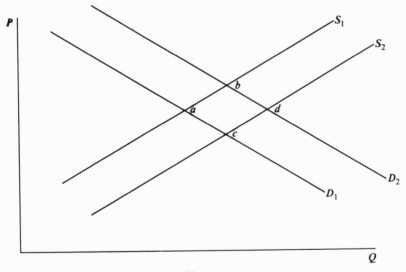

Figure 2.1

Production costs of exports are defined as their costs at the port of origin. For colonial exports these included costs incurred at the production site together with land transportation costs to move the goods to a colonial port or distribution center. These costs are reflected in the F.O.B. supply schedule (S_{FOB} in Figure 2.2), which shows the various quantities per time period that the colonists were willing to market at various prices in the colonies. The C.I.F. supply schedule

(S_{CIF}), which shows the various quantities that the colonists were willing to market at various prices in the overseas market, is obtained by adding the per unit costs of distribution to the F.O.B. supply curve. These costs include packaging, inventory, insurance, water transport, information, risk, and other similar transaction costs; they are given as the vertical distance (ab) between S_{FOB} and S_{CIF}. At price b in the overseas market, the quantity of colonial exports equals the quantity demanded there. At this price the demand and supply schedules (D_{CIF} and S_{CIF} respectively) intersect, which denotes a position of equilibrium. It should be noted that in equilibrium Q_1 is produced and receives price a (equal to average production costs) at the colonial distribution center, and is sold for price b (equal to average production costs plus average distribution costs) in the overseas market.

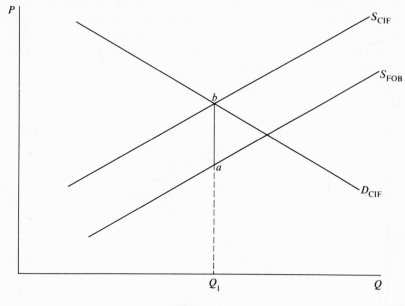

Figure 2.2

In this section of the analysis we focus on production costs in the colonies, and examine the causes and effects of shifts in the F.O.B. supply curves of colonial goods (i.e. changes in the costs of colonial production including land transportation costs). To do this we presume for the moment that per unit distribution costs are fixed and do not change. Consequently, any shifts in S_{FOB} will result in equal corresponding shifts in S_{CIF}.

The framework, presented in its simplest form, contains two regions, Great Britain and the colonies; three factors of production, labor, capital, and natural resources; and two types of goods, manufactured and agricultural goods.[1] Manufactured goods require capital, labor, and raw materials for their fabrication, but raw materials are an insignificant part of the costs of manufacturing. Above a minimum efficient scale, the production function exhibits constant returns to scale (constant average costs). That is, average costs fall over a certain range and then become constant thereafter. Agricultural goods require labor, capital, and substantial amounts of natural resources for their production. Some agricultural goods require specific resources such as land and climate of a unique type, which are inelastic in supply, and the production of these goods is subject to diminishing returns (increasing costs).

We assume initially that Great Britain is characterized as a diversified economy producing all classes and types of commodities, both agricultural and industrial. It is well endowed with capital and labor, but has relatively smaller quantities of natural resources. Levels of income and density of population in Great Britain are sufficiently high to provide a wide market for manufactures, and hence the production of manufactures is at a sufficiently high level to permit long-run minimum costs. In contrast, various agricultural commodities have rising supply curves due to the limited availability and inelasticity of supply of certain essential resources, such as high quality land and appropriate climate. Consequently, as population and income increase over time, and the demands for various manufactures and agricultural items increase, there is a relative increase in the costs (and prices) of natural-resource-intensive goods.

In contrast to Great Britain, the colonies initially are unpopulated, with no labor or capital. It is known that there is an abundance of natural resources in the colonies, but the initially high costs (especially subjective risks and uncertainties) of colonial enterprise and settlement discourage migration and development.

The long-run costs of production of various natural-resource-intensive goods (for example, fur, fish, tobacco, rice, wheat, Indian corn, lumber, and so forth) in Great Britain may be viewed in the long-run supply curve given in Figure 2.3. Because of an inelastic supply of appropriate types of land and climate, the costs of such commodities sharply increase after certain low levels of production are reached. The demand for these goods changes as population, income, and perhaps tastes change over time, and the effect of these shifts in demand is to raise prices secularly. Measuring vertically from the horizontal axis, prices move from *a* to *c* to *d* in the long run, but prices may rise (to *b*)

---

[1] We could include services in the model, but with the exceptions of shipping, insurance, and mercantile services, they were not traded internationally and thus would add little to the analysis at this point. These types of services are important in the analysis of distribution costs, and are treated explicitly below.

more sharply in the short run because of the time required to bring new lands or other fixed factors into production.

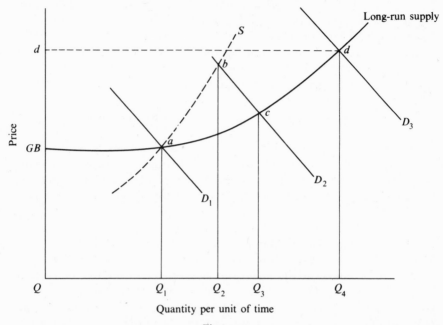

Figure 2.3

The long-run cost conditions of producing natural-resource-intensive goods (hereafter called colonial staples) in the colonies are given in Figure 2.4. These costs, which are reflected in the long-run supply curve (LRS_1), decline over a limited range, remain constant as long as new 'best quality' lands are available near cheap water transport, and finally begin to rise as lower quality lands and interior lands facing higher land transportation costs are brought into production. As a result, the long-run supply curve of colonial staples eventually becomes upward-sloping. The short-run supply curves $(\hat{S})$ given in Figure 2.4 are upward-sloping, reflecting diminishing returns to the variable factors, labor and capital, in the short run.

Now suppose in fact that demand did actually shift over time and that the demand curves, D_1, D_2, and D_3, in Figure 2.3 reflect these shifts. The result was the expansion of production from Q_1 to Q_3 to Q_4 and so on, and over this range many potential colonial staples were produced in Great Britain (some, such as sugar and rice, were not, of course). However, as prices reached and exceeded Od, some initial attempts to produce these goods in the colonies were undertaken.

The anticipated costs of production in the colonies, reflected in the supply curve $\hat{S}_1$ (Figure 2.4), were relatively high because of high risks.

The initial uncertainties created by Indian resistance, the uncertainties of land quality, climate, and the problems associated with knowing

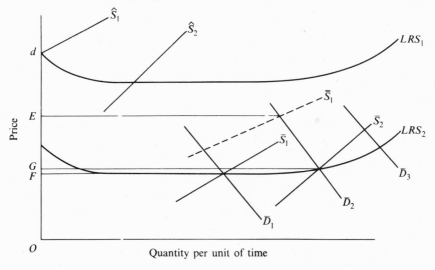

Figure 2.4

what to produce profitably in unfamiliar areas, and the difficulty of attracting a labor force into such an environment were a few of the risks faced by early colonial entrepreneurs. Nevertheless, as prices reached and exceeded *Od*, the migration of capital and labor to the colonies began, and the production of colonial staples was initiated. The anticipated costs reflected in $\hat{S}_1$ may be viewed originally as the short-run opportunity costs of colonial staple production. However, after a period of trial and error, the incipient risks of enterprise declined, and as initial uncertainties were eventually eliminated, the costs of production were reduced.[1]

The effects of these cost reductions were downward shifts in both the short-run supply curves ($\hat{S}_1$ to $\hat{S}_2$) and the long-run supply curves (LRS_1 to LRS_2). Extensive growth (that is, the process of settlement and increased total output) in the colonies consequently had significant effects on productivity by reducing uncertainties and the risk of enterprise. Moreover, as production increased and time passed, improved methods of production resulted from learning through experience what could profitably be produced for market and how such commodities

[1] Of course, the importance of reductions of uncertainties and risks differed substantially depending on the region and type of export. For a number of important exports, such as fish, lumber, furs, deerskins, and iron, the role of discovery was crucial. Also, in the case of other items, like rice, indigo, and tobacco, ways had to be found to use the resources known to be available. In these cases, the costs of search as well as existing risks explain the high level of the short-run supply curve.

should be produced. Entrepreneurial talents were stimulated and more efficient scales of production were achieved. As resource markets improved and institutions such as slavery and indentured servitude developed, the problems of acquiring a labor force and necessary capital were eventually solved.

Reductions in the costs of production of colonial staples undoubtedly did not occur in an orderly fashion. A process of trial and error preceded the discovery of many of the colonial staples, but the process of settlement itself reduced the risks of migration and enterprise. Thus, these factors tended to reinforce one another. In some instances (such as rice production), economies of scale led to further cost reductions. Learning by doing was also an essential aspect of early settlement and commercial development. As the supply of colonial staples increased, their relative prices declined, and their production in Great Britain was diminished (provided they had been produced there in the first place). British restrictions against production of some staples, such as tobacco, of course reinforced these tendencies. Ultimately, these goods were produced almost entirely in the colonies, in much larger quantities and at significantly lower costs than in Great Britain.

It seems appropriate at this point to consider the effects of demand shifts on factor movements, the process of settlement, the allocation of labor and capital among alternative uses, and the determination of long-run equilibrium in the colonies. The above-mentioned sources of cost reductions causing supply shifts were influential over much of the colonial period, particularly in areas of new settlement. At this point in the analysis, however, we wish to turn and look at the effects of increasing demand on colonial development, and for this purpose we assume that supply does not change.

Assume a long-run equilibrium of the demand and supply of a colonial staple, such as the intersection of $\bar{D}_1$ and $\bar{S}_1$ at price OF in Figure 2.4. Suppose a shift in demand such as from $\bar{D}_1$ to $\bar{D}_2$ with price increasing and approaching OE in the short run. Because land in production was relatively fixed in the short run, increases in variable factors resulted in diminishing returns (indicated by a movement along $\bar{S}_1$). In addition, because of an inelastic supply of variable factors in the colonies, wages and capital costs increased, resulting in a shift of the short-run supply curve from $\bar{S}_1$ to $\bar{S}_1$.[1] As long as price was above the long-run costs OG (at the quantity indicated by the intersection of $\bar{D}_2$ and LRS_2), migration continued because remunerations were higher to labor and capital in the colonies than in Great Britain. The increased

---

[1] The implication is that the long-run supply of variable factors is quite elastic, but the short-run supply of these factors is relatively inelastic. The increased demand for variable factors results in a short-run increase in wages and returns to capital, but little or no change in the remunerations in the long run.

supply of factors, however, lowered their costs and shifted the short-run supply curve to the right (to $\bar{S}_2$), and a new long-run equilibrium was eventually achieved. When labor (and capital) received the same returns on both sides of the Atlantic, migration stopped.[1]

Incoming labor and capital were allocated to minimize costs of production, and thus located on lands of highest quality and nearest to distribution centers. First settlements were on high quality land along the seaboard and waterways, with subsequent increases in production coming on less fertile land near waterways and on high quality lands further inland. Given a random distribution of high quality land, population densities would have been greater near available water transport. Land of similar quality along waterways and near ports and harbors was first settled because of the advantage of location, and these areas received higher rents than land of the same quality further inland. The higher cost of land transport to producers located further inland resulted in lower rents and explains, in part, the upward slope of the long-run supply curve. At some point, rents became zero because of the high cost of land transportation, and this may be viewed as a boundary of feasible market production. It may also be viewed as determining equilibrium in the long run. When this boundary was reached, no new lands were cleared and planted, and migration halted. Production for market beyond this boundary did not occur because this would have resulted in avoidable losses.

Now assume another shift in the demand curve, from $\bar{D}_2$ to $\bar{D}_3$. This resulted in disequilibrium, a shift of the boundary of feasible market production further inland, and new migration. The increased supply of colonial staples came from using land already in cultivation more intensively, as well as from additions of new lands. Attempts to expand production in the colonies, by utilizing available resources more intensively and extensively, raised the demand for labor and capital and bid up wages and increased the returns to capital. Once again, migration was induced and continued until equality of remuneration was achieved geographically and a new equilibrium was reached.[2]

In the process, the international economic environment became quite different. From a world in which no trans-Atlantic trade existed, a substantial amount of trade developed. Colonists produced and exported staple goods and imported various manufactured and finished

---

[1] Migration costs, geographical preferences, ignorance of the differentials, and differences in risks (geographically), of course, would have precluded exact equality in remunerations to the respective factors between regions. Because of these influences, wages in the long run were typically higher in the colonies than in Great Britain.

[2] It should be noted that the displaced capital and labor in Great Britain either joined the process of migration to the colonies or changed to the production of other goods in Great Britain. Submarginal land used to produce staples in Great Britain became idle or was used in other endeavors. Also, the qualifications given in the preceding note still apply here.

goods. Although a colonial market for manufactured goods developed as the colonies became populated, the domestic market was too limited to support large-scale colonial production of manufactures on a commercial basis. Given increasing returns over a range of low levels of production, manufactures were produced more cheaply in Great Britain than in the colonies.

The result of specialization and these other improvements was increased per capita output. The migration of labor and capital to the colonies (to the extent that such migration was based on economic factors) indicated that in the short run they received (or expected to receive) higher incomes in the colonies than in Great Britain. The result in the long run was a reduction in the world price of colonial staples. The extent of the price reduction depended on a number of factors: (1) differences in the quality of natural resources between Great Britain and the colonies, (2) subsequent effects of the various sources of improved productivity as production increased, and (3) the price and income elasticities of the demand for colonial staples. These factors determined the relative portion of colonial staple production which occurred in the colonies and the subsequent decline of price and production of these staples in Great Britain. In this example, the total amount of such production ultimately occurred in the colonies, and all consumers of these goods were better off. Real incomes, appearing in the form of rents to owners of colonial land producing for market, were raised.

The attainment of new equilibrium implies the cessation of migration and the reduction of the growth rate in the colonies to zero. Further growth depended upon an increase in the demand for colonial staples, the development of other types of natural-resource-intensive goods which were produced for export, or further cost reductions which led to supply shifts. As discoveries of other types of natural-resource-intensive goods were made, new migration increased land use and the expansion of trade resulted. Growth in total income occurred in the colonies, and rising per capita incomes were enjoyed in both areas.

It should be emphasized that demand plays a crucial role in our analysis of colonial development. No attempt is made to explain or determine the timing of the shifts in the demand for various colonial exports, and it is merely assumed that demand increased secularly over the period. This key role was to raise temporarily the price of natural-resource-intensive goods, thus attracting mobile factors to the natural-resource-abundant colonies.[1] This effect, in conjunction with learning by doing and the reduction of risks which lowered production costs,

---

[1] Higher money returns to the mobile factors are not necessarily maintained in the long run, but rents are increased secularly in addition to the reduction in cost of living caused by lower prices of natural-resource-intensive goods.

expanded markets for colonial exports and sustained colonial development.

DECLINING COSTS OF DISTRIBUTION

In this section of the analysis we focus on the effects of reductions in distribution costs. The assumption of fixed distribution or transaction costs is replaced with the assumption that production costs (per unit) and demand did not change. In other words, in this part of the analysis we assume that the F.O.B. supply schedule and the C.I.F. demand curve remain unchanged.

The effects of reductions in distribution costs are given in Figures 2.5 and 2.6. Consider the case of colonial staple production with the major market being in Europe. The initial equilibrium position given in Figure 2.5 is the quantity Q_1, which was produced in the colonies at per unit cost (F.O.B. price) $\bar{P}_1$ and sold in Europe at price (C.I.F. price) P_1, the difference AB being the per unit costs of ocean transportation and distribution. The supply curve of colonial staples in Europe (S'_{CIF}) is drawn vertically parallel to S_{FOB} and passes through A. From the point of view of the European purchaser, a decline in distribution costs from AB to CE appeared as a shift in supply (S'_{CIF} to S''_{CIF}). From

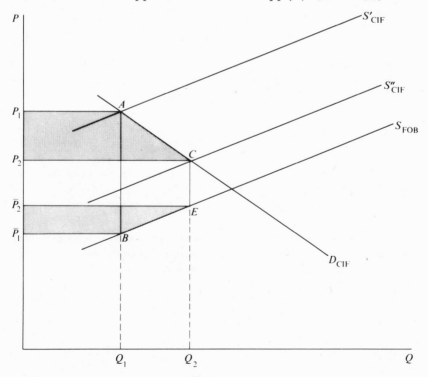

Figure 2.5

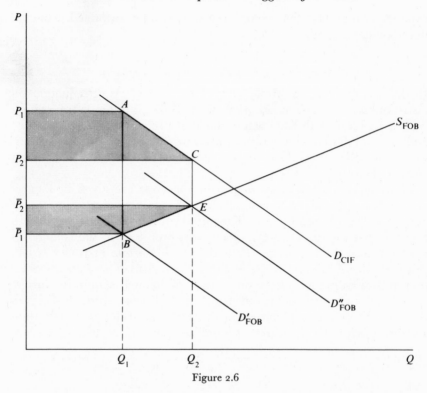

Figure 2.6

the point of view of the colonial producer (as given in Figure 2.6), it appeared as an increase in demand (the F.O.B. demand is obtained by subtracting the per unit transaction costs from D_{CIF}). Given the reduction in distribution costs, Q_2 was produced and purchased, and both the consumer and producer were better off. Consumers enjoyed more of the goods at a lower price and producers expanded production and received higher returns, mainly in the form of rents. The relative slopes of the curves determined the relative benefits received from the falling costs of shipment. These can be viewed approximately as the relative areas P_1P_2CA (consumers' surplus) and $\bar{P}_2\bar{P}_1BE$ (producers' surplus or rents).

Besides the very important effect of lowering C.I.F. prices to consumers, declining transaction costs increased the cultivation of lands. As in the earlier analysis, colonial staple producers who were near good ports and waterways were closer to the market in terms of transportation costs than producers who were located further inland. Consequently, lands of equal quality further inland received lower rents. At some point, rents became zero because of the high costs of land transportation, and once again we can view this as a boundary of feasible market production, with producers beyond this boundary not producing for the market. One of the effects of falling transaction costs was to shift this boundary inland and introduce new growing regions to the market economy. Similarly, it induced more intensive use of the land already under cultivation, and increased the demand for labor and capital. Migration continued until the new equilibrium position was attained.

The decline of distribution costs was an important aspect of the growth of trade and the development of an integrated market economy. Improvements in shipping were an especially important aspect of this development, but reductions in the costs of inventories, packaging, insurance, and information about markets contributed as well. Declining distribution costs more clearly brought into focus the relative comparative advantages in production among regions with widely different factor endowments. The consequence was advancing regional specialization and division of labor, which increased output and raised living standards.

RELEVANCE, QUALIFICATIONS, AND LIMITATIONS
OF THE FRAMEWORK

Agriculture and other natural-resource-intensive activities such as fishing and lumber production were the dominant forms of economic activity in the colonies. The large majority of the population lived in rural areas and were predominantly engaged in such activities. Most of the remainder (probably less than ten per cent) were engaged in commercial activities, with commercial manufacturing being a very small part of the economy. Consequently it follows that whatever improvements occurred in productivity in commercial manufacturing, such improvements could not have made a large contribution to overall growth. Thus, sources of productivity change in colonial manufacturing need not require stress.

The low levels of manufacturing activity stemmed primarily from two sources: the abundance of land relative to labor and capital, and the limited size of the market. The abundance of land and natural resources attracted labor and capital as complementary factors in the production of natural-resource-intensive commodities. The low labor–land ratio resulted in high wages and a comparative advantage in agriculture. Also if economies of scale of production existed in manufacturing, potential colonial manufacturers could not produce on a large enough scale to reach the position of minimum costs enjoyed by English manufacturers who faced a larger market. An important aspect of this was the lack of division of labor in colonial manufacturing, about which Benjamin Franklin made the following comment:

Manufactures, where they are in perfection, are carried on by a multiplicity of hands, each of which is expert only in his own part, no one of them a master of the whole; and if by any means spirited away to a foreign country, he is lost without his fellows. Then it is a matter of extremist difficulty to persuade a complete set of workmen, skilled in all parts of manufactory, to leave their country together and settle in a foreign land. Some of the idle and drunken may be enticed away, but these only disappoint their employers, and serve to discourage the undertaking. If by royal munificence, and an expense that the profits of the trade alone would not bear, a complete set of good and skillful hands are collected and carried over, they find so much of the system imperfect, so many things wanting to carry on the trade to advantage, so many difficulties to overcome, and the knot of hands so easily broken by death, dissatisfaction, and desertion, that they and their employers are discouraged altogether, and the project vanishes into smoke.[1]

High wages and the limited division of labor resulted in the importation of manufactures rather than their domestic production.[2]

Because technological change (advances in knowledge) appears to have contributed insignificantly to improvements in agriculture,[3] the predominant economic activity of colonists, we suggest that technological change was not an important source of growth in the colonies. This conclusion is further supported by the evidence presented in Chapter 5 on sources of productivity change in shipping and other commercial activities. Reduced risks, improvements in economic organization, and greater degrees of regional specialization, appear to have been the main factors leading to productivity change and higher levels of per capita income in the colonies.

Because most of the population was engaged in agricultural activities, which included not only self-sufficient production but also production for the market, we believe that the above framework is relevant and a

---

[1] 'The interest of Great Britain in America,' cited by George J. Stigler, 'The division of labor is limited by the extent of the market,' *Journal of Political Economy*, LIX, 3 (June 1951), p. 193; and V. S. Clark, *History of Manufactures in the United States, 1607–1860* (Washington, D.C.: The Carnegie Institution of Washington, 1916), I, p. 152. Clark adds: 'In these words Franklin was but reciting the history of the more important colonial attempts to establish a new industry or to enlarge an old one with which he was personally familiar.'

[2] It should be noted that household manufacturing, shipbuilding, iron production and flour milling stand as several exceptions to this general characteristic.

[3] See P. W. Bidwell and J. I. Falconer, *History of Agriculture in the Northern United States, 1620–1860* (Washington, D.C.: Carnegie Institution of Washington, 1925); and Lewis C. Gray, *History of Agriculture in the Southern United States to 1860* (Washington, D.C.: Carnegie Institution of Washington, 1933), 2 volumes. Bidwell and Falconer state: 'The eighteenth century farmers showed little advance over the first settlers in their care of livestock.' (p. 107); and 'Little if any improvement had been made in farm implements until the very close of the eighteenth century.' (p. 123).

useful one with which to view colonial economic development.[1] The framework is particularly useful in understanding the continued exploitation of natural resources, the forces leading to migration of labor and capital from Europe, and the particular patterns of development that took place in the colonies. Certain important deficiencies and qualifications regarding the framework, however, should be clearly stated.

First, as stated above, it is important to keep in mind the importance of overseas trade and the market economy as a source of colonial income,[2] as opposed to self-sufficient or subsistence economic activities. While overseas trade and market activity may not have comprised the major portion of all colonial economic activity, the importance of the market was that of improving resource allocation. Our interest in the market is due to the fact that it later came to occupy a central position. We argue that while subsistence agriculture provided an important base to colonial incomes and was a substantial share of average per capita income, changes in incomes and improvements in welfare came largely through overseas trade and other market activities. Not only did improvements in productivity occur primarily through market activities, but the pattern of settlement and production was determined by market forces. This pattern changed slowly and unevenly, spreading from the waterways and distribution centers along the Atlantic seaboard into the interior. The geographical location of the population near available water transport resulted primarily from the wide differences in the costs of transportation by water and by land. Few settlers were completely independent of the market, and most colonists were engaged, at least part-time, in production for markets. Furthermore, the costs of transportation in the colonies were particularly important for such items as tobacco, rice, indigo, fish, wheat, lumber, and others, which were typically high bulk items in relation to their value. In fact, there were few goods that could bear the costs of overland shipment of any great distance, and, as a result, resources

---

[1] We wish to stress that this is a framework suggested to view and to aid in the explanation of the broad patterns of colonial economic development – it is not a theory to be tested in this book.

[2] The term 'colonial income' also must be acceptably defined and clarified. The term 'colonial income' is analogous to the present meaning of national income. The difficulty is that the use of the adjective 'national' is not really proper for the colonial period. For present purposes, colonial income can be divided into two categories: (1) the value of goods and services that were produced and exchanged in market trade (the market sector of the economy), and (2) the value of goods and services that were consumed by the producing unit, whether a plantation, a family farm, or an urban household (the subsistence sector). That part of colonial income which originated in the market sector can be further broken down into: income which originated in market trade that took place only within a colony (intracolonial trade); income which originated from market trade between colonies (intercolonial trade); and income which originated from trade between the colonies and overseas areas (overseas trade).

responded to market forces and production and exchange centered near cheap water transport.

Secondly, no very exact figures of levels or rates of change of real per capita output exist for the American colonies. Consequently, any arguments about the pace of development or periods of acceleration or deceleration in the rate of growth must remain largely conjectural. Nonetheless, some evidence about the pace and pattern of colonial development does exist. It is to an examination of this evidence that we now turn.

CHAPTER 3

COLONIAL ECONOMIC DEVELOPMENT
AND TRADE: AN OVERVIEW

In this chapter we review the existing historical literature which has contributed to our understanding of the broad outlines of colonial economic development and growth. We begin by considering the evidence and speculation concerning trends in total and per capita output in the colonies. Population growth and immigration are then examined. Finally, rough estimates of the magnitudes of eighteenth-century overseas trade are presented, and from this evidence conclusions regarding the patterns and degrees of regional specialization are drawn.

TRENDS IN COLONIAL OUTPUT

Unfortunately, comprehensive data on output in the eighteenth century do not exist. It was not until the nineteenth century that output data began to be collected for the United States. Consequently, students of the colonial period have been forced to rely upon fragmentary and qualitative evidence concerning economic conditions and living standards in the colonies, the result of which has been prolonged debate and disagreement about the course of colonial development.[1]

---

[1] This debate has been carried into the early national period up to 1840, as well. The estimates of Robert F. Martin (*National Income in the United States, 1799–1938* (New York: National Industrial Conference Board, 1939)) suggested a decline in per capita output between 1800 and 1840. Despite support from Douglass C. North ('Early national income estimates of the United States,' *Economic Development and Cultural Change*, IX, 3 (April 1961), pp. 387–96) and George Rogers Taylor ('American economic growth before 1840: an exploratory essay,' *Journal of Economic History*, XXIV, 4 (December 1964), pp. 427–44), Martin's estimates have come in for heavy criticism from Simon Kuznets ('Current national income estimates for the period prior to 1870,' *Income and Wealth of the United States, Trends and Structure* (Cambridge, England: Bowes & Bowes, 1952), pp. 221–41) and recently from Paul David ('The growth of real product in the United States before 1840: new evidence, controlled conjectures,' *Journal of Economic History*, XXVII, 2 (June 1967), pp. 151–97). David's estimates, based on evidence of labor productivity, the proportion of the labor force engaged in agriculture and labor force participation rates, suggest there was no decisive up-turn in the rate of growth of per capita output between 1790 and 1840. See Ralph L. Andreano (*New Views on American Economic Development* (Cambridge, Mass.: Schenkman Publishing Company Inc., 1965), pp. 121–67) for a summary of the debate about the period 1790–1840. See also Andreano, pp. 41–56, and Robert E. Gallman ('The pace and pattern of American economic growth,' *American Economic Growth: An Economist's History of the United States*, ed. William N. Parker (New York: Harper & Row, 1972)) for a summary of the debate about growth in the colonial period.

There is little doubt that total output expanded rapidly over the colonial period. Such indicators as the rapid rate of population growth (see Figure 3.1 below) and the growth of trade (as indicated by the increase in exports and imports, or the aggregate tonnage of vessels entering and clearing colonial ports) suggest a rapid rate of growth of aggregate output. The rapid growth of total output tells us nothing, however, about the path of per capita output. Qualitative evidence suggests that colonial living standards and real per capita output did improve over the colonial period. Surely per capita output in the eighteenth century was above that of the earliest settlers. As Bruchey states:

> At the outset of the colonial experience the settlers in Virginia went through a 'starving period:' by January of the second year of Jamestown's settlement, 67 of the original 105 colonists were dead of disease and malnutrition. But in 1663 the Reverend John Higginson of Boston could observe that 'we live in a more plentifull and comfortable manner than ever we did expect.' And by the 1740's Benjamin Franklin could remark that 'The first drudgery of settling new colonies, which confines the attention of people to mere necessaries, is now pretty well over; and there are many in every province in circumstances that set them at ease...'[1]

Some speculation about the secular trend in real per capita output has been made, and widely varying opinions have been reached. The average annual increase in real national product per head was 1.6 per cent for the period 1839–1960, and as Raymond W. Goldsmith has pointed out, if average real per capita output in 1760 was not less than half the level of 1860, the average annual rate of growth of per capita output from 1760 to 1839 would have been 0.6 per cent.[2] Furthermore, if the rate of growth after 1839 is extrapolated back into the period before 1839, unrealistic figures are soon reached.

> If the trend observed since 1839 had been in force before that date, average income per head in today's prices would have been about $145 in 1776, $80 in 1739, and less than $30 in 1676. It takes only a little consideration of the minimum requirements for keeping body and soul together, even in the simpler conditions prevailing in colonial America, to conclude that at present prices for individual commodities an average level of income below $200 is fairly well ruled out for 1776 or even the early eighteenth century.[3]

[1] Stuart Bruchey (ed.), *The Colonial Merchant: Sources and Readings* (New York: Harcourt, Brace & World, Inc., 1966), p. 1.
[2] 'Long period growth in income and product, 1839–1960,' reprinted in Andreano, p. 354.
[3] Goldsmith, *op. cit.*, reprinted in Andreano, p. 355.

If real output per head in the colonies had risen at about the same rate as in England during the eighteenth century up to 1785, then the average annual increase would have been about 0.3 per cent, according to Deane and Cole.[1] Growth rates in the colonies need not necessarily have been the same as in England, but others have suggested that they were probably similar.

Using statistical fragments and qualitative evidence, George Rogers Taylor has suggested that the growth of real per capita output before 1710 was slow and irregular, and that between 1710 and 1775 it averaged 'slightly more than one per cent per annum.'[2] Taylor goes on to say that 'by 1836–1840, the level of living had, I believe, risen to (or somewhat above) the average reached in 1770–1774 and 1799–1804.'[3] His conclusions, however, are admittedly 'largely speculative.'[4] Alternatively, Andreano, by taking hypothetical figures on investment for the colonial period, concludes 'that the average per capita per annum increase in national output must have been below one per cent, and more than likely in the range of zero to 0.5 per cent per annum.'[5]

Recently, Robert Gallman[6] has concurred with the belief that average annual rates of growth in eighteenth-century colonial America were a good deal less than 1 per cent (he places them between 0.3 and 0.5 per cent for the period 1710–1840). He surmises that colonial output per capita was lower, but not much lower, than the English level of £8 to £9 in current prices early in the eighteenth century; that the eighteenth century up to 1775 was a period chiefly of extensive growth (although some growth in per capita output occurred); and that the level of real per capita output in 1790 was about the same as had existed in 1775. Furthermore, Gallman believes that Taylor's opinion that per capita output in 1775 was as high as that which prevailed in 1840 (about $90 in 1840 prices) errs on the high side; and that in 1774 per capita output was more likely in the range of $60 to $70 (in prices of 1840). If Gallman is correct, then average annual output in the late colonial period was approximately in the range of £11 to £12½ (pounds sterling in 1774 prices, which were lower than prices of 1840).[7]

[1] Phyllis Deane and W. A. Cole, *British Economic Growth, 1688–1959: Trends and Structure* (London: Cambridge University Press, 1964), p. 80.
[2] Taylor, p. 437.
[3] *Ibid.*
[4] *Ibid.*
[5] Andreano, p. 50.
[6] Gallman, *op. cit.*
[7] The adjustment has been made using the Warren and Pearson wholesale price index, U.S. Bureau of the Census, *Historical Statistics of the United States, Colonial Times to 1957* (Washington D.C.: U.S. Government Printing Office, 1960), pp. 115–16 (hereafter cited as *Historical Statistics*). Gallman's estimate of per capita output for 1774 is founded partly upon an estimate he made of factor supplies, which in turn is based upon wealth estimates for that year made by Alice Hanson Jones which are discussed below.

Two other conjectures about the range of colonial per capita output have recently been made. One, by Alice Hanson Jones from her research concerning private wealth in the colonies, is based upon wealth estimates constructed from detailed inventories of personal property of decedents in colonial probate records.[1] By assuming wealth–output ratios of between three and five to one (approximate ratios that have been observed by Goldsmith and Gallman for some nineteenth-century dates, and for some developing countries today), Mrs Jones suggests a probable range of per capita output for 1774 of approximately £8½ to £14 (pounds sterling in current prices).[2] David Klingaman, using another approach, suggests a range of probable per capita output of £6½ to £19.[3] Klingaman's range is based upon estimates of the value of average per capita consumption of basic foodstuffs (grains and meats) around 1770, and the assumption that these plus other expenditures on foodstuffs would not have been less than 40 per cent nor greater than 70 per cent of per capita income (a range of expenditure on foodstuffs which he finds encompasses many countries at different stages of development today).[4] Neither the ranges, nor the midpoints, of Gallman's, Jones', or Klingaman's estimates for per capita output in the late colonial period are exactly congruous, but the similarity is striking. No matter how probabilistic and rough-hewn these estimates may be, they do shed some important light on questions about colonial output and growth.

Clearly, the weight of opinion and evidence places average annual growth rates in colonial America at relatively low levels. They were probably well under 1 per cent during the eighteenth century to 1775, with stagnation (or decline and recovery) from 1775 to 1790. When possible sources of productivity change are considered, it is not surprising that growth rates in the colonies are believed to have been low.

---

[1] Alice Hanson Jones, 'Wealth estimates for the American middle colonies, 1774,' *Economic Development and Cultural Change*, XVIII, 4, Supplement (July 1970), p. 129. Her wealth estimates are based upon private wealth holdings including land, but excluding cash, servants, and slaves.

[2] Mrs Jones suggests a range of $43–71 (in 1792 dollars) for per capita income, or $201–335 in 1967 dollars. This translates to the approximate range of 8½–14 pounds sterling in 1774 prices.

[3] David Klingaman, 'Food surpluses and deficits in the American colonies, 1768–1772,' *Journal of Economic History*, XXXI, 3 (September 1971), pp. 553–69.

[4] His estimate places average per capita expenditure on basic foodstuffs of grains and meats at £2.625 in Philadelphia wholesale prices (converted to sterling) for the years around 1770. In order to lessen any doubt that this estimate is too low and to allow for regional price variations and retail mark-ups, he then assumes this figure should be inflated by one-third to £3½ per capita. He assumes next that between £1 and £4 sterling is spent on all other foodstuffs, and that from 40 to 70 per cent of average per capita income is spent on all foodstuffs. This results in the probable range of £6½ to almost £19 for per capita income. Klingaman thinks £6½ is too low, and £19 is too high, to be very realistic; and that the true figure for per capita income lies somewhere between these extremes.

Approximately 85–90 per cent of the labor force was engaged in agriculture and other primary types of production. The period does not appear to have been a time of rapid technological change in the production of such commodities. Consequently, although no precise statements can be made about the pace of early American development, it appears that growth was relatively slow. It is doubtful that David's conclusions about the period 1790–1840 can be extended back into the pre-1790 era.[1] Gradual improvement did occur and growth did take place (as we shall see in the following chapters on shipping and distribution), but such improvements did not result in modern rates of economic growth for the American colonies.

POPULATION GROWTH

American population growth during the colonial and early national periods has been viewed consistently as a unique demographic experience; American population grew at extremely rapid rates. As Thomas Malthus put it, 'a rapidity of increase, probably without parallel in history.'[2] Malthus used the early United States as his example of a population that was growing virtually unchecked – a population that was doubling about every twenty-five years.

There can be little doubt that the growth of American population in the colonial period was very rapid, but deficiencies in the data limit our knowledge about the following specific questions: What contribution did natural increase make to population growth as compared to immigration? What were birth and death rates, and net migration? What was internal migration? What was the age and sex composition of the population? Various estimates (by decade) of colonial population do exist for the thirteen colonies, beginning in 1610;[3] the trends are shown in Figure 3.1. Despite justifiable concern about the accuracy of these estimates, they surely portray the broad trends in American population growth within reasonable bounds of accuracy. The rate of total population growth (which includes both free and slave immigration as well as natural increase) appears to have been very rapid in the earlier decades of the seventeenth century with a slowing in the rate appearing as early as 1640. From 1660 to the Revolution the rate of growth appears to have fluctuated only slightly, and the trend appears to have been fairly stable. Potter puts the average rate of increase at

---

[1] David, *op. cit.*

[2] Quoted in J. Potter, 'The growth of population in America, 1700–1860,' *Population in History*, eds. D. V. Glass and D. E. C. Eversley (London: Edward Arnold, 1965), p. 631.

[3] These estimates are reproduced in *Historical Statistics*, p. 756. The estimates are based on tax and militia lists and sporadic censuses taken in various colonies, and thus raise serious questions about their accuracy. These questions are discussed in the above source, and in Potter, *op. cit.*

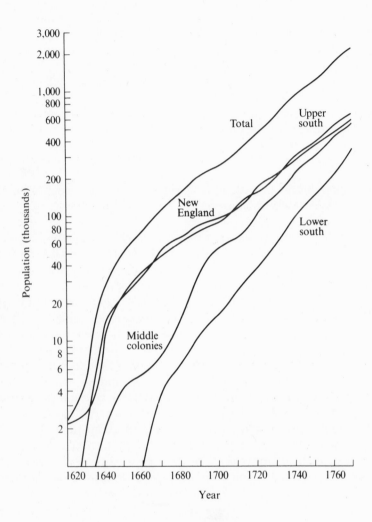

Figure 3.1. Population growth of the thirteen colonies. New England: New Hampshire, Massachusetts, Rhode Island and Connecticut; the middle colonies: New York, New Jersey, Pennsylvania and Delaware; the upper south: Maryland and Virginia; the lower south: North Carolina, South Carolina and Georgia. Other regions, not included in Figure 3.1, are the northern colonies: Newfoundland, Nova Scotia, Island of St Johns and Quebec; and East and West Florida, the Bahamas, and Bermuda. This six-part regional division is used repeatedly throughout the study. Source: U.S. Bureau of the Census, *Historical Statistics of the United States, Colonial Times to 1957* (Washington, D.C.: Government Printing Office, 1960), p. 756.

34 per cent per decade for the period 1660 to 1790.[1] From 1700 to 1770
population increased from about 250,000 to over 2,100,000 for the
thirteen colonies. Certain regional differences are apparent from Figure
3.1. After 1650 New England and the upper south grew at slower rates
than did the middle colonies, which grew especially rapidly from
about 1670 to 1690, and the lower south, a late-starter, which grew
at consistently higher rates up to the Revolution than any other
region. Despite their less rapid rates of growth, however, the upper
south and New England (in that order) were still the most populous
regions in 1770. The population of the northern colonies, which later
became Canada, was small over the entire period compared with any
of the more populous regions of the thirteen colonies. The white population of these colonies was less than 1,000 at the middle of the seventeenth
century, only about 17,000 in 1701, and approximately 105,000 in
1771.[2]

Without reliable data on colonial immigration – both slave and
free – it is difficult to make any firm statements about the contribution
of immigration versus that of natural increase to this increase in
population. Limited evidence does exist, however, with regard to the
importation of slaves. The bulk of this importation took place in the
eighteenth century; the number of slaves in the colonies in 1700 was
small, probably in the range of 5,000 to 20,000.[3] According to Potter,
the 'inflow was uneven, the biggest decennial importation being in the
1760s, when about 75,000 were imported.'[4] Data on slave importations
into New York, Virginia, and Charleston are available for most of the
eighteenth century (the average annual numbers imported by decade
are given in Table 3.1). Although these three colonies were not the
only ones importing slaves, they were the destination of a large proportion of the incoming slaves (for the years 1768–72, New York imported
50 per cent of the slaves entering the middle colonies and New England,
Virginia brought in 76 per cent of the slaves entering the upper south,
and 78 per cent entering the lower south were imported through
Charleston). By assuming that the same percentages held for these
regions over the rest of the eighteenth century prior to 1770, average

[1] Potter, p. 640, note 19. The estimates of population for the thirteen colonies used in Figure
3.1 exhibit annual rates of increase of 3.1 per cent for both the periods 1660–1770 and
1660–1790 (in fact, this rate of increase holds for the entire period 1660–1860); see 'Employment and population trends in perspective,' *Federal Reserve Bank of St Louis Review*, XLVII,
11 (November 1965), p. 6.
[2] Dominion Bureau of Statistics, Canada, *Seventh Census of Canada, 1931*, Vol. 1 (Ottawa,
1936), p. 100. Quebec, of course, was the most populous of these colonies, having about
15,000 people in 1700, 82,000 in 1759 when it fell to the English, and 70,000 in 1765 (see
pp. 133–53 of this source). Newfoundland's British population was 11,000 to 12,000 during
the late 1760s and early 1770s. The remainder (20,000 to 25,000) was composed of settlers
of British and French origin in the various parts of Nova Scotia.
[3] Potter, p. 641.
[4] *Ibid.*

TABLE 3.1.   *Estimated average annual numbers of slaves entering the thirteen colonies, by decade, 1701–70*

Decade	New York	Virginia[a]	Charleston, S.C.	Estimated total[b]
1701–10	50	725	67	1,100
1711–20	159	762	322	1,700
1721–30	158	912	624	2,300
1731–40	126	1,674	1,754	4,700
1741–50	21	1,136	585[c]	2,300
1751–60	65	1,366	1,966	4,400
1761–70	120	1,388	1,844	4,400

Source: *Historical Statistics*, pp. 769–70.

[a] Years for which African slave imports were unavailable were excluded. Hence these are averages of total slave imports from the West Indies and Africa combined. The 1701–10 annual average only includes African slave imports, however.

[b] See text for explanation of method of estimating total slave imports. These estimates have been rounded to the nearest hundred.

[c] This is an average of the slave imports for the years 1739, 1749, 1750, and 1751.

annual imports into all thirteen colonies have been estimated and are presented in Table 3.1. The average number of slaves did change from decade to decade, but the estimates are supported by Nettels, who states that the annual imports of slaves averaged 3,500 during the period 1715–70,[1] and by Potter, who states: 'Importations between 1700 and 1790...probably amounted to between 250,000 and 300,000.'[2] Almost all of these slaves, of course, went to the southern colonies.

Evidence on white immigration is even more sparse. It is usually assumed that despite the fact that absolute numbers of immigrants were greater in the eighteenth century than in the seventeenth, immigration contributed proportionately less to total population growth in the eighteenth than in the seventeenth century.[3] However, widely varying views about the magnitudes of this immigration are to be found. Nettels cites one of the highest estimates: 'the eighteenth century was preëminently the century of the foreigner: in 1760 the foreign-born represented a third of the colonial population....'[4] 'At the other extreme, one finds the view that immigration was insignificant, with a suggested figure of about 10 per cent foreign born in 1790.'[5]

According to Abbot E. Smith, the trends of colonial immigration can be summarized as follows:

[1] Curtis P. Nettels, *The Roots of American Civilization* (2nd ed.; New York: Appleton-Century-Crofts, 1963), p. 419.

[2] Potter, p. 641. Our estimate for the 1760s of 44,000 in Table 3.1 and Potter's above statement of 75,000 for this decade do not agree; but our estimates for 1700–70 and his for 1700–90 are in rough agreement.

[3] *Ibid.*, p. 644.

[4] Nettels, p. 383, quoted from Potter, p. 645.

[5] Potter, p. 645.

(1) After about 1689 there was a great falling off in migration from Britain, which lasted until 1768. At the latter date it began to pick up once again, and the greatest English emigration of the colonial period was that from 1770 to 1775.

(2) Beginning in 1728, a vastly increased movement from Ireland began, and by far the greatest number of servants and redemptioners came from that country during the eighteenth century.

(3) The German migration, second in volume only to the Irish, began also about 1720, reached its height in the middle of the century, and did not, like the English and Irish, increase during the 1770s.

(4) During every period of war there was a marked falling off in migration.[1]

Smith avoided making any quantitative estimate of this immigration, but various others have done so. The volume of the Irish migration, which consisted mostly of Ulster Scots (the Scotch-Irish),[2] has been placed as high as 150,000 up to 1775,[3] although a recent careful assessment of the evidence suggests a somewhat lower range of 100,000 to 125,000 for the period 1718–75.[4] The other sizable group, the Germans, amounted to possibly 100,000 over the course of their immigration into the colonies.[5] Smith put the number of Germans entering Pennsylvania, the destination of the majority, at 75,000 between the 1720s and the Revolution.[6] As suggested in the above-quoted trends, migration from Britain to the colonies during the eighteenth century was at relatively low levels until the late 1760s. In Chapter 8 the evidence concerning British emigration during the late colonial period is reviewed; we conclude that immigration into the colonies was in the range of 15,000 to 20,000 from England, and about 25,000 from Scotland, from the Treaty of Paris to the Revolution. Based on this fragmentary evidence, a reasonable guess would put white immigration into the colonies during the eighteenth century in the range of 250,000 to 300,000. Potter's conjecture that it was 350,000 from 1700 to 1790 (an average of less than 3,900 per year) may well be close to the mark when one considers that he was speculating about a longer period.[7] This is considerably less than the figure suggested by the Beards of an

[1] Abbot E. Smith, *Colonists in Bondage: White Servitude and Convict Labor in America, 1607–1776* (Chapel Hill, N.C.: University of North Carolina Press, 1947), pp. 335–6.

[2] R. J. Dickson, *Ulster Emigration to Colonial America, 1718–1775* (London: Routledge & Kegan Paul, 1966), especially pp. 66–7.

[3] Ian C. C. Graham, *Colonists from Scotland: Emigration to North America, 1707–1783* (Ithaca, N.Y.: Cornell University Press, 1956), p. 19.

[4] Dickson *op. cit.* We believe this range sums up fairly accurately the various statements Dickson makes with regard to the numbers emigrating from Ulster over this period.

[5] Max Savelle and Robert Middlekauff, *A History of Colonial America* (rev. ed.; New York: Holt, Rinehart & Winston, 1964), p. 453.

[6] Smith, p. 323.

[7] Potter, p. 645.

inflow of 750,000 Europeans between 1660 to 1770.[1] The lower figure suggested by Potter is consistent with various combinations of birth and death rates, but the most plausible seem to suggest crude white birth rates of 45 to 50 per thousand of population and moderate death rates of 20 to 25 per thousand.[2] In Chapter 8, estimates of immigration are placed between 11,000 and 19,000 annually for the period 1768–72. As pointed out there, however, it is possible that as many as 50,000 to 100,000 immigrants arrived during this short period, which, according to the above trends, was a time of relatively heavy immigration. Clearly, white immigration averaged much less than this over the rest of the eighteenth century to 1775. The weight of the evidence suggests that the contribution of immigration to the total increase in the white population was moderately small – as low as 15 per cent, and no more than 20 per cent as a generous estimate. These proportions were much higher in the black population, in which slave imports formed one-third to two-fifths of the increase between 1700 and 1790.

If the above suggestions about immigration can be accepted, then the natural rate of growth of population in the colonies seems to have been in the range of 26 to 30 per cent per decade in the eighteenth century.[3] This is a rate slightly below Malthus' supposed doubling of population every twenty-five years (due to natural increase); nevertheless, this high rate is consistent with his views. Potter, for example, suggests that the contemporary view that this rapid growth of population was due to early marriage may hold some truth (the evidence suggests that the average age of marriage was lower in colonial America than in Europe), but that 'the high productivity of American agriculture indeed appears as the key to American population growth.'[4] In particular, this high agricultural productivity resulted in lower infant mortality rates by sustaining the health of women of child-bearing age.[5] This rate of natural increase is considerably higher than that found in England at any time in the eighteenth and nineteenth centuries. In any event, this natural increase was the main component of population growth in eighteenth-century colonial America, and it was this rapid rate of population growth which in turn supported the extensive growth that took place in the colonial economy.

THE EXPANSION OF OVERSEAS TRADE

Only for the five years 1768–72 do complete statistics exist for the

[1] *Ibid.*, p. 645, n. 29.
[2] *Ibid.*, p. 646. It should be kept in mind that these rates are only conjecture. A higher estimate of immigration would be consistent with lower birth rates and/or higher death rates.
[3] *Ibid.*, p. 662.
[4] *Ibid.*, p. 663.
[5] *Ibid.*

overseas legal trade of the British North American colonies. A wealth of data exists, however, for trade in earlier years, even though it is of questionable accuracy and some is of a fragmentary nature that does not furnish a complete picture.[1] It is possible, however, to obtain from these data some rough estimates of the magnitudes of trade in earlier years and to examine the changing composition of trade. It is also possible to get some ideas about the colonial balance of payments for the earlier years in the eighteenth century.

We begin with the British Isles because the customs records that were kept there recorded trade with the colonies.[2] Statistics of trade with other overseas areas are fragmentary and come mostly from lists kept by naval officers in the various colonial ports, who were required to record entries and clearances of ships, their cargoes, and their origins and destinations.[3]

THE TRADE OF THE COLONIES WITH THE BRITISH ISLES

The English customs records began in 1696; they recorded quantities and official values of both commodity imports into England and commodity exports to the colonies. These records are examined in detail in Appendix II, and it is concluded that the official values, especially in the earlier years of the eighteenth century, were not too far different from the actual values. In Figure 3.2, these values for the thirteen colonies are plotted along with the official values from the Scottish customs records, which began in 1755. These values furnish a good picture of the growth of English trade with the colonies over the eighteenth century. Exports from the thirteen colonies grew from an annual average of £289,081 in 1697–1700 to £1,452,476 in 1771–5.[4] The official value of exports to England grew fairly steadily except during some of the war years, when they tended to stagnate or fall. The official values of imports into the colonies from England fluctuated more widely during the earlier years of the century, averaging £336,545 during 1697–1700, then grew fairly steadily to £830,433 in 1748, rapidly increased to £1,230,386 in 1749 and remained at about that level until the beginning of the Seven Years' War in 1755. They then began to increase to a peak of £2,611,764 in 1760, averaged £1,711,012 during 1761–5, rose to £2,157,218 in 1768, and fell drastically in 1769

---

[1] The largest collection of these data in one place can be found in *Historical Statistics*, Chapter Z, prepared by Lawrence A. Harper, University of California, Berkeley.

[2] London, Public Record Office, Customs 3, Customs 14, and Customs 15. The English records began in 1696, the Scottish in 1755, and the Irish in 1698.

[3] *Historical Statistics*, p. 743. Only a few of the Naval Office Lists have survived, and most of these are from the eighteenth century. Some of the gaps are very serious; for example, none of the lists from Philadelphia exist. See Appendix 1 and *Historical Statistics*, p. 743, for a further description of these data.

[4] These official values can be found in *Historical Statistics*, p. 757.

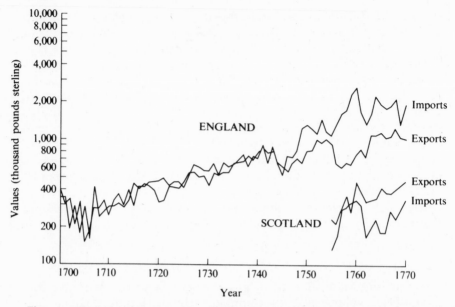

Figure 3.2. Exports and imports of the thirteen colonies to England, 1700–70, and Scotland, 1755–70 (official values). Source: *Historical Statistics*, p. 757 and Customs 14, Public Record Office, London.

due to the non-importation agreements. In 1771, after the non-importation agreements were ended, imports flooded into the colonies and reached their peak of £4,202,472 for the colonial period. They then fell off somewhat until 1775, when they were abruptly cut to a trickle with the non-importation acts of that year.

The composition of colonial exports to England for the five years 1768 through 1772 is examined in detail in Chapter 6. The staples of the southern colonies, tobacco and rice, formed the bulk of the exports during this later period – as they did for the entire eighteenth century, although their relative shares changed over the century. The official values of tobacco and rice exported to England as a percentage of the total official value of exports to England from the thirteen colonies during the following periods were:[1]

	Tobacco	Rice
1697–1705	83%	less than 1%
1721–30	61%	12%
1746–55	59%	16%
1766–75	35%	24%

[1] These percentages have been constructed from values computed from the quantities of tobacco and rice exported to England (*Historical Statistics*, pp. 765 and 768), and the official rates used in the English customs records to value these two commodities. In the years 1697–1705, the official rate for tobacco from Virginia and Maryland varied between 1½d. and 2d. per pound. For these years we have valued the quantities at the average rate of 1.79d. per pound. For following years the rate became standardized at 2.25d. per pound. The official rate of 15s. per hundredweight was used for rice for all the periods.

Tobacco thus declined in relative importance as an export to England,[1] and rice, which had just begun to be grown in the lower south at the turn of the century, increased in relative importance. The Rice production in South Carolina and Georgia expanded rapidly during the late colonial period. As a source of labor for the expansion of plantation agriculture, over three times as many slaves were being imported into the Carolinas and Georgia during the five years 1768–72 as were imported into Virginia and Maryland.[2]

Other exports to England included indigo, which was introduced into South Carolina in the late 1730s and became an export of some importance after Parliament granted a bounty of 6d. per pound on it in 1748. Other southern exports to England included deerskins, bar and pig iron (from the upper south), naval stores (mostly from North Carolina), and staves. Exports from the middle, New England, and northern colonies to England were never large (relative to imports from Britain, or compared with exports from the southern colonies). At the beginning of the eighteenth century their exports were several times greater than exports from the Carolinas, but these colonies to the north of Maryland never found products, such as tobacco, rice or indigo, for which a large demand existed, or developed, in England. Their exports to England included bar and pig iron (mainly from Pennsylvania); potash and pearlash; staves; beeswax; lumber and masts (from New England); whale oil; fish (from New England and Newfoundland); and furs (especially from Quebec and Hudson's Bay). A few re-exports such as logwood, mahogany, and cotton largely made up the remainder of exports to England.

It is clear from Figure 3.2 that by the late colonial period exports from the colonies to Scotland were a sizable share of total exports to Great Britain. The Act of Union of 1707 had placed Scotland within the trading empire of Great Britain, and Scottish traders took advantage of this opportunity by stepping into the tobacco trade in Virginia and Maryland, especially in the Piedmont region into which tobacco growing was expanding during the eighteenth century.[3] From 1755 through 1774, the total official value of colonial exports to Scotland was 40 per cent of the official value of exports to England[4]. The great bulk of

---

[1] Exports of tobacco to Scotland, of course, increased in relative importance (see the discussion below). Also, see David Klingaman, 'The significance of grain in the development of the tobacco colonies,' *Journal of Economic History*, xxix, 2 (June 1969), pp. 268–78.

[2] Table 8.2.

[3] See Jacob M. Price, 'The rise of Glasgow in the Chesapeake tobacco trade, 1707–1775,' *William and Mary Quarterly*, 3rd Ser., xi (April 1954), pp. 179–99; and J. H. Soltow, 'Scottish traders in Virginia, 1750–1775,' *Economic History Review*, 2nd Series, xii, 1 (August 1959), pp. 83–98.

[4] The official value of colonial exports to Scotland was £7,170,574 in the Scottish customs records (Customs 14) for 1755 through 1774 (not including 1763 and 1769, the records for which are not in the Public Record Office). The official value of colonial exports to

these exports to Scotland (about 88 per cent) during the 1760s and early 1770s[1] was from the upper south. Tobacco, which comprised 83 per cent of the official value of colonial exports to Scotland in 1768 and 1770–2, rose from a quantity of 1 million pounds in 1708, the year after Union, to a peak of 47 million pounds in 1771.[2] Scotland's share of colonial tobacco exports to Great Britain rose from about 3 per cent in 1708 to 15 per cent during 1721–30 to almost 20 per cent from 1741 through 1747. This share had further climbed to nearly 30 per cent during 1752–60, and to over 45 per cent during the last ten years of the colonial period (1766–75).[3]

Although Scotland had obtained nearly a 30 per cent share of the export trade from the colonies to Great Britain by the mid-1750s, mainly by dominating the tobacco exports from the Piedmont regions, its share of the import trade never increased accordingly. The official value of imports from Scotland into the colonies was 11 per cent of the total official value of both the English and Scottish customs records for the period 1755–74[4] (this share was roughly constant over this period).

The composition of imports from Great Britain did not change significantly over the eighteenth century. Woolens, British and Irish linens, hardware and metal products of all sorts, along with re-exports from England, such as tea, spices, drugs, and German linens, dominated British exports to the colonies. The share of exports of British manufacture and re-exports in total exports also remained roughly constant over the century.[5]

THE TRADE OF THE COLONIES WITH SOUTHERN EUROPE AND THE WEST INDIES

Trade with southern Europe and the West Indies began in the middle of the seventeenth century, and by the end of the colonial period it had

England from the English customs records (Customs 3) is £17,882,571 (not including 1763 and 1769). The English values are for the thirteen colonies only. The Scottish figure includes exports from Canada, Newfoundland, St Johns Island, and Honduras totalling £101,293 for the years 1762 through 1774.

[1] The official value of exports to Scotland from Maryland and Virginia was £4,374,005 for 1762 through 1774 (not including 1763 and 1769). The Scottish records did not give a breakdown by colony for years earlier than 1762. This compares with the total official value of exports to Scotland from all colonies of £4,974,594 for these years.

[2] *Historical Statistics*, p. 766.   [3] *Ibid.*

[4] The official value of Scottish exports to the colonies was £4,655,104 for the years 1755 through 1774 (not including the missing years 1763 and 1769). This compares with the total official values of exports from England to the colonies of £37,559,690 for the same years.

[5] This was also true of exports from England to all overseas areas (see Elizabeth B. Schumpeter, *English Overseas Trade Statistics, 1697–1808* (Oxford: The Clarendon Press, 1960), pp. 15–16). Exports of English manufacture declined slightly from about 70 to 65 per cent of the total official value of English exports. In terms of actual values, however, they undoubtedly increased, since the prices of re-exports fell over the century, and prices of exports of British manufacture probably rose slightly up to the Revolution.

grown to sizable proportions (as shown in Chapter 6). Trade with these areas had particular importance for the colonial balance of payments because of the surpluses earned in these trades. The question which we would like to answer at this point is: How fast did these trades grow and what were the magnitudes involved? Unfortunately, only fragmentary evidence has survived regarding these trades prior to 1768. Appendix I describes this evidence and presents export data in Tables 1 and 2 for some of the more valuable commodities which comprised a substantial proportion of these trades (these data are given for years and ports for which records have survived).

If one is willing to assume that the relative values of commodities exported by each colony were roughly the same in earlier years as they were during 1768–72, then by such extrapolation we can suggest the total magnitudes of exports to these areas. On the basis of such calculations (see Appendix I for details), one would place colonial exports to southern Europe in the 1720s and 1730s at £50,000 to £60,000 per year, and exports to the West Indies in the range of £125,000 to £150,000 annually for these same decades. During the 1750s, exports to southern Europe probably averaged about £125,000 to £150,000, and £175,000 to £200,000 in the West Indian trade.

One must admit that such calculations are very rough, but probably they are not too high, and they do permit us to make the following statements about the colonial balance of payments in the earlier years of the eighteenth century. If one grants that invisible earnings would also have been earned by the colonists, it is probable that these trades produced surpluses of £150,000 or more in the 1720s and 1730s (assuming imports and invisibles bore roughly the same relation to exports that they did in 1768–72), and £250,000 or more by the 1750s.

THE COLONIAL BALANCE OF PAYMENTS
DURING THE EIGHTEENTH CENTURY

If one looks just at the official values of imports and exports, trade with England appears to have been very nearly balanced for the first decade of the century, and from 1711 through 1740, on the average, the colonies earned surpluses. Certain adjustments must be made, however, for the purposes of looking at the colonial balance of payments. Exports were over-valued by the official rates, and imports must be converted to C.I.F. values in the colonies. If exports are adjusted by a price index calculated from Bezanson's Philadelphia prices for tobacco, and imports are increased in value by 8 per cent (the costs of shipment and distribution from England, as suggested in Appendix II), the annual average adjusted figures by decade (in pounds sterling) are:

	Annual average exports	Annual average imports	Annual average deficit
1721–30	£442,000	£509,000	£67,000
1731–40	559,000	698,000	139,000
1741–50	599,000	923,000	324,000
1751–60	808,000	1,704,000	896,000
1761–70	1,203,000	1,942,000	739,000

These estimates can be compared with an average annual deficit of about £189,000 estimated by Nettels for the period 1698–1717 (which includes payments of £60,000 for slaves and indentured servants).[1] Clearly, the deficits were relatively small in the earlier years. From the official values in Figure 3.2 we can see that deficits from the English trade did not become consistent until 1745, and it was not until 1755 that they became relatively large. In 1755 exports declined, partly due to the loss of European markets (especially the French market for tobacco) at the beginning of the Seven Years' War. Imports rose sharply at this time, probably due to the war effort in the colonies.

If one considers the above magnitudes of the deficits in the English trade prior to 1745 and the debits due to the importation of slaves and indentured servants,[2] it seems likely that the surpluses earned in the southern European and West Indian trades, plus whatever expenditures were made by the British government in the colonies,[3] completely

---

[1] Curtis P. Nettels, *The Money Supply of the American Colonies before 1720* (New York: Augustus M. Kelley, 1964), Chapters 2 and 3. Nettels' estimate was intended to be a lower bound to the actual deficit, and pertained to the New England colonies, New York, Maryland, Virginia and South Carolina.

[2] From the estimates of annual average number of slaves imported given above (Table 3.1) and prices given by Nettels (*The Roots*, p. 419), it is possible to compute the estimated values of slaves imported into the thirteen colonies (Nettels' prices are cited on p. 141, note 2). Our estimates of slave prices for 1768–72 (see Table 8.3), however, indicate that Nettels' prices are probably too high. Accordingly, the following lower average prices have been used:

1700–40	£25
1741–50	30
1751–70	35

The estimated average annual values, by decade, of slaves imported into the thirteen colonies are thus:

1701–10	£28,000	1741–50	£69,000
1711–20	43,000	1751–60	156,000
1721–30	58,000	1761–70	155,000
1731–40	118,000		

Other debits were due to the immigration of indentured servants. Due to the lack of evidence, however, little more can be said about this factor. Nettels (*The Money Supply*, p. 52) puts this debit against Maryland and Virginia alone at £30,000 per year early in the eighteenth century. In view of the above evidence on white immigration, however, this figure is too high, especially before the years of heavier Scotch-Irish and German migration.

[3] These expenditures were made by Great Britain for the purposes of paying certain costs of civil government in the colonies and providing defense. See Nettels, *The Money Supply*, Chapter 7. The amount of these expenditures for earlier years is not known (see Chapter 8).

offset these deficits and that either no, or relatively small, capital inflows occurred from 1700 to 1745.

After 1745, the deficits became relatively large, but several factors must be remembered at this point. One is that trade with Scotland began to be important by 1745, and imports from Scotland were consistently less than exports to Scotland (see Figure 3.2). This surplus averaged about £45,000 annually from 1755 through 1760.[1] A small part of the increasing deficits to England would thus have been offset by surpluses in the Scottish trade. Second, defense expenditures by Great Britain in the colonies increased significantly after the War began, and these were high during wartime even in the early years of the century. Nettels, for example, states that Britain spent £414,000 on the defense of the commerce and the coast of the mainland colonies in the four years 1708–11.[2] Third, trade with southern Europe and the West Indies increased during these decades, and so did the surpluses earned in trade with these areas. These surpluses may well have been greater than the estimates of £250,000 to £300,000 made in Appendix 1. We conclude that no deficits, or relatively small ones, existed on the colonies' current account during the eighteenth century up to the Revolution. It appears that by the beginning of the eighteenth century the colonies (the thirteen colonies, at least) were economically self-sufficient. Both Britain and the colonies complemented each other in those goods which they produced, and both stood to gain from trade. The colonies apparently were not subsidized by Britain to any extent, with the important exception of the provision of defense, nor does British investment in the colonies appear to have been significant after 1700. Capital formation in the colonies was financed almost exclusively by domestic saving during the eighteenth century.

THE IMPORTANCE OF TRADE: EMPIRICAL FINDINGS

It is apparent that population grew more rapidly than exports to Great Britain during the eighteenth century. The annual average per capita values of exports to Britain (computed for five-year periods) fluctuate, but they do exhibit a downward trend.[3] When exports to southern Europe and the West Indies are added to exports to Britain, however, the resulting annual average per capita commodity export values indicate no clear trend:

[1] The total official value of exports to Scotland from the colonies during this period was £1,816,318, and the value of imports was £1,546,621 for this same period (Customs 14).
[2] Nettels, *The Money Supply*, p. 195.
[3] These values are based on the English official values plus the Scottish official values for 1758–62. Exports to Scotland for the earlier periods have been based upon tobacco exports to Scotland (*Historical Statistics*, p. 766). Exports for 1768–72 have been taken from Chapter 6. Population figures are from *Historical Statistics*, p. 756. These values pertain only to the thirteen colonies.

	To Great Britain	To all areas
1698–1702	£1.21	—
1708–12	0.97	—
1718–22	1.08	£1.40
1728–32	1.02	1.34
1738–42	0.89	1.14
1748–52	0.83	1.09
1758–62	0.69	0.89
1768–72	0.72	1.31

Thus the increased export earnings from the southern European and West Indian trades tended to offset the decline (relative to population) of exports to Britain.

Whether or not these per capita export values can be interpreted as meaning that overseas trade was of declining relative importance to the colonies during the eighteenth century depends upon levels of per capita output. If per capita output did not rise over the eighteenth century, then no such conclusion is justified. But if per capita output rose, as was suggested above, then overseas trade was a declining proportion of total economic activity over the century. If per capita output rose from levels of £8–9 at the beginning of the century to £11–12½ by the 1770s, then commodity exports as a percentage of total output declined from somewhere around 14–18 per cent at the beginning of the century to 11–12 per cent by the Revolution. When invisible earnings for 1768–72 (from Chapter 7) are added to earnings from commodity exports, then earnings from overseas trade rise to 14–15 per cent of total output. If invisible earnings were the same proportion of commodity trade at the beginning of the eighteenth century as they were during 1768–72, then total earnings from overseas trade would have been around 18–22 per cent of total output. Such percentages for the early eighteenth century, however, may overstate the proportion of total output accounted for by overseas trade because levels of per capita output may have been greater, or, as was probably the case, because invisible earnings were not as large relative to commodity trade at the beginning of the century. Nevertheless, the conclusion is inescapable that the proportion of colonial economic activity devoted to production for overseas markets was relatively large at the beginning of the eighteenth century, and, though it declined over the century, it remained a substantial portion of total output.

PATTERNS AND DEGREES OF REGIONAL SPECIALIZATION

As we pointed out in Chapter 2, an important effect of market forces was the significant degree of regional specialization that took place. Development in the colonies and the magnitudes of trade with overseas areas depended on such factors as geographical differences in the cost of production (which in turn depended upon a colony's particular resource endowments), transportation costs, and other costs of distribution, on the supply side; and, on the demand side, demand in overseas markets for colonial products, and demand in the colonies for imported goods.

The patterns of colonial trade discussed above gave rise to various patterns of regional specialization in the colonies. In general, these patterns reflected the comparative advantages held by the colonies in the production of various primary products. Newfoundland and Nova Scotia were exporting dried and pickled fish and whale oil; Quebec exported wheat and furs; New Hampshire's exports were mainly forest products; Massachusetts sold forest products, fish, and shipping and mercantile services to overseas areas; Connecticut, Rhode Island, and the middle colonies exported primarily foodstuffs, especially grains and grain products from New York and Pennsylvania, and invisible earnings were important to the latter two colonies; the exports of the upper south were dominated by tobacco, although wheat was increasing in importance in the later colonial period; naval stores came from the sandy pine forests of North Carolina along with some foodstuffs; rice, indigo, and deerskins from the back country were produced for export in South Carolina and Georgia; and, finally, the beginnings of rice and indigo exports were seen in Florida, which was only just beginning to be settled by the late colonial period.

This description of the patterns of regional specialization, however, lends little insight into the degree of such specialization in the various colonies. Per capita exports, by colony, can be estimated from the data underlying the estimates of exports for the period 1768–72 made in Chapter 6, and from the estimates of colonial population discussed above in this chapter. These estimates are presented in Table 3.2 and they suggest that overseas trade was of greatly varying importance to different regions and colonies by the late colonial period. As expected, the per capita values of commodity exports were relatively low from New England, somewhat higher from the middle colonies, and highest from the southern colonies.

Within each region, however, there were surprisingly large variations (with the exception of the upper south). New Jersey and North Carolina stand out as having had exceptionally low exports relative to their population. This result must be qualified to the extent that their products were exported from other colonies, as was to some degree the case (some North Carolina tobacco was said to have been exported from Virginia, and some commodities produced in east and west New Jersey were exported through New York and Philadelphia, respectively). Nevertheless, it would appear that the proportion of total output of these two colonies destined for overseas markets was low. It would also seem that plantation agriculture (if its existence can be indicated by a sizable slave-labor force) was not necessarily correlated with a heavy concentration of production for export markets, because at this time 35 per cent of North Carolina's population was black.

The other southern colonies, as noted above, did have relatively high per capita exports, but still there are noticeable differences. For example, the estimates for South Carolina and Georgia stand out as having been exceptionally high. Furthermore, if one views these exports relative only to the white population, this tendency is even more pronounced. Such a view is legitimate because the slave population's claim against output was essentially for a subsistence level of income. An examination of the coastal trade for this period shows that the southern colonies were self-sufficient in the production of foodstuffs,[1] so a large portion of this subsistence income must have been produced within each colony. For practical purposes, therefore, export earnings can be viewed as accruing to the free population. If this is done (as in Table 3.2), South Carolina, whose population was less than 40 per cent white in 1770, appears to have been heavily engaged in plantation agriculture, producing mainly rice and indigo for export. Indeed, export earnings per white resident come to more than three-quarters of the above conjectural estimate of per capita output for the late colonial period.

From these estimates, Newfoundland appears to have been the colony most heavily oriented to producing for overseas markets. Perhaps this is not so surprising; cod fishing was virtually the sole economic activity, and most foodstuffs and other necessities had to be imported. This estimate for Newfoundland must be qualified, however. Exports consisted mostly of dried cod to southern Europe (82 per cent of all Newfoundland's exports during this period went directly to southern European markets). The recorded exports may have included the catch of the west country fishermen from Britain in addition to that of the resident population. There is no way of knowing for certain (the source gives no indication), but probably the British catch was included because the cod were dried ashore. On the other hand, the source did state that these were exports from St Johns only; therefore, total exports from Newfoundland may have been even greater. Newfoundland stands in sharp contrast to Quebec, which, even with its fur trade, was below the average for all the colonies.

These estimates provide a rough indication of the degree of production for markets relative to subsistence production in the colonies. Because trade took place among the colonies, as well as within each colony, these estimates represent only a lower bound to the ratio of

---

[1] See Klingaman, 'Food surpluses', and Max G. Schumacher, 'The Northern Farmer and His Markets during the Late Colonial Period' (unpublished Ph.D. dissertation, Department of History, University of California, Berkeley, 1948).

market production to total output. Whether production for markets was less in colonies such as North Carolina and New Jersey depends, of course, upon the magnitudes of this intercolonial and intracolonial trade. Although there is little evidence about trade within each colony,

TABLE 3.2. *Average annual commodity exports of the British North American colonies, by colony and region, 1768–72* (pounds sterling)

	Total[a]	Per capita[b]	Per white resident
Newfoundland	131,000	11.47	—
Quebec	67,000	0.92	—
Nova Scotia	10,000	0.48	—
Northern colonies	208,000	1.98	—
New Hampshire	47,000	0.65	0.66
Massachusetts	265,000	0.99	1.01
Rhode Island	83,000	1.43	1.52
Connecticut	94,000	0.51	0.53
New England	489,000	0.84	0.86
New York	191,000	1.17	1.33
New Jersey	2,000	0.02	0.02
Pennsylvania	361,000	1.50	1.54
Delaware	18,000	0.51	0.53
Middle colonies	572,000	1.03	1.10
Maryland	398,000	1.96	2.87
Virginia	783,000	1.75	3.02
Upper south	1,181,000	1.82	2.97
North Carolina	76,000	0.39	0.60
South Carolina	463,000	3.73	9.44
Georgia	75,000	3.21	5.88
Lower south	614,000	1.78	3.24
Total, above colonies	3,064,000	1.37	—

Source: based on the detailed estimates by James F. Shepherd, 'Commodity exports from the British North American colonies to overseas areas, 1768–1772: magnitudes and patterns of trade,' *Explorations in Economic History*, VIII, 1 (Fall 1970), pp. 5–76.

[a]The total value of exports from each of the thirteen colonies and Nova Scotia was estimated in the same manner as exports from each region in Chapter 6. Because this method would have understated exports from Quebec, those commodities in the source for which values were computed were added to the estimated value of fur exports from Quebec in 1770 of £28,433 (*Historical Statistics*, p. 762). Also, because exports from Newfoundland were primarily codfish, the estimate of total exports from there was based only upon those commodities for which values were computed in the source.

[b]Population estimates for Newfoundland, Quebec, and Nova Scotia were based upon statements about early Canadian population found in Dominion Bureau of Statistics, Canada, *Seventh Census of Canada, 1931* (Ottawa, 1936), I, pp. 133–53. Newfoundland was said to have had 11,418 British residents in 1770 (*ibid.*, p. 143). The populations of Quebec and Nova Scotia *circa* 1770 were assumed to have been 72,500 and 21,000, respectively, in order that the total population for the three colonies approximate 105,000 (see *ibid.*, p. 100, and note 2, p. 33).

some does exist with regard to the coastal trade. Further research therefore will shed some light on this question. One can safely conclude at this point, however, that for some colonies (South Carolina and Newfoundland are the outstanding examples), production for overseas markets comprised a large proportion of total output.

CHAPTER 4

COLONIAL TRADE, DISTRIBUTION COSTS, AND PRODUCTIVITY CHANGE IN SHIPPING

At this point we examine the trades described in Chapter 3 and review the actual patterns of commerce that existed. Following this, we analyze the magnitudes of total costs of distribution incurred in these different trades. From this analysis we illustrate how these costs and their major component, shipping costs, changed over time, and how they helped shape the particular patterns of commerce.

The traditional description of colonial commerce found in nearly every textbook on the history of the American economy[1] portrays the southern colonies engaged in a direct shuttle-type trade with Great Britain, while the middle colonies and New England had more complex routes which were epitomized in the well-known triangles of trade. Traditionally, the picture of the southern trade is that of a basic transfer of southern staples (tobacco, rice, indigo, and naval stores) to Great Britain for manufactured commodities. One important exception was the direct trade of rice to southern Europe, which after 1730 normally amounted to roughly one-half the annual rice crop.

The more complex trade patterns of the middle colonies and New England are generally described as the famous triangles of trade. The most well-known triangle is the one from New England to Africa where rum and trinkets were exchanged for slaves; the slaves were then taken across the famous 'middle passage' to the West Indies where they were traded for sugar, molasses, coin, and bills of exchange; and on the final leg returned to New England where the molasses was manufactured into rum, thus allowing the cycle to be repeated. Another famous triangle was the shipment of foodstuffs and wood products from the middle colonies or New England to the West Indies. These goods were exchanged there for sugar and other tropical and semi-tropical goods,

---

[1] Too many sources exist to list them all here, but for example see Dudley Dillard, *Economic Development of the North Atlantic Community* (Englewood Cliffs, N.J.: Prentice-Hall, Inc., 1967), pp. 197–8; Ross M. Robertson, *History of the American Economy* (2nd ed.; New York: Harcourt, Brace & World, Inc., 1964), pp. 80–1; Robert C. Albion, 'Colonial Commerce and Regulation,' *The Growth of the American Economy*, Harold F. Williamson (ed.) (2nd ed.; Englewood Cliffs, N.J.: Prentice-Hall, Inc., 1951), pp. 50–1; Edward Kirkland, *A History of American Economic Life*, (4th ed.; New York: Appleton-Century-Crofts, Inc., 1969), pp. 65–9; or Chester W. Wright, *Economic History of the United States* (New York: McGraw-Hill, Inc., 1941), pp. 153–4.

which were then carried to England where they were sold to buy manufactures for the return voyage (or sometimes the ship was sold in England). Lastly, a ship might carry fish, wheat, and wood products to southern Europe to be exchanged for wine, salt, fruits, and cash; then sail to England to exchange these for manufactures; and return to the colonies.

Also common in the literature about New England commerce is the irregular pattern of voyages undertaken. The New England shipper is generally portrayed as a 'jack-of-all-trades' type who frequently switched among routes in search of trade. Supposedly, his was 'a peddling and huckstering business, involving an enormous amount of petty detail, frequent exchanges, and a constant lading and unlading as the captains and masters moved from port to port.'[1] One contemporary observer, Benjamin Franklin, speaking to a Parliamentary committee in 1766, mentioned the 'circuitous voyages' of Pennsylvania merchants.[2]

A recent quantitative analysis of colonial commerce indicates that this traditional view of the shipping activity of New England and the middle colonies is incorrect, either in emphasis or in fact.[3] For instance, out of the annual average of 107,285 tons that cleared New England, 1768–72, only 1,023 of these tons were destined for Africa – less than 1 per cent of the total.[4] This route was even less important to the middle colonies. The attention typically given to the African route has resulted in a significant distortion of the descriptions of the commerce of these regions.

It is also apparent that the triangle between either New England or the middle colonies, the West Indies and Great Britain did not engage many colonial vessels. Out of hundreds of vessels which have been traced from New England and the middle colonies to Barbados and Jamaica and outward from these islands, only a few departed to Great Britain.[5]

The third triangle most often described was the one from New England or the middle colonies to southern Europe, Great Britain, and the return. The existence of this triangle cannot explicitly be subjected to a test because the necessary evidence is lacking. However,

---

[1] Charles M. Andrews, 'Colonial commerce,' *American Historical Review*, xx (October 1914), reprinted in *Readings in United States Economic and Business History*, eds. Ross M. Robertson and James L. Pate (Boston: Houghton Mifflin Company, Inc., 1966), p. 137.

[2] Quoted from Harold U. Faulkner, *American Economic History* (8th ed.; New York: Harper & Brothers, Publishers, 1960), p. 81.

[3] Gary M. Walton, 'New evidence on colonial commerce,' *Journal of Economic History*, xxviii, 3 (September 1968), pp. 363–89.

[4] *Ibid.*, p. 366. The relative unimportance of the African route is also supported by the evidence of commodity trade in Chapter 6 as well as the tonnage of vessels clearing to overseas areas given in Table 7.2.

[5] *Ibid.*, p. 371.

the close similarity of the clearances and entries (shown in Table 7.2, Chapter 7, for 1768–72) between both New England and the middle colonies and southern Europe supports our hypothesis that a shuttle pattern prevailed.

In general, the emphasis given to these triangular trades appears unwarranted. Although New England and middle colonial shippers frequently undertook multilateral voyages, the available evidence suggests that shuttle patterns and route specialization were more common to these shippers than were multilateral routes and route switching.[1]

Another important characteristic of colonial commerce and shipping was the division of ownership on different routes. In general, British-owned shipping dominated the routes between Great Britain and the southern colonies, as well as between Britain and the West Indies, whereas colonial-owned ships outnumbered those of British ownership in intercolonial trade and on routes between the colonies and most overseas areas other than the British Isles.[2]

These aspects of colonial commerce were determined primarily by the relative costs of providing marketing and shipping services. Of particular importance were the high risks encountered, the difficulties of acquiring and responding to information about changing market conditions, and the relatively high costs of labor. These factors also determined, in part, the particular forms of business arrangements of the period.

The marketing and shipping of goods were often undertaken by one merchant, and they were not separate and distinct operations as they usually are today. As Nettels states:

> The freighting and marketing of goods in those days were simply aspects of a single operation, and freights and profits were frequently indistinguishable. Often a merchant owner shipped his goods in his own vessel. Other traders dispatched consignments to designated ports, paying the freight to the owner. By a third method, a group of merchants chartered a vessel, in whole or in part, paying a monthly charge determined by the space hired rather than by the quantity of the goods shipped and the length of the voyage.[3]

The methods of marketing were principally of two types: consignments to ship captains who would sell, trade, and buy goods for the merchant;

[1] *Ibid.*, pp. 382–3.

[2] *Ibid.*, pp. 369–71. The exception to this was the British dominance of the route between the lower south and southern Europe. Colonial-owned ships were dominant between Great Britain and New England and the middle colonies, however.

[3] Curtis P. Nettels, *The Money Supply of the American Colonies Before 1720* (Madison, Wis.: University of Wisconsin Studies in the Social Sciences and History, No. 20, October 1934), p. 70.

and consignment to factors located in the markets who would make the transactions. Merchants were highly dependent on their factors or ship captains, the person to whom the consignment was made. This dependency of merchants on their selling agents and the concomitant degree of risk involved explain in part why colonial merchants favored colonial ships and colonial ship captains. The greater the familiarity between merchant and agent, the lower the risks of trade. Consequently, the frequency of contact and the speed of communications between merchants and their marketing agents partially determined the degree of risk, and thus importantly entered into the costs of trade over various routes.

Nearness to market was important because of the rudimentary forms of communication and transportation. For instance, in the tobacco trade New England shippers could not acquire information on the changing conditions in both markets (the southern colonies and Europe) as easily and as efficiently as British shippers and merchants were able to acquire it. On the other hand, in the West Indies–New England trade colonial shippers and merchants were closer to the market and could respond more quickly to market fluctuations. This type of flexibility was fundamental in permitting some shippers and merchants lower risks and reduced costs of information than their competitors.[1]

Finally, crews on board British vessels remained on board and were paid while in colonial ports.[2] They were dispersed only at the end of the voyage, after returning to Great Britain. Likewise, colonial shippers were able to discharge their crews upon returning to the home port. This significantly reduced total labor costs since the times generally spent in port were of lengthy duration. For instance, British crews were paid for the time at sea and the time spent in port in the southern colonies. Colonial shippers (except those resident in the southern colonies) faced larger labor costs over this route since wages had to be paid for the time spent in port in Great Britain, as well as the time at sea and in the Chesapeake. For analogous reasons, colonial shippers had lower labor costs than British shippers on routes between their home ports and the Caribbean.

For similar reasons, specialized routes and shuttle patterns, rather

---

[1] Michael Atkins, a British shipowner, in a letter to the Philadelphia merchant, John Reynell, in 1751 stated: 'Traders at the Northern Colonies have all the West India business to themselves, Europeans can have no encouragement for mixing with them in the commodities of provisions and lumber. You time things better than we and go to market cheaper.' See Richard Pares, *Yankees and Creoles* (London: Longmans, Green & Co., 1956), p. 8.

[2] With rare exceptions, seamen were hired by the voyage out and return. See Ralph Davis, *The Rise of the English Shipping Industry* (London: Macmillan & Co., 1962), p. 116, or the many wage contracts among the records of the High Court of Admiralty, Public Record Office, London.

than multilateral or triangular patterns of trade, were the dominant characteristics of shipping movements. It is true that efforts were made to keep vessels as fully loaded as possible, but in moving from port to port to do so, there were large and offsetting costs. For instance, with respect to the West Indies trade, where a ship's captain typically was the selling agent, one of the objectives of the master was to locate the best markets for the particular commodities he carried. To achieve this goal might require several voyages among the islands. Also, difficulties of agreeing on prices and the medium of exchange to be used, as well as the problem of settling past debts, all lengthened the period required for transactions. If bartering was the means of transaction, or there were various media of exchange used, prices were especially difficult to determine. Facing such difficulties, ships did not generally venture where trade was unfamiliar, for this would result in lengthy port time, which was an important form of under-utilization. Clearly, the problems of making transactions were difficult enough, even for merchants and captains who were familiar with each other. The risks of default were great and credit facilities were limited. Also, because of poor communications it was easy to misread unfamiliar markets. Given these many problems, it is understandable why it was exceptional for a vessel to vary from its regular run between a limited number of regions.[1]

Lastly, the practice of discharging crews while in the home port made shuttle rather than multilateral patterns more favorable. Shuttle patterns resulted in an increase in the percentage of port time spent in the home port. This reduced the overall costs of port time, and, of course, total costs.

DISTRIBUTION COSTS: SOME EXAMPLES AND MAGNITUDES

In view of the dramatic increase in trade, were solutions to the above types of problems found which had a favorable effect on the growth of an Atlantic trading community? Did the costs of distribution, such as transportation, packaging, inventory, and other transactions costs, decline? By how much did they decline? How important were these reductions? What caused them, and what was their significance?

Although the growth of trade was substantial, not all goods could be efficiently exchanged within a market system. The reason was that for many goods and services the benefits from exchange did not exceed the costs of trade; in other words, the costs of production plus distribu-

---

[1] English vessels generally engaged in little tramping and remained on regular runs 'simply because among their most valuable assets were the master's and owners' connections in particular ports overseas.' See Davis, pp. 196–7. For more supporting evidence and information on the risks of colonial trade, see Stuart Bruchey, 'Success and failure factors: American merchants in foreign trade in the eighteenth and early nineteenth centuries,' *Business History Review*, XXXII, 3 (Autumn 1958), pp. 272–92.

tion were greater than the revenues that could be received from selling them in the market. The benefits of using the market stem primarily from productivity advances due to specialization based on comparative advantages in certain types of production, the division of labor and economies of large-scale production, or some combination of these.[1] The degree of specialization depends, of course, upon the extent of the market, which is limited by distribution costs. In some cases, even where lower production costs could be obtained through specialization these gains may be precluded by prohibitively high distribution costs.

As stated in Chapter 2, these costs of distribution may be looked upon as the total differential between a producer's selling price and the price paid by the consumer. For purposes of illustration we will focus upon transactions in overseas trade and use the term 'total differential' to refer to the difference between the wholesale price of a commodity in the colonies and the price in an overseas market. Although shipping costs were typically the largest part of this differential (except for tariffs on a few commodities), other types of distribution costs such as inventory costs, insurance, commission and handling charges, and the costs of other functions performed by merchants, made up an important share of the total differential. Reductions of these costs had the same effects on trade and development as did reductions of transportation costs.

It is important to keep in mind that eighteenth-century markets functioned quite imperfectly in the economic sense. If we define a market for a particular good as a collection of buyers and sellers (actual or potential) of that good, the degree of imperfection of the market is determined at any given time by the degree of price variance among regions, not including transportation and other distribution costs. There is abundant evidence which indicates that prices varied in different areas by more than can be explained by differences in these costs.[2] This imperfection in markets can be explained primarily by high information costs about prices and changing market conditions. For instance, our heritage of colonial merchants' accounts and correspondence shows sharp fluctuations of prices as ships arrived with cargoes. They also reveal the continuous exchange of information about market conditions, prices, and expectations. As stated above, supply response to changes in demand was hindered by uncertainty, slow communica-

[1] For a discussion of the effects of trade on growth, see Chapter 2. The benefits of exchange are well illustrated in Charles P. Kindleberger, *International Economics* (3rd ed.; Homewood, Ill.: Richard D. Irwin, Inc., 1963), Chapters 5 and 6.

[2] In discussing the West Indian trade, Herbert C. Bell states: 'Thanks to the smallness of the islands and their extreme dependence on outside supplies, any kind of American produce was apt to command very different prices in any two of them at the same time. For the same reasons prices fell and rose sharply with the arrival of fresh consignments or the nonappearance of those expected.' 'The West India trade before the American Revolution,' *American Historical Review*, XXII, 2 (January 1917), p. 284.

tion, and incomplete information on the part of buyers and sellers. These made for high costs of information and a greater degree of risk for market participants than would otherwise have existed.[1] In general, these costs acted as a natural barrier, or tariff, to trade. The differential between the producer's selling price and the overseas price, which included the risks associated with imperfect markets, narrowed the possibilities for engaging in trade, and increased self-sufficient economic activities.

Merchants' accounts which have survived the passage of time provide some evidence on the numerous charges incurred in trade. Some of the explicit charges given in these accounts are illustrated in Tables 4.1

TABLE 4.1.   *Accounts of sales, charges and net proceeds on 252 barrels of pitch in London, 1775*

	£	s.	d.
Gross sales	203	9	6
Freight	71	17	6
Primage	2	1	8
Pierage	1	3	5
Duty	11	9	0
Sufferance and duplicate	0	3	6
Landwaiters and weighers	1	10	0
Oath	0	1	0
Weighers and henekens	0	2	0
Post entry on two barrels	0	3	0
Land Surveyors for certificate	1	5	0
Passing certificate in the custom house	1	1	0
Clerk at the Navy office	0	2	6
Heneken for wharfage	4	4	0
$\frac{1}{4}$ discount allowed as per agreement and custom	2	10	10
Brokerage for attendance at weighing and making entries at 1%	2	6	0
Commission on gross sales at $2\frac{1}{2}$%	5	1	8
Total charges	105	2	1
Net proceeds	98	7	5

Source: Account and Invoice Book, Wallace, Davidson and Johnson, Maryland Hall of Records, Annapolis, Maryland.

[1] For instance, letters from the colonies to London typically took two months for delivery and adding to this the time needed to respond to the described market conditions (of two months earlier), the total time response must surely have been $3\frac{1}{2}$ to 4 months at a minimum. During this time conditions could sharply change and turn a profitable venture into a failure. It is difficult to say anything very explicit about changes in information costs over the colonial period. Ship speeds did not increase over the period, but the speed of communications probably increased somewhat, due to an increased number of ships moving between various locations and an increased regularity in vessel movements. Besides the increased regularity and volume of ships, a greater number of merchants in trade centers plus a growing understanding of trade and the art of doing business in colonial markets probably resulted in more and better information and reduced the risks of trade. It is impossible to assess quantitatively how important these improvements were, however. For a description of the many difficulties facing eighteenth-century merchants, see W. T. Baxter, *The House of Hancock* (Cambridge, Mass.: Harvard University Press, 1945), especially Chapters 11 and 16.

TABLE 4.2.   *Accounts of sales, charges and net proceeds on 617½ quarters of wheat and 79 barrels of flour in London, 1775*

	£	s.	d.
Gross sales 200 quarters of wheat at £2 10s. 0d. per qtr.	500	0	0
417½ quarters of wheat at £2 8s. 0d. per qtr.	990	6	0
79 barrels of flour at 16s. per cwt.	128	5	10
Total gross sales	1,618	11	10
Freight on wheat	247	0	0
Freight on flour	19	15	0
Primage	5	5	0
Duty on 617½ qtrs. of wheat at 6d. per qtr.	15	8	9
Entry and fees	1	15	6
Meters bill into lighter on wheat	10	13	7
Lighterage, screening, turning and delivery on wheat	10	4	2
Duty on flour	1	7	0
Entry and officers landing and attendance	0	10	6
Lighterage, lading, weighing and delivery of flour	3	12	5
Cooper bill paid	0	5	6
Brokerage on wheat	30	12	6
Brokerage on flour	3	4	0
Commission on gross sales at 2½%	40	9	4
Total charges	390	3	3
Net proceeds	1,228	8	7

Source: see Table 4.1.

TABLE 4.3.   *The charges of purchasing, transporting and marketing one hogshead of tobacco from Maryland to London, 1737*

	£	s.	d.
Purchase of one hogshead (790 pounds net) at 1½d. per pound (in Maryland)	4	18	9
British duties[a]	16	18	2
Maryland export duty	0	2	9
Freight	1	15	0
Primage and petty charges	0	2	1
To entry inwards etc.	0	1	6
To entry outwards etc.	0	2	0
To cooperage etc.	0	2	0
To porterage etc.	0	1	0
To warehouse rent	0	3	6
To brokerage	0	2	0
To postage of letters	0	1	0
To drafts (4 pounds of tobacco)	0	0	9
To loss of weight (allowing 14 pounds for natural loss on shipboard 44 pounds of tobacco)	0	8	3
To commission of 2½% on duties and on selling price	0	12	0
Total charges	20	12	0
Total value in London	25	10	9

Source: Lewis C. Gray, *History of Agriculture in the Southern United States to 1860* (Washington, D.C.: Carnegie Institution of Washington, 1933), 1, p. 224.

[a] British duties were rebated upon re-export from England and would not be included in the total differential between the planter's price and the buyer's price on the continent. Any foreign duties on tobacco would have to be added, however.

through 4.3. These charges do not reflect the complete difference between the planter's selling price and that paid by British or European merchants. The net proceeds item is the payment for the product inclusive of colonial inventory costs, packaging, insurance, and the returns to the colonial merchant for his services and assumption of risk. Consequently, these explicit charges understate total distribution costs.

Of course, the importance of the total differential varied significantly among commodities. It was generally a larger percentage of the value of low-valued, high-bulk items, as were most colonial exports, and a smaller percentage of expensive, low-bulk wares, such as manufactured goods imported from Britain. From Table 4.1 we see that for pitch the explicit charges alone amounted to more than one-half the value of gross sales, and these charges on wheat and flour (Table 4.2) were approximately one-quarter of gross sales. Table 4.3 indicates that these charges (not including English duties) were over 75 per cent of the cost of a hogshead of tobacco in the colonies in 1737. From the accounts of Wallace, Davidson and Johnson, an Annapolis firm exporting tobacco in 1774, we see that charges (exclusive of English duty) averaged 64 per cent of the net proceeds received by the colonial consignee of this tobacco.[1] If these were typical cases, this indicates some improvement in the marketing of tobacco over this period. At any rate, colonial exports were generally of high bulk in relation to their value (like the above items), and the explicit charges on these examples are probably a reasonable indication of similar charges on most of the major exports.

An alternative lower bound estimate of the total differential can be obtained by a comparison of the total value of services in trade to the value of imported goods. For instance, for each trade, it is possible to construct a ratio of the value of invisible earnings to the wholesale value of commodities.[2] For 1768, invisible earnings on exports as a percentage of their value in the overseas market were 24 per cent in the trade to Great Britain and Ireland, 30 per cent in the trade with southern Europe, and 35 per cent in the West Indian trade.[3]

Because most imports were typically low-bulk (relative to their

---

[1] Tobacco Sales Book, Wallace, Davidson and Johnson, Maryland Hall of Records, Annapolis, Maryland.

[2] This ratio is $T_i/(E_i + T_i)$ or T_i/I_i where:
    $T_i = S_i + N_i + P_i = $ total invisible earnings on the ith route;
    $S_i = $ total earnings on shipping services (colonial and English) on the ith route;
    $N_i = $ insurance costs on the ith route;
    $P_i = $ mercantile profits on the ith route;
    $E_i = $ value of exports (value F.O.B.) on the ith route;
    $I_i = $ value of imports (value C.I.F.) on the ith route.

[3] The values of exports are given in Chapter 6, and total invisible earnings can be derived from the estimates in Chapter 7. S can be derived by taking freight rates times ship tons times rates of utilization, and P and N are given for each route.

value), the total differential on imports was less, particularly on the trade from Great Britain and Ireland. In the import trade from Great Britain and Ireland in 1768, the transactions costs were probably in the neighborhood of 8 per cent of the colonial wholesale price.[1] In the West Indies and southern Europe trades they were approximately 27 per cent and 62 per cent, respectively. Transactions costs were a more important share of the final delivered price on these imports because, like colonial exports, they tended to be of low value relative to their bulk. It is important to note that these mark-ups do not reflect observed differences in actual wholesale prices. Most colonial importers and merchants engaged in a combination of retail and wholesale market activities, and it is doubtful that colonial wholesale prices on imports from overseas areas can be clearly distinguished from retail prices, after allowing for merchant profits. Nonetheless, the above measures of the total differentials are definitely lower bound measures.

These measures strongly suggest that the costs of distribution were high relative to the costs of production in 1768. Evidence on earlier periods indicates that distribution costs were relatively higher before 1768. For example, in the first decades of the 1700s, Nettels states: 'Reports from New England stated that the price of English goods there was between 150 and 225 per cent higher than in England; while at New York it was commonly said that foreign goods at twice their English prices were considered cheap.'[2] Probably such statements referred to the retail prices of English goods in the colonial currency, which would have included the exchange differential between New England currencies and sterling, as well as the mark-up of the colonial merchant (after adjusting for the exchange differential, these colonial prices were 80 to 140 per cent higher than in England). Such mark-ups tended to be substantial. J. H. Soltow has suggested that Scottish traders in Virginia priced goods which cost £100 sterling in Britain at £175 in Virginia currency during the late colonial period (this included an exchange differential of between 15 to 25 per cent as well as freight and other charges).[3] Adjusting for the exchange differentials, this would suggest that British goods were selling at prices from 40 to 50 per cent higher in Virginia than their cost in Britain. Evidence from a Philadelphia merchant's accounts from 1748 to 1750 suggests he was selling British goods in Pennsylvania currency for two-and-a-half to

---

[1] The values of imports are given in Chapter 6, and in the English trade we have used the mark-ups given in Appendix 11 to estimate *T*. In the import trade from the West Indies and southern Europe, shipping earnings, insurance, and mercantile profits derivable from Chapter 7 are used to estimate *T* for each respective route. These measures are extremely rough and indicate little more than a general order of magnitude.

[2] Curtis P. Nettels, 'England's trade with New England and New York, 1685–1720,' *Publications of the Colonial Society of Massachusetts*, 28 (February 1933), p. 326.

[3] J. H. Soltow, 'Scottish traders in Virginia, 1750–1775,' *Economic History Review*, XII, 1 (August 1959), p. 93.

three times (the average probably being closer to three) their sterling cost to him.[1] Again adjusting for the exchange differential, this suggests that he was selling British goods from 45 to 75 per cent higher than their sterling cost to him. If the statements about the earlier eighteenth century are correct, the evidence suggests that the distribution costs from the British manufacturer to the colonial consumer declined substantially during the century.

It is possible to view an overall trend in the costs of distribution for tobacco, at least, by comparing tobacco prices in Philadelphia with those in Amsterdam. By the use of exchange rates and prices given in the sources to Figure 4.1,[2] it is possible to convert Philadelphia and Amsterdam prices to English sterling price equivalents for Virginia

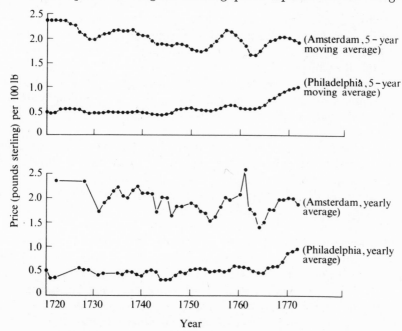

Figure 4.1. A comparison of Amsterdam and Philadelphia tobacco prices, 1720–72. Source: N. W. Posthumus, *Inquiry into the History of Prices in Holland* (Leiden: E. J. Brill, 1946), I, pp. 202–3 and 597–602, and Anne Bezanson, *et al., Prices in Colonial Pennsylvania* (Philadelphia: University of Pennsylvania Press, 1935), pp. 422 and 432. (See note 2 below.)

[1] Samuel Powel, Jr, Invoice and Day Book, 1748–50, The Historical Society of Pennsylvania (Philadelphia, Pennsylvania).

[2] Philadelphia prices of leaf tobacco and exchange rates between Pennsylvania currency and English sterling are given in Anne Bezanson, *et al., Prices in Colonial Pennsylvania* (Philadelphia: University of Pennsylvania Press, 1935), pp. 422 and 432, respectively. Amsterdam prices of Virginia leaf tobacco are given in N. W. Posthumus, *Inquiry into the History of Prices in Holland* (Leiden: E. J. Brill, 1946), I, pp. 202–3. Rates of exchange between schellingen and English sterling are given in *Ibid.*, pp. 597–602 for the years 1722–72, and 20 schellingen equalled 6 guilden (*Ibid.*, p. liv).

leaf tobacco. Figure 4.1 shows the differences between Amsterdam and Philadelphia prices, and clearly shows the convergence of tobacco prices between these areas. For each five-year period, the average difference between the Amsterdam and Philadelphia price as a percentage of the Amsterdam price was:

1720–4	82%	1750–4	67%
1725–9	76%	1755–9	72%
1730–4	82%	1760–4	70%
1735–9	77%	1765–9	65%
1740–4	77%	1770–4	51%
1745–9	76%		

This evidence clearly indicates that substantial improvements in distribution occurred in the tobacco trade during the eighteenth century.

Although the costs of using the market were still quite high on the eve of the Revolution, these barriers to trade were declining and were much less than in earlier decades. Additional independent evidence on shipping costs supports the conclusion that distribution costs fell dramatically over the one-hundred-year period preceding American Independence.

By piecing together rates from published and primary sources, seven series of freight rates have been constructed: wine, southern Europe to London (1640–1783); sugar, Barbados to London and Jamaica to London (1678–1717); tobacco, Chesapeake to London (1630–1775); oil, Boston to London (1700–74); bullion, New York to London (1699–1789); and flour, New York to Jamaica (1699–1768). Except for the sugar rates in Table 4.4 below, these rates are given in Appendix III and provide the basis for an analysis of productivity change in overseas shipping. The decline in rates varied among routes, but the general downward trend was unquestionable and suggests that freight costs fell by approximately one-half over the hundred years 1675–1775. These reductions in shipping costs were real gains to market participants and not part of a general price decline. They resulted from productivity advances in shipping. It is important to measure carefully how much productivity change occurred in shipping over the period, because as stated above, shipping costs were the most important part of total distribution costs.

MEASURES OF PRODUCTIVITY CHANGE

Total factor productivity change is the rate of change of physical output per unit of inputs with each input appropriately weighted. To state this algebraically, let

P_Q = price of the output

Q = quantity of the output

P_K = price of capital

K = quantity of capital

P_L = price of labor

L = quantity of labor.

The fundamental identity that the value of output is equal to the value of inputs for each accounting period is given as:

$$P_Q Q = P_K K + P_L L. \tag{1}$$

By differentiating (1) with respect to time and dividing both sides of the equation by total value we can show the identity of the growth of output price and quantity and the weighted average of the growth of input prices and quantities:

$$\frac{\dot{P}_Q}{P_Q} + \frac{\dot{Q}}{Q} = \alpha\left(\frac{\dot{P}_K}{P_K} + \frac{\dot{K}}{K}\right) + \beta\left(\frac{\dot{P}_L}{P_L} + \frac{\dot{L}}{L}\right), \tag{2}$$

where dots denote time derivatives and α and β are the base year shares of total costs of capital and labor respectively.

Useful indexes of input changes and input price changes can be derived from (2). These are, respectively:

$$\frac{\dot{I}}{I} = \alpha\frac{\dot{K}}{K} + \beta\frac{\dot{L}}{L} \tag{2a}$$

and

$$\frac{\dot{P}_I}{P_I} = \alpha\frac{\dot{P}_K}{P_K} + \beta\frac{\dot{P}_L}{P_L}, \tag{2b}$$

where I is the index of inputs (K and L weighted by their respective base year prices) and P_I is the index of input prices (P_K and P_L weighted respectively by the base year shares of capital and labor in total costs). Total factor productivity, P, is the ratio of the quantity of output to the quantity of total inputs:

$$P = \frac{Q}{I}; \tag{3}$$

and total factor productivity change is the rate of growth of P:

$$\frac{\dot{P}}{P} = \frac{\dot{Q}}{Q} - \frac{\dot{I}}{I} = \frac{\dot{Q}}{Q} - \alpha\frac{\dot{K}}{K} - \beta\frac{\dot{L}}{L}. \tag{3a}$$

A partial measure of productivity change would be $\frac{\dot{Q}}{Q} - \frac{\dot{K}}{K}$ for output changes per unit of capital and $\frac{\dot{Q}}{Q} - \frac{\dot{L}}{L}$ for output changes per unit of labor. Such measures, however, have limited usefulness, and we shall employ a total factor productivity measure.

It should be emphasized that to use price weights in (3a) necessarily assumes competition in the industry. It is also a necessary assumption for the measures used below. While market imperfections did exist, the large flows of tonnage and movement of vessels with a wide dispersion of ownership give the strong impression that the industry was competitive. This is true both in the sale of shipping services (the product market) and in the purchase of capital and hire of labor (the factor market) by shippers.

Unfortunately, data limitations often prevent such a measure (3a) of total factor productivity and this is the case for shipping in the colonial period. However, an alternative measure is to compare output price, our freight rates, to an index of shipping input prices (weighted by the input's share of total shipping costs).[1] In this form:

$$P = \frac{P_I}{P_Q},\tag{4}$$

and the rate of growth of P is:[2]

$$\frac{\dot{P}}{P} = \frac{\dot{P}_I}{P_I} - \frac{\dot{P}_Q}{P_Q}.\tag{4a}$$

It should be noted that if input (factor) prices do not change, changes in undeflated rates appropriately measure the productivity change that occurred.

---

[1] For a discussion of this method of estimating total factor productivity change, see Dale Jorgenson, 'The embodiment hypothesis,' *Journal of Political Economy*, LXXIV, 1 (February 1966), pp. 1–17.

[2] Another possible alternative measure is to compare freight rates with the general price level. The justification for this is the expectation that changes in the general price level will mirror the trend of input prices in the industry. If this can be accepted, this alternative of P is

$$P = \frac{P_G}{P_Q},$$

where P_G is an index of the general price level and the rate of growth of P is

$$\frac{\dot{P}}{P} = \frac{\dot{P}_G}{P_G} - \frac{\dot{P}_Q}{P_Q}.$$

Although we need not rely on this somewhat crude measure, the best major index of English prices indicates that although the general level of prices fluctuated, the trend is neither up nor down, between 1675 and 1775 (certainly this is true for the particular beginning and ending dates for the time series being considered); thus freight rate declines were due to productivity gains rather than monetary effects. See B. R. Mitchell and Phyllis Deane, *Abstract of British Historical Statistics* (London: Cambridge University Press, 1962), pp. 468–9; or the foldout sheet presenting this index in Phyllis Deane and W. A. Cole, *British Economic Growth, 1688–1959* (London: Cambridge University Press, 1964); and the discussion of eighteenth-century prices in Appendix II.

The use of undeflated rates appears to give a lower bound measure. Although the input prices of seamen's wages remained steady,[1] as did the costs of ship repair and maintenance,[2] other input prices moved upward between 1675 and 1775. These other costs which rose are shipbuilding costs and victualling costs, but the specific effects of these rising input prices on our productivity measures will be treated more thoroughly below. For the present, we will attempt to measure productivity change by assuming that no input prices rose; thus, we obtain lower bound measures by the use of undeflated rates, and then we can adjust these measures upward by including the effects of rising input prices in the final estimates.

The use of undeflated freight rates is not free of difficulties and problems of interpretation. Caution is required because of commercial practices in the colonies and the way the freight charge was levied. Freight rates were generally expressed as a charge per 'ton', but the 'ton' by custom usually meant a particular number of hogsheads, or barrels, or bundles, and these units changed in weight and size over the period. Consequently, a shipping ton of fish did not necessarily equal a shipping ton of flour, or sugar, or hemp. Therefore, freight series must not include different goods, even though the term 'ton' is explicitly specified as the unit. Moreover, as these units changed over time, a shipping ton of a particular good in an early period no longer equalled this same ton as time passed. For instance, an average hogshead of tobacco doubled in weight and increased in volume over the period. Nevertheless, the freight charge remained at four hogsheads to a ton. Consequently, the actual changes in the costs of shipment differed from those expressed by the nominal freight rates. It is only by combining the changes in the nominal rates with the changes in the weights (or volume) of the various items that made up the shipping ton that the actual effective change in costs can be determined.

---

[1] Wartime fluctuations aside, the peacetime wages of able seamen remained unchanged at 25s. per month from the end of the seventeenth century to American Independence; see Davis, *The Rise of the English Shipping Industry* (London: Macmillan & Co., 1962), p. 137. Corroborating evidence is given in G. M. Walton, 'A Quantitative Study of American Colonial Shipping' (unpublished Ph.D. dissertation, University of Washington, 1966), pp. 156–7.
[2] Davis, p. 370.

LOWER BOUND MEASURES OF
PRODUCTIVITY CHANGE BY ROUTE

The series of freight rates given in Appendix III indicate the decline in the nominal peacetime rates. Bullion rates (New York to London, 1699–1789) fell by one-half over the eighteenth century, thus implying that shipping became 100 per cent more productive over this route.[1] Freight rates on flour (New York to Jamaica, 1699–1768) fell from an average of between £5 and £5 10s. per ton near the turn of the century to between £3 17s. 6d. and £4 10s. per ton by the mid-1720s. By the late 1760s this rate was £3 10s. These figures suggest an increase in productivity on this route of somewhere between 43 per cent and 57 per cent, or an average of 50 per cent, in about seventy years. The peacetime rates on oil (Boston to London, 1700–74) declined from between £3 10s. and £4 per ton in 1700–1 to between £2 and £2 10s. per ton just prior to the Revolution. This decline indicated a change in productivity for this route ranging between 60 per cent and 75 per cent, or an average increase of approximately 67 per cent, in seventy-four years. Likewise, the rates on wine (southern Europe to London, 1640–1783) were approximately £2 10s. to £3 10s. per ton in the seventeenth century, while by the late eighteenth century this rate had fallen to between £1 10s. and £2 per ton. This decline suggests an average increase in productivity of approximately 71 per cent in a little more than a century.

These series of nominal freight rates were expressed as a charge per ton (the bullion series excepted) where the ton of flour equalled sixteen half-barrels, the ton of oil equalled eight barrels, and the ton of wine equalled two pipes. It is assumed that these units did not change in weight or size. For instance, if the weight of the half-barrel of flour had increased, the effective cost of shipment on flour would have fallen by more than the decline indicated by the nominal rates. Consequently, if the average weight and volume of these units did increase, these measures understate the real decline in costs.

---

[1] Productivity change by commodity route is measured as the percentage change in quantity (volume or weight) that can be shipped for a given real cost. Stated algebraically, let P_t = the cost to freight Q_t, where $t=1$, initial period, and 2, terminal period. Hence, the amount that can be shipped in period $t=1$ for P_1 is Q_1, in period $t=2$ for P_2 is Q_2, or for P_1 is P_1 (Q_2/P_2).

Now let Q_{12} = the percentage change in quantity, $(Q_2-Q_1)/Q_1$, for some P (P_1 in this case) between periods 1 and 2,

$$Q_{12}=\frac{P_1(Q_2/P_2)-Q_1}{Q_1},$$

or

$$Q_{12}=\frac{P_1Q_2-P_2Q_1}{P_2Q_1}.$$

Thus, where $Q_1=Q_2$ (the quantities are held constant between periods), this measure can be calculated simply as $(P_1-P_2)/P_2$. It should be noted that this is the same measure as 4*a* where undeflated rates are used.

By far the best time-series available on freight-rate data is that on tobacco. This time-series is greater both in the length of time covered and in the number of observations given. Despite the general availability of these rates, difficulties in interpretation have prevented scholars from using them to reflect declining costs of shipment and rising productivity of shipping between the Chesapeake and Great Britain. The rate was expressed as a charge per ton, where four hogsheads, regardless of weight, customarily were called one 'ton.' It is well known that tobacco hogsheads increased greatly in weight and size over the period 1675–1775. Since the average hogshead roughly doubled in weight, and the freight rate during peacetime held steady at £7 per ton, the cost per pound of shipping tobacco to Great Britain fell by one-half. The increased weight of the hogshead resulted from tighter compression of the tobacco and from increasing the size of the hogshead. Hence the increase in weight per hogshead was proportionately greater than the increase in volume. Consequently, it has not been determined whether declining costs of shipment resulted from increased efficiencies in packing or in shipping. Clearly, these two sources of falling costs must be separated before these freight rates can be used to mirror increased efficiency in shipping.

First, we must specify how the charge was levied on tobacco. When the space occupied by a cargo was large relative to its weight, the freight charge was on volume rather than weight. As Lane has said:

> The problem of equating a weight with a space occupied arose first in connection with setting freight rates. If the cargo was as heavy as wine or heavier than wine, it paid so much per ton by weight, but the shipowner would not accept at that rate a lighter cargo such as cotton for he then would collect little even from a full ship. To persuade the ship to take a cargo lighter than wine, a shipper had to pay approximately as much for the space his cargo occupied as did the shipper of wine casks. In England the space obtained by paying for a ton of freight became standardized fairly early at 40 cu. ft. This was the freight ton. But 40 cu. ft. was only about two-thirds or at most four-fifths of the space which the 2,240 lbs. cask really 'occupied' or used up.[1]

For the period when size and weight are changing we must determine whether or not the average number of cubic feet of space occupied by four hogsheads weighed more or less than the same volume of water.

In the early period before 1676, it is not known if the hogshead changed in size or weight. Freight rates, however, were definitely levied on volume rather than weight.[2] Assuming that volume held

[1] Frederic C. Lane, 'Tonnages, medieval and modern,' *Economic History Review*, XVII, 2 (December 1964), p. 220.
[2] Davis, p. 228.

steady, or at least did not decrease, what can be said? In the 1630s freight rates on tobacco from Virginia to London were generally £12 per ton. By the third quarter of the century the typical peacetime rate had fallen to £7 per ton, reflecting a significant increase in shipping productivity. This decline suggests an increase in productivity of 71 per cent in forty-five years.[1] However, by the third quarter of the seventeenth century, peacetime rates from Maryland held steady at £7 per four hogsheads right up until the Revolution. Though the money rate did not fall, the effective rate did decline, since the amount of tobacco carried (per ton) increased as hogsheads swelled in size and weight.

We cannot be too precise with regard to the actual average size of the hogshead at different periods, but some inferences can be drawn from the legislation relating to the hogshead. To give some indication of the changes of tobacco hogsheads between 1675 and the Revolution, we can profitably quote Lewis C. Gray:

> The hogshead was an object of much colonial legislation, particularly its size. The fact that colonial export taxes and various handling and marketing charges were rated on the hogshead as a unit and that transport charges were based on the assumption of 4 hogsheads to the ton stimulated a steady increase in size of hogsheads, an increase not checked by laws fixing the maximum. It is probable that in 1661 hogsheads did not average above 350 pounds net weight. In 1657/8 a Virginia law fixed the maximum size at 43 inches in height by 26 inches in diameter of the head, 'bulge proportionable,' and in 1676 Maryland increased the maximum diameter of the head to 27 inches, requiring that hogsheads should not be less than 42 inches by 26 inches. In 1692 Maryland found it necessary to increase maximum legal dimensions to 44 by 31 inches, and two years later to 48 by 32 inches, which was continued by various acts in 1699, 1700, and 1704. In 1695 and again in 1705 Virginia provided for maximum dimensions of 48 by 30 inches.[2]

The increased size of the hogshead reduced shipping income from freights, since increased volume reduced available cargo space. This effective reduction in the freight rates resulted in much dissatisfaction by merchants and authorities in Great Britain, and pressures were

---

[1] We view this measure as extremely rough because it is based on the assumptions of a stable price level and unchanged factor prices before 1675. Accordingly, we do not include this measure in the general index of productivity change below.

[2] Lewis C. Gray, *History of Agriculture in the Southern United States to 1860* (Washington, D.C.: Carnegie Institution of Washington, D.C., 1933), 1, pp. 220–1. For a lengthy detailed description of tobacco regulations in Maryland in the seventeenth and eighteenth centuries, see Vetrees J. Wyckoff, *Tobacco Regulations in Maryland* (Baltimore: The Johns Hopkins Press, 1936).

placed on the colonists to reduce the gauge of the hogshead. Marylanders argued that they could not compress their Oronoko tobacco as tightly into the hogshead as could Virginians with their sweet-scented tobacco. Hence they felt justified in maintaining a larger hogshead in order to ship the same weight, despite the will of British authorities. Gray states:

> In that year the Maryland Assembly finally conformed to Her Majesty's command by fixing the gauge of hogsheads at 48 by 30 inches, but in 1716 the original diameter of 32 inches was restored, the act asserting the great hardships on account of the previous act, which had been widely evaded. The new act was vetoed by the Proprietor on account of objections to revenue provisions, but it was passed again the next year with necessary modifications and renewed from time to time until passage of the inspection law of 1747.[1]

Assuming that the increase in the average hogshead in Maryland between 1676 and 1747 was approximately that portrayed by the maximum gauges in these two periods, some inferences can be made. Using the formula of a cylinder ($\pi r^2 \times$ height) to approximate the volume of a hogshead, the increase in volume was from 13.2 cubic feet in 1676 to 22.2 cubic feet by mid-century. These computed volumes understate the true absolute size of the hogshead. But since the change was with the 'bulge proportionable,' the relative change in size can be approximated by these volumes. The increase in volume was 68.2 per cent, not of insignificant proportions, and thus substantiating the concern of British authorities and shippers.

Since the weight of the hogshead increased more than the volume, because of tighter packing, one must account for the possibility that at some point weight, not volume, became the relevant factor in reducing the effective freight rate. However, for the entire period, the average weight of four hogsheads of tobacco was considerably less than the weight of water (or wine, the traditional unit of a shipping ton) that would occupy this same volume. If for the purpose of the freight charge, 40 cubic feet is equal to one ton of water (2,240 lb), then 1 cubic foot of water equals 56 lb. Since the hogshead of tobacco weighed between 350 and 500 lb (not 739 lb, or 13.2 × 56 lb) in 1676 and around 1,000 lb (not 1,243 lb, or 22.2 × 56 lb) in 1750, it can be safely concluded that the relevant factor in reducing the effective freight rate was volume, not weight. When we consider the increased volume of the bulge and the space between hogsheads, instead of simply the volume of a cylinder, our conclusion is further supported.

Summarizing the tobacco trade, freight rates in the very early period

[1] Gray, p. 221.

fell significantly, showing an increase of productivity of approximately 71 per cent. After 1676 the effective rate was again reduced as a result of increasing the volume of the hogshead while the money rate was held constant. The increase in volume of approximately 68.2 per cent reflects the increased productivity of shipping after 1676 for this route.

A similar mode of analysis can be applied to freight rates on sugar between Jamaica and Great Britain. Davis reports that:

> There is a special difficulty over sugar freight rates. Sugar (like tobacco) grew up with a trade convention of charging freight on a ton of four hogsheads. These hogsheads in fact varied in size from place to place; and in the course of time they grew far beyond the five hundred-weight on which the standard was originally based, commonly reaching ten to twelve hundred-weight...at Nevis 14 cwt. casks are recorded in 1730.[1]

Table 4.4 gives average peacetime freight rates on sugar, Barbados to London and Jamaica to London. Over this period of roughly forty

TABLE 4.4.   *Freight rates on sugar* (per ton)

	Barbados			Jamaica		
	£	s.	d.	£	s.	d.
1678–82	3	19	0	6	4	0
1683–8	4	11	0	5	4	0
1698–1702	3	1	0	8	1	0
1714–17	3	12	0	9	6	0

Source: Ralph Davis, *The Rise of the English Shipping Industry*, p. 284.

years, the increase in the money rate by 50 per cent on the Jamaica–London route would suggest a decline in efficiency. However, assuming that the hogshead approximately doubled in weight, there was actually an increase of productivity of nearly 33 per cent for this period.[2] A similar weight conversion is not applicable to the Barbados route, despite a doubling in the average size of the sugar hogshead there. In approximately 1700, the freight charge on sugar from Barbados became standardized for a ton of twenty hundredweight.[3] Assuming the average hogshead weighed approximately five hundredweight near 1680, we can measure productivity by viewing the nominal rates alone. The decline in nominal rates appears to be from an average of 85s. per twenty hundredweight to an average of 65s. per twenty hundredweight,

---

[1] Davis, p. 282.
[2] The relevant factor on sugar is weight, since for comparable volumes, sugar is heavier than water.
[3] Davis, p. 284.

or an increase of productivity of approximately 31 per cent, between 1678 and 1717.

A GENERAL INDEX OF PRODUCTIVITY ADVANCE PER YEAR

The above lower bound measures of productivity change indicate significant but differential advances among routes and periods. These advances are summarized in Table 4.5, column 2, in terms of compounded yearly rates of change, and show a range of increases from 0.4 per cent on the wine route to 0.7 per cent on the sugar, bullion, and oil routes. Because these estimates of productivity change are lower bound estimates, it seems appropriate at this point to attempt a measure closer to the true productivity change that occurred.

A more accurate measure of productivity change can be obtained by reconsidering measure (4a):

$$\frac{\dot{P}}{P} = \frac{\dot{P}_I}{P_I} - \frac{\dot{P}_Q}{P_Q}.$$

Using undeflated rates, we in effect measured

$$\frac{\dot{P}}{P} = - \frac{\dot{P}_Q}{P_Q},$$

and the estimates in column 2, Table 4.5 were derived from this measure. A 'more accurate' measure of $\dot{P}/P$ requires that we add the rate of change of input prices, $\dot{P}_I/P_I$ (appropriately weighted), to the lower bound measures given in column 2, Table 4.5; thus, we consider changes in input prices, $\dot{P}_I/P_I$, as well as changes in output prices, $-\dot{P}_Q/P_Q$.

As stated above, the input prices of seamen's wages and ship repair

TABLE 4.5. *Changes in shipping productivity by commodity route*

Route	Good	Period	(1) Lower bound increase by period (%)	(2) Lower bound increase per annum (%)	(3) 'More accurate' increase per annum (%)
New York–London	Bullion	1700–89	100	0.8	1.0
New York–Jamaica	Flour	1699–1768	50	0.6	0.8
Boston–London	Oil	1700–74	67	0.7	0.9
So. Europe–London	Wine	1650–1770	71	0.4	0.6
Virginia–London	Tobacco	1630–75	71	1.2	—
Maryland–London	Tobacco	1676–1776	68	0.5	0.7
Barbados–London	Sugar	1678–1717	31	0.7	0.9
Jamaica–London	Sugar	1678–1717	33	0.7	0.9

Source: see text.

costs remained stable over the period (p. 63, notes 1 and 2). However, shipbuilding costs approximately doubled in England (and similarly rose in the colonies) over the years 1675–1775, which indicates a rise in the price of this input by 0.7 per cent, compounded annually.[1] Likewise, evidence on victualling costs of seamen in the colonies suggests a rise of almost 60 per cent during 1720–75, or a compounded annual rise of between approximately 0.8 and 0.9 per cent.[2] A reason-

[1] Any analysis of seventeenth- and eighteenth-century shipbuilding costs poses significant problems of interpretation. Some cost figures referred only to the hull; others included hull, masts, and yards; and others included all of these plus the rigging and outfitting of the ship. Very seldom do the costs properly distinguish between these stages of completion. Davis indicates that the costs of a standard-sized merchant vessel in London rose from £5 per measured ton in 1675 to between £8 and £9 per measured ton in 1775. (Davis, p. 374). His calculations, however, are somewhat impressionistic, although probably fairly accurate. The best time series of shipbuilding costs available are those by Robert G. Albion, in his *Forests and Sea Power* (Cambridge, Mass.: Harvard University Press, 1926), pp. 92–3, where he gives a time series of the costs in England of a standard-type Navy vessel:

> The cost per ton of a third rate (usually a seventy-four in the eighteenth century), built in a merchant yard, including hull, mast, and yards, but not rigging or stores, can be traced through two centuries and a half, making allowances for the uncertain basis of comparison.... In 1600, it was about £5 10s. and in 1675, as quoted above, it was £9. By 1693, it had risen to about £11 5s. Between 1719 and 1741, the cost gradually rose from £12 to £13. During the Seven Years' War, it was £16 or £17. This increased to over £20 in the American Revolution and between 1793 and 1802, £20 or £21 was the usual cost.

Albion's figures are quite high, absolutely, because they refer to Navy vessels and do not reflect peacetime costs. Nevertheless, they are very useful for viewing the trend of costs. While they suggest more than a doubling of costs between 1675 and 1775, Davis suggests slightly less than a doubling of costs over this period. We accept a doubling of shipbuilding costs as an approximation.

Unfortunately, there are no similar reliable time series of colonial shipbuilding costs. Colonial-built ships were generally of a poorer quality and were built at costs substantially below those in England (see Davis, p. 375). In 1784, several informed contemporaries suggested that the costs of a 200-ton (measured) vessel in New York and Philadelphia were £6 8s. to £7 19s. per ton and in New England were £3 18s. to £5 9s. per ton (*ibid.*, p. 375). Hutchins suggests prices of £3 to £4 per ton in North America during the colonial period generally (John G. B. Hutchins, *The American Maritime Industries and Public Policy, 1789–1914* (Cambridge, Mass.: Harvard University Press, 1941), p. 153), but by 1775 the costs per ton probably exceeded £4. For instance, in 1771 a 130-ton (full rig) vessel cost £4 12s. 4d. per ton in New England and in 1774 a 168-ton (full rig) vessel cost £4 10s. 7d. per ton in New England (Baker Library, John Hancock Papers, Vol. 25). Weeden gives numerous costs of shipbuilding in New England, 1661–1711, in local currency, which if converted to sterling suggest costs in the range of £2 to £3 per ton (William B. Weeden, *Economic and Social History of New England*, Vol. 1, pp. 367–8). As stated above, the comparability of these (colonial) costs is open to question, but the evidence does indicate a substantial rise in the costs of shipbuilding in the colonies. For more information on shipbuilding costs in the late colonial period, see Appendix VI. Ideally, the price of capital should be for a flow of capital rather than a stock of capital. Construction prices are for a stock of capital and are influenced by the expected life of the vessel as well as the interest rate. The average life of a ship did not change over the period, but interest rates declined somewhat. Therefore a part of the rise in ship construction prices was due to this decline in interest rates. Nevertheless, the rate of change of ship construction prices is a reasonable proxy for changes in the price of capital expressed as a flow.

[2] A good proxy of victualling costs is the index of wholesale prices of beef, bread, corn, flour, molasses, pitch, pork, rum, salt, sugar, tar and wheat, 1720–75, given in Bezanson *et al.*,

able measure of $\dot{P}_I/P_I$ requires that we weight these several inputs according to their share of total costs. Approximate shares of total costs can be derived from the recent study of ocean shipping by North.[1] These weights are very rough, but for an average voyage shipbuilding costs comprised somewhere between 10 per cent and 15 per cent of costs, and victualling costs were 15–25 per cent. Assuming that only victualling costs and shipbuilding costs rose over the period, a conservative estimate of the rate of growth of input prices is 0.1 (0.7 per cent) + 0.15 (0.8 per cent) ≈ 0.2 per cent. Consequently, our final estimates of productivity change by route, which are the addition of 0.2 per cent to each lower bound measure in column 2, Table 4.5, are also estimates containing downward biases. These 'more accurate' estimates are given in column 3, Table 4.5, and are a better indication of the true productivity change which occurred in shipping.

Lastly, it is of general interest to know what overall advance in productivity took place in shipping in colonial waters between 1675 and 1775. Of course, to derive a general index of productivity change requires that appropriate weights be given to the individual series. Ideally, each series should be weighted by its share of total shipping earnings. For example, oil should be weighted by total earnings obtained in carrying oil from Boston to London in a base year. Alternatively, weights could be based on the ship tonnage utilized in carrying each type of good over the particular route for a particular year. The needed data are not available to obtain these weights with any marked precision, but by piecing together information from various sources and applying some qualitative evidence, they can be approximated. This approximation comes by way of estimating tonnage utilization by goods and route for a representative base year.[2]

---

p. 427. This arithmetic index rises from 79.9 in 1720 to 128.7 in 1775, or by about 60 per cent. Bezanson also gives a twenty-commodity index, but the additional eight goods are not foodstuffs for the most part, and, in any case, it rises at almost the same rate as the above twelve-commodity index.

[1] See Douglass C. North, 'Sources of productivity change in ocean shipping, 1600–1850', *Journal of Political Economy*, Vol. 76, No. 5 (September–October 1968), pp. 953–70. North gives weights for two base years, 1600–25 and 1814 (*ibid.*, p. 965) which we have averaged in an attempt to locate a base year weight near 1700. Because North's weights are not very different, our averaging has little influence on our final estimates. North gives labor costs at sea between 0.550 and 0.344, capital costs at sea between 0.065 and 0.121, and other costs at sea between 0.385 and 0.535. Similarly, for costs in port they were 0.498 to 0.245, 0.104 to 0.246, and 0.398 to 0.509, respectively. The average of North's 1600–25 base and the 1814 base indicates costs at sea equal to costs in port; thus, labor costs equalled about 41 per cent of total costs, capital costs were roughly 14 per cent of total costs, and other costs were the remainder of 45 per cent. Shipbuilding costs were almost all of the capital costs and victualling costs were probably about one-half of the labor costs. We have chosen what we believe to be lower bound weights for shipbuilding and victualling costs in order to derive a conservative estimate of the rate of growth of the index of input prices.

[2] The general index of productivity increase per annum can be viewed as $\Sigma_i P_i W_i / \Sigma_i W_i$, where P_i = productivity change per annum on the ith commodity route and W_i = base year tonnage employed on the ith commodity route.

These weights are given in Appendix III, and their derivations are explained in detail there. Briefly summarized, they are 288 tons for bullion; 303 tons for flour; 550 tons for oil; 8,568 tons for wine; 5,661 tons for tobacco (1676–1776); and 8,783 tons for each sugar route. Early base years were chosen: 1716 for bullion, flour, and oil; 1686 for wine and both sugar routes; and 1690–1700 for tobacco. Applying these weights to the individual series gives an index indicating a general overall advance of at least 0.8 per cent per year for the 100-year period preceding the Revolution.[1] Certainly this information leaves little doubt that this industry was undergoing important changes which were a significant aspect of colonial development.

---

[1] The recent article by North (*op. cit.*, pp. 953–70) suggests a lower measure of 0.45 per cent per annum for the period 1600–1784. His evidence, however, is derived entirely from the period 1675–1775, and, in fact, North implicitly assumes zero productivity change for the period 1600–75 and 1775–84. When his information is correctly addressed to the period from which it is taken (1675–1775), his measure slightly exceeds 0.8 per cent per annum.

CHAPTER 5

SOURCES OF PRODUCTIVITY CHANGE
IN SHIPPING AND DISTRIBUTION

The substantial decline in freight rates and our estimates of productivity advance leave little doubt that the real costs of shipping dramatically fell over the period 1675–1775. The unanswered question, however, is what caused the decline in costs and what were the sources of productivity change in colonial waters. The improvements revealed by the freight rates are also reflected in the cost determinants of shipping, and an analysis of the cost determinants provides the answer to the question of causality. The evidence indicates that most of the observed increase in productivity can be attributed to improvements in market organization and the decline of risks associated with piracy, privateering, and similar hazards. Technological change, which is often an important source of productivity advance, appears to have played a minor role, and economies of scale as reflected in average ship size operating in colonial waters also appear to have been unimportant.

The primary emphasis of this chapter is on sources of productivity change in colonial shipping. Sources of reductions in other distribution costs are so analyzed, but the evidence on these costs is fragmentary and it is not possible to give precise quantitative measures or to reach firm conclusions.

THE COST DETERMINANTS OF SHIPPING

The analysis of sources of productivity change is best undertaken by first separating the cost determinants of shipping and then examining them individually. For the sake of simplicity let us assume a standard vessel of a given size and a standard route.[1] First, consider the costs of a single voyage. Labor costs, in general, were a function of crew size, of the average monetary wage of seamen, and of victualling costs. Capital costs consisted of the initial outlay for construction and outfitting of the ship, plus interest, repair, and maintenance costs; and these can be amortized over the expected life of the ship. The other costs incurred were for insurance and port charges.

[1] This analysis is not completely comprehensive, since the costs of shipping were partially a function of ship size, or carrying capacity. However, as will be shown, average ship size varied little in colonial waters prior to the Revolution.

To determine the costs of the voyage it is necessary to examine changes in the length of the voyage and changes in its time components. The length of the voyage consisted of three periods: the number of days spent in the home port, the time spent at sea, and the port time in foreign waters. Any decrease in sea time reduced both labor and capital costs directly by reducing the number of days a crew was paid (both monetary wages and victualling costs) and the number of days of capital amortization. Decreases in foreign port time had precisely the same result: decreases in home port time resulted in a reduction of capital costs (days of amortization), but not of labor costs, since, typically, crews were discharged (the captain excepted) upon arrival in home waters. Finally, insurance costs were generally a charge per voyage, not including the stay in the home port, so changes in the voyage time or its components did not affect insurance charges; consequently, these other costs were invariant with respect to voyage time.

The annual costs of this standard vessel are the product of individual voyage costs multiplied by the average number of trips made per year. Ideally, estimates of productivity change should be composed of estimates of changes in output (the quantity of cargo and the distance of its carriage, usually measured in tons and miles) and changes in inputs. Increases in output (ton-miles of carriage) with no increase in total costs represent lower per-unit costs of carriage, and thus increased productivity. The data are not sufficient, however, to measure the output of shipping directly, because we do not know what changes in load-factors, or utilization, took place over the period. We assume that utilization remained unchanged; hence output is reflected by aggregated (ship) tonnage flows, and this compared with input changes permits us to arrive at conclusions about sources of productivity changes.

Limited data dictate what can and cannot be examined. Adequate data exist to allow an analysis of the following cost determinants: (1) ship size, (2) crew size, (3) seamen's wages, (4) victualling costs, (5) armaments, (6) shipbuilding costs, (7) insurance costs, (8) ship speed, and (9) port time. Some comment can be given on depreciation and interest rates, but little can be said about changes in utilization.[1] In the following pages it is shown that (of the above factors) crew size, armaments, and port times declined precipitously; moderate reductions occurred in insurance costs; and, in contrast, ship size, seamen's wages, and ship speed remained stable, while shipbuilding costs and victualling costs rose over the period. The analysis of trends in input prices such as

---

[1] During this period, the pattern of utilization of vessels was that of fully-laden vessels sailing from America to the Old World and to the Caribbean and only partially laden vessels returning. The changes taking place in the backhauls are not known; therefore, for this analysis, load factor is assumed to have been constant over time. Estimates of utilization are made in Chapter 7 for the period 1768–72, but data that would be needed to construct earlier estimates do not exist.

seamen's wages, victualling costs, and shipbuilding costs was presented above in Chapter 4.

TONS, GUNS, MEN, AND INSURANCE COSTS

An important aspect of shipping in general has been the effect of ship size on costs per ton-mile. Where trade was well organized and the market large, economies of scale in shipping existed. Though vessels of larger size carried larger crews, the tons per man (carrying capacity per unit of labor) were significantly greater. In other words, crew size (and labor costs) grew less than proportionately to tonnage as vessels increased in size. As Figure 5.1 clearly indicates, the ton–men ratio of small ships (50–99 tons) was less than half that of vessels exceeding 300 tons.[1] One would certainly expect that such obvious economies in labor would result in a growth in average ship size over the period. On some routes, such as those into the Baltic and noticeably on the timber trade to Norway, very large vessels (with high ton–men ratios) were employed by the early seventeenth century. However, the average size of vessels employed in the Caribbean and the western Atlantic showed little secular increase prior to the Revolution. Despite fluctuations, the information on ship size in Appendix III indicates no upward trend in average ship size over time. One might argue that average ship size

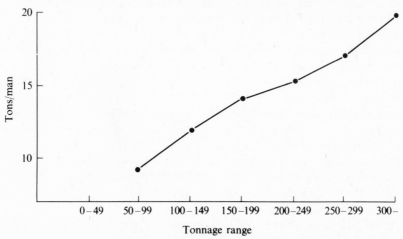

Figure 5.1. Tons per man by size of ship in 1764. Source: Lloyd's Register of Shipping, 1764.

[1] It should be noted that these tons are measured, not registered, tons and thus not strictly comparable to the ton–men ratios discussed below. The lack of comparability of absolute size is unimportant, however, to show the rate of increase of ton–men ratios as ship size increased. For corroborating evidence of this effect using registered tons, see Ralph Davis, *The Rise of the English Shipping Industry* (London: Macmillan & Co. Ltd., 1962), p. 73. For most routes to London, vessels about 100 tons had ton–men ratios only two-thirds those of vessels about 300 tons.

increased slightly at Boston, but a slight decrease appears to have occurred for the Chesapeake. For the colonies as a whole there was no significant or noticeable trend.

The reason that economies of scale in shipping were not enjoyed in colonial waters is that the numerous small and scattered markets offset the labor-saving benefits of large vessels. The larger the vessel, the greater was the probability of its being under-utilized, and, as is shown for Philadelphia shipping (Appendix III), the longer its average port time (by more than twice for a ship, snow, or brig, compared to a schooner or sloop). This meant that the average number of miles travelled per ton was greater for small than for large vessels. Consequently, though economies of scale in shipping were realized in some trade areas, these potential economies were precluded in the colonies by limited market size and by colonial commercial practices which gave rise to high risks of under-utilization for large-sized ships.

Despite the lack of secular increase in average ship size, manning requirements declined significantly over the period. As the information on ton–men ratios in Appendix III indicates, tons per man on vessels trading at Boston, New York, Virginia, Barbados, and Jamaica increased greatly; hence, crew sizes were falling for vessels of a given size. For instance, in Boston this meant that a vessel of 50 tons employed approximately seven men in 1716; by 1765 the labor requirement for a 50-ton vessel trading there was only five men. Similarly, for New York a 50-ton vessel would employ eleven men in 1716 and only seven men by 1764.[1]

Also, a precipitous decline in armaments on merchant vessels occurred in the eighteenth century. Gunning requirements varied among routes, being mainly a function of the degree of risk associated with war hazards, piracy, and privateering. Typically, vessels owned in Great Britain were more heavily protected than colonial vessels. However, initial differences in gun–men ratios diminished, and protection characteristics of both British and colonial vessels were very nearly the same by the Revolution. This information on gun–men ratios is also given in Appendix III and clearly reveals the sharp decline in armaments and the fact that by the end of the period guns were seldom carried on merchant vessels.

Another feature of the period was a moderate decline in insurance

---

[1] Further evidence of the striking changes in ton–men ratios over time for numerous routes is given in Davis, p. 71.

Another factor that would have influenced ton–men ratios was the possible occurrence of changes in the relative prices of capital and labor. It appears that the relative prices changed insignificantly, however, and they may have remained unchanged. Ship construction costs and victualling costs appear to have risen at about the same annual rate (see Chapter 4, p. 70, notes 1 and 2) and monetary wages and repair costs remained steady (see p. 63, notes 1 and 2).

costs. First, an important change in insurance practice took place, which lowered the effective rate of premiums by approximately 10 to 20 per cent. In the seventeenth century the customary payment in case of loss varied between 75 per cent and 90 per cent of the sum insured. However, prior to the mid-eighteenth century, insurers increased coverage to within 1 or 2 per cent of the loss, thus lowering the effective charge.[1] Second, although most trans-Atlantic routes had reached the common peacetime rate of 2 per cent (one way) by the 1720s, routes into Jamaican waters had rates well above normal peacetime rates elsewhere, because of the higher incidence of piracy. The typical outward rate from London was between $2\frac{1}{2}$ per cent and 3 per cent in the 1720s, and the return rate was 4 per cent.[2] By 1765–75 the rate from Jamaica to London and other English ports was between 3 per cent and $3\frac{1}{2}$ per cent.[3] Likewise, the round-trip rate between New York and Jamaica was 5 per cent in 1720, whereas by 1773 the normal rate was 4 per cent.[4] Finally, a decline was seen on some routes from New England to certain West Indian islands, specifically Nevis and St Thomas, where peacetime rates fell roughly by one-half between 1700 and 1770.[5]

Little can be said with regard to depreciation, but Davis suggests that the average life of English ships held steady over the period.[6] It seems reasonable to assume that this was true for colonial vessels as well. Also, interest rates were falling in England; thus capital costs were lowered somewhat to shippers as well as to investors generally.[7]

THE TIME COMPONENTS OF VOYAGES

Turning now from the general inputs of a single voyage, it is of particular interest to determine changes in the time components of voyages and the average number of voyages undertaken per year. First, consider the question of changing ship speed and sea time. Throughout the entire period there is no discernible upward trend in speed. Appendix III shows average speeds in nautical miles per hour (and sea time in days), some of which are faster and others slower in 1686–8 than on voyages accomplished much later. By combining

---

[1] A. H. John, 'The London Assurance Company and the marine assurance market of the eighteenth century,' *Economica*, xxv, 18 (May 1958), p. 140.

[2] Rough Journals of the London Assurance Company, London, England (hereafter referred to as Rough Journals).

[3] William Walton's Insurance Book, New York Chamber of Commerce Library, New York; and Ezekiel Price's Policy Books, Boston Athenaeum, Boston, Massachusetts.

[4] Rough Journals and William Walton's Insurance Book.

[5] C. 104–16, Public Record Office, London; and Ezekiel Price's Policy Books and William Walton's Insurance Book.

[6] Davis, p. 376.

[7] T. S. Ashton, *The Industrial Revolution* (Oxford: The Clarendon Press, 1948), pp. 9–10.

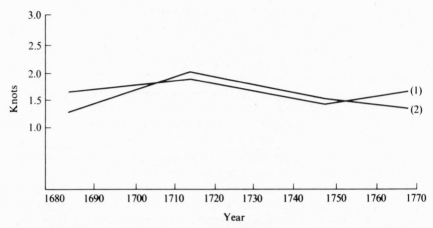

Figure 5.2. Average knots, 1686–1765: (1) New England and New York–Jamaica and Barbados; (2) Jamaica and Barbados–New England and New York. Source: see text and Appendix III.

observations for the routes between New England, New York, and the Caribbean, some of the cyclical fluctuations are dampened. Figure 5.2 indicates that there was no increasing secular trend in ship speed. On the leg of the route going to the West Indies, the average knots were 1.67, 1.97, 1.60 and 1.80 for the respective periods 1686–8, 1715–19, 1742–8, and 1764–5. On the return run they were 1.31, 2.09, 1.59, and 1.50 for the same respective dates. Clearly, vessels sailing over these routes were not traveling significantly faster on the eve of the Revolution than they were nearly one hundred years earlier.[1]

Despite the constancy of ship speed, round-trip voyage times did decline. Figure 5.3 portrays average port times for key ports in the American and West Indies colonies; with the single exception of Boston, these port times fell markedly. Such declines, which are also shown in Appendix III, were certainly significant because at that time a very large proportion of a ship's life was spent in port.

Consider, for example, the Chesapeake trade. On the average, vessels engaged there were in port over twice as long in 1694–1701 as they were in 1762–8.[2] An important aspect of this change was the introduction of Scottish factors into the Chesapeake after 1707. The distinct relative growth of the Scottish tobacco trade certainly indicates

[1] It is a curious fact that if the ship speeds for the years 1686–8 and 1715–19 are combined and those of 1742–8 and 1764–5 are combined there is an apparent decline in speed. Average knots to the Caribbean fell from 1.86 to 1.73 and from the Caribbean they fell from 1.95 to 1.52 for these combined periods. See Appendix III, p. 197, for the discussion of qualifications of the entrance and clearance data from the Naval Office Lists.

[2] V. J. Wyckoff ('Ships and shipping of seventeenth century Maryland,' *Maryland Historical Magazine*, XXXIV (1954), p. 355) states that out of 213 ships (1690–2), 42 per cent were in port longer than 105 days, with only 18 per cent clearing in less than 44 days.

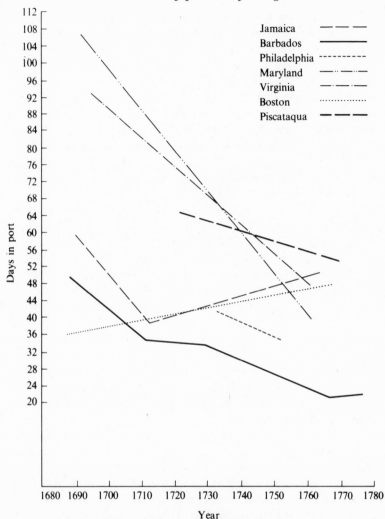

Figure 5.3. Average port times. Source: Appendix III.

that Scottish traders were more efficient than their predecessors. It is quite likely that their methods of gathering the tobacco crop and inventorying it in barns and warehouses, from which it could be quickly loaded upon arrival of their vessels, had a significant impact on port times in the Chesapeake. These practices, along with the shorter route north of Ireland, allowed Scottish traders to make two voyages a year on an average rather than just one – which according to Davis was typical for the English tobacco shipper.[1]

Similarly, in Barbados, port times fell by more than half over the

[1] Jacob M. Price, 'The rise of Glasgow in the Chesapeake tobacco trade, 1707–1775,' *The William and Mary Quarterly*, XI, 2 (April 1954), p. 187; and Davis, p. 190.

period. The reasons for such declines are better understood when one considers the many problems faced by shipmasters acting on behalf of their merchants. The limited size of the many scattered markets resulted in considerable variation in prices, both among the different islands and even for the same island over short intervals, as ships came and went. One of the objectives of the master was to locate the best markets for the particular commodities he carried. To achieve this goal might require several voyages to different islands, which could lengthen his stay in the Caribbean significantly. Also, difficulties in agreeing on prices and on the medium of exchange to be used, plus the problem of settling past debts, all lengthened the period required for transactions. Often bartering was the means of transaction; and even when various forms of exchange were used, prices were not easy to determine, since the value of different currencies and bills of exchange (with varying degrees of risk) was by no means certain.[1] In the meantime, no doubt, the ship was being loaded as well as unloaded, but the problem of collecting cargoes added to the length of stay, and when harvests were poor, port times were lengthened even more. The general growth of a more systematic market economy which provided solutions to these problems was a main factor in reducing port time.

TECHNICAL CHANGE, PIRACY, AND TECHNICAL DIFFUSION

It seems appropriate at this point to assess the importance of technological change in reducing shipping costs.[2] In general it appears that advances in knowledge were not an important factor in lowering costs. Our period preceded the era of iron and steam, and such basic features as the materials and techniques used for ship construction and the source of power remained unchanged over the period. The increasing complexity of sail and rig and the alteration of hull shapes were not significant changes reflecting advances in knowledge. If they had been, one of their major effects would have been to increase ship speed, but the data reveal no upward trend in average ship speed. It might be argued that crew reductions stemmed from technical improvements, but this assertion can be refuted by the fact that during the early seventeenth century the Dutch flyboat possessed the essential characteristics of design, manning, and other input requirements found on the most efficient and modern vessels in the 1760s and 1770s.

---

[1] For a more complete treatment of the many problems encountered in the West Indies trade, see Herbert C. Bell, 'West India trade before the Revolution,' *American Historical Review*, XXII, 2 (January 1917), pp. 282–6.

[2] Technological change is defined to be an advance of knowledge that enables fewer inputs to produce a given output. Technical diffusion is viewed as the process by which actual techniques in the industry approach the best-practice techniques. W. E. G. Salter, *Productivity and Technical Change* (London: Cambridge University Press, 1960).

The argument presented here is that crew reductions were made possible by the elimination of piracy and privateering. This hypothesis will be explicitly tested, and an explanation will also be offered of why imitations of the flyboat did not quickly spread to the Caribbean and the western Atlantic in the seventeenth century. Our analysis views piracy as an obstacle to technical diffusion, and as this obstacle was eliminated, prototypes of the flyboat were adopted and armaments and crew sizes declined.

The most significant change in technology which was to affect seventeenth- and eighteenth-century shipping came in approximately 1595, when the Dutch first introduced the flyboat (or flute).[1] Sharply different from other contemporary ships, the flyboat was a specialized merchant vessel with a design favourable to the carriage of bulk commodities. Its bottom was nearly flat, it was exceptionally long compared to its width, it was lightly built because armament, gun platforms, and reinforced planking were eliminated, and it was known for the simplicity of its rig.[2] In contrast, English and colonial vessels were heavily built, gunned, and manned to meet the dual purpose of trade and defense. They cost more per ton to build because of heavy construction and armaments, and they used more men per ton because of more complex sail patterns, for manning armaments, and for additional protection in the event of attack.

Despite these advantages in cost, which permitted the Dutch to charge peacetime rates in some waters which were '$\frac{1}{3}$ to $\frac{1}{2}$ lower than English for the same voyage,'[3] the input characteristics of the flyboat were not adopted quickly by the English. The primary reason was that English and colonial shippers frequented waters infested with pirates and privateers. In the rich trades into the Mediterranean and to the East Indies the English were effective competitors, but in the bulk trades, where freight charges were an important part of the final delivered prices, and where the dangers of attack were low, the Dutch clearly were dominant. Consequently, the flyboat engulfed the bulk trades of the Baltic and dominated the English coal trade,[4] areas which had been cleared of pirates early in the seventeenth century.

As stated above, prohibitively high risks in other waters prevented these economies. In fact, one of the most notable features of seventeenth-century shipping was the widespread use of armaments on trading vessels, and in certain waters defensible ships were still used throughout

---

[1] The term 'flyboat' is used interchangeably with 'flute', to refer to the Dutch vessel.

[2] For a valuable discussion of the flyboat and seventeenth-century shipping see Violet Barbour, 'Dutch and English merchant shipping in the seventeenth century,' *Economic History Review*, II (1930), pp. 261–90.

[3] *Ibid.*, p. 285.

[4] The results in these trades were low-cost shipping and ton–men ratios that approached and leveled off at approximately 20 to 1 in the mid-1600s.

much of the eighteenth century. For instance, before 1750 in the Caribbean, and especially near Jamaica, unarmed vessels over 100 tons were seldom seen and even small vessels often carried arms.[1]

The need for protection and armaments in the Caribbean is clearly described by Barbour:

> There the sea was broken by a multitude of islands affording safe anchorage and refuge, with wood, water, even provisions for the taking. There the colonies of the great European powers, grouped within a few days' sail of one another, were forever embroiled in current European wars which gave the stronger of them excuse for preying on the weaker and seemed to make legitimate the constant disorder of those seas. There trade was rich but settlement thin and defense difficult. There the idle, the criminal, and the poverty-stricken were sent to ease society in the Old World. By all these conditions piracy was fostered, and for two centuries throve ruinously, partly as an easy method of individual enrichment and partly as an instrument of practical politics.[2]

Privateering, like piracy, added to the disorder. The policy of granting letters of marque to private citizens was a means used by various nation-states to harass their rivals.[3] Privateering commissions were issued without constraint in wartime, and even in peacetime they occasionally were given for the purpose of redress to citizens who had suffered loss from subjects of an offending state. These commissions were obtained easily: 'The English and Dutch, French and Portuguese peddled letters of marque freely to one another, and regularly to the disadvantage of Spain, the rich prey in those parts.'[4] Moreover, privateers frequently went outside the constraints of their commissions because enforcement was often lax. The effects of privateering, consequently, were not much different from the effects of piracy.

The proliferation of these sea hazards was reinforced by other government policies as well. The supply of actual and potential privateers and pirates was enlarged by the policy of populating the islands with

[1] See Appendix III.

[2] Violet Barbour, 'Privateers and pirates in the West Indies,' *American Historical Review*, XVI (April 1911), p. 529.

[3] Letters of marque were the legal papers making a privateer distinct from a pirate. Piracy was merely robbery or other criminal act of violence on the sea, independent of any governmental or political authority. Privateering was an act of warfare (or redress in peacetime) where private owners, officers, and crews were commissioned by a belligerent government to attack enemy vessels. Besides rendering harm to the enemy, the granting government typically received 10 to 15 per cent of the value of prizes taken. For an example, see John F. Jameson, *Privateering and Piracy in the Colonial Period: Illustrative Documents* (New York: The Macmillan Company, 1923), Item 127, pp. 355–6.

[4] Barbour, 'Privateers,' pp. 531–2.

convicts. As late as 1718, the Governor of Jamaica complained of this policy and stated its effect of sea disorders:

> Several People have been lately sent over out of the gaols in England, upon the Encouragement of An Act of Parliament pass'd the last sessions... those people have been so farr from altering their Evil Courses and way of living and becoming an Advantage to Us, that the greatest part of them are gone and have Induced others to go with them a Pyrating and have Inveglied and Encouraged Severall Negroes to desert from their Masters and go to the Spaniards in Cuba, the few that remains proves a wicked Lazy and Indolent people, so that I could heartily wish this Country might be troubled with no more of them.[1]

At present, no precise quantitative figures of the extent of piracy and privateering in the Caribbean are available, but apparently it was quite extensive according to the qualitative evidence. In a letter dated 1700 to the Council of Trade and Plantations, Colonel Query of Virginia wrote: 'All the news of America is, the swarming of pirates not only on these coasts, but all the West Indies over, which doth ruin trade ten times worse than a war.'[2] A year earlier a Jamaican wrote: 'There are many pirates about our seas, and the French make us no restitution nor the Spaniards spare anything they can master, so that we are in an ill case with our hands bound and must stand still to be buffeted.'[3] Barbour reports that 'in 1724 England was still trying to quell these pirates by administering semi-occasional chastisement with a man-of-war' and that it was not until 'the latter part of the eighteenth century, [that] the imperative demand for security in trade brought about gradually a systematic and adequate policing of the seas.'[4]

In the new world, encounters with pirates were not limited to the waters of the Caribbean. The illustrated documents given in the collection by Jameson[5] indicate that piracy openly (almost respectfully) flourished along the entire Atlantic seaboard, and the study by Hughson gives a detailed account of pirating activity in the Carolinas.[6] Residing safely in the inlets of North Carolina, pirates regularly raided and looted vessels trading at Charleston, and in 1718 it was reported that 'every month brought intelligence of renewed outrages, of vessels

---

[1] Lawes to Board of Trade, September 1, 1718, C.O. 137:13, p. 19, printed in Frank W. Pitman, *The Development of the West Indies, 1700–63* (New Haven, Conn.: Yale University Press, 1917), pp. 55–6. Similar supporting statements are given on p. 381, and also in Barbour, 'Privateers,' p. 591.

[2] This letter was dated June 5, 1700; see Barbour, 'Privateers,' p. 566.

[3] *Ibid.*, p. 565.

[4] Both statements are from *ibid.*, p. 566.

[5] Jameson, *op. cit.*

[6] S. C. Hughson, 'The Carolina pirates and colonial commerce (1670–1740),' *Johns Hopkins University Studies in Historical and Political Science*, XII (1894).

sacked on the high seas, burned with their cargo, or seized and converted to the nefarious uses of the outlaws.'[1] Local traders, shippers, and government officials in the Carolinas made numerous pleas to the Board of Trade for protection, but their requests were largely ignored. Finally, in 1719, Carolina inhabitants acted through their local government to rid their seas of pirates, and their Assembly voted to appropriate funds to support private vessels against the pirates.[2] These funds were used to help finance several initial expeditions, where the private gains of captured prizes were not expected to cover the private costs. Despite problems of low private rates of return, expected (and ultimately realized) social returns were sufficiently high to warrant action, and finally even England supported these efforts by sending a man-of-war to police the Carolina coast. Because of these efforts piracy was greatly reduced, and by 1742 'the pirates on the coast had been completely exterminated, and vessels came and went, unarmed and unguarded without fear of interruption.'[3]

As the need for self-protection declined, armaments were abandoned and crews were reduced. The evidence on ton–men and gun–men ratios indicate that these adjustments came only gradually, however, rather than suddenly. Hostilities were not eliminated simultaneously in all waters, and vessels trading in unsafe seas, even if only part-time, maintained their armaments. Also, guns and heavy ship construction were characteristically fixed costs that were only gradually eliminated from the stock of tonnage as vessels were scrapped or overhauled.[4] Crew sizes, of course, fell more rapidly, because labor was a variable cost. As Davis states: '. . .as the dangers declined, so crews were reduced gradually towards levels determined by the requirements of serving the ships; curiously enough, the number of guns carried was little if at all reduced, though they could no longer be fully manned.'[5]

The reductions in piracy and privateering, armaments and crew sizes, of course, could be independent and coincidental changes, and their correlation does not necessarily denote causality. Nevertheless, the above qualitative evidence strongly suggests that the decline of piracy did cause armament reductions, and we draw this conclusion. However, did it also lead to crew reductions, or were other sources of labor savings responsible? The mutual decline of armaments and crew sizes suggests piracy was responsible, but added evidence is obtained by viewing armed and unarmed vessels of a given size. Assuming that armament characteristics were determined by piracy, differences in crew sizes between armed and unarmed vessels – all other characteristics

[1] *Ibid.*, p. 123.   [2] *Ibid.*, p. 124.   [3] *Ibid.*, p. 133.
[4] Besides these reasons, it is quite possible that the opportunity to undertake privateering expeditions during wartime contributed to the maintenance of armaments, even after pirates were eliminated.
[5] Davis, p. 58.

being the same – can also be attributed to piracy. The differences in ton–men ratios for armed and unarmed vessels are given in Appendix III, and for 41 out of 45 comparisons, armed vessels had lower ton–men ratios than unarmed vessels. Statistical *t*-tests have been applied to determine whether or not the means in each classification are from the same population and their differences due to chance or random events. The null hypothesis is that the true difference in the means of each classification is zero. Applying *t*-tests to the means of the totals indicates that out of the fourteen comparisons (there were no unarmed vessels at Jamaica over 150 tons) eight of the differences are statistically significant at the 5 per cent confidence level. These eight statistically significant differences are for the following tonnage classes: Jamaica, 20–49, 50–99, and 100–149; Barbados, 20–49 and 50–99; Charleston, 20–49, 50–99, and 100–149. To the extent that crews were reduced more rapidly than guns were eliminated (as Davis indicates), the differences revealed here understate the effect of armament reductions on crew sizes. It appears that the decline of piracy and privateering and armaments and crew sizes is more than coincidental. The qualitative evidence suggests that piracy and privateering declined substantially in the early eighteenth century. The quantitative evidence reveals a sharp decline in armaments and crew sizes, and the effect of armaments on crew sizes has been statistically shown. These changes were a process of technical diffusion. As the obstacles of piracy and similar hazards were eliminated, specialized cargo-carrying vessels, possessing the design characteristics of the flyboat, were adopted. In the process, the costs of shipping were substantially reduced, and this had a favorable impact on the development of a trading Atlantic community.[1]

[1] It should be noted that the decline in the costs of protection to private shippers possibly overstates the true decline in social costs, and consequently, that our measure of productivity change is too large. This would be true to the extent that the decline in private protection costs was offset by additions to naval costs. Economies of scale in law enforcement, however, would result in some cost reduction, and it is likely that naval forces were not enlarged because of action taken against piracy. For the most part, it probably represented the peacetime use of otherwise underutilized naval resources.

It is of considerable interest to consider why deliberate action to reduce piracy and privateering was not taken much earlier, for instance in the seventeenth century. The dangers of attack forced traders to carry armaments for defense, but individual merchants had little, if any, incentive to initiate attacks against pirates or privateers. The latter were generally better prepared for combat, and rather than use guns, it was in the merchant's best interest, when possible, to try and outsail the attacker (which partially explains the more complex rig of English and colonial vessels compared with the flyboat). However, the main reason why individual acts against the pirates were not undertaken was because an important share of the gains (lower labor and capital costs as well as insurance costs) would have gone to other shippers in the form of external economies. Moreover, shippers, merchants, and other concerned parties did not volunteer revenues (or vessels) to eliminate pirates because of organizational difficulties and because the gains to individuals were independent of their personal contribution. It is a classic case of a public good where the exclusion principle cannot be applied. While some local community action did develop (like that in the Carolinas), the effective reduction of piracy required the specialized action of the Royal Navy.

SOURCES OF REDUCTIONS IN OTHER DISTRIBUTION COSTS

To the sources of improvements in shipping which have been analyzed above, we now add evidence on improvements in other types of distribution services. Unfortunately, our analysis is based only on fragments of information about packaging, inventorying, insurance, and other costs. The evidence on reductions of these types of costs is indirect for the most part, but an analysis of it does provide some insights into the types of improvements which were taking place. Because the evidence is fragmentary, it is not possible to give precise quantitative measures of the reductions of costs or advances in productivity, and the discussion is meant to be suggestive rather than conclusive.

First, there is evidence that packaging costs were declining. The average size of containers for some of the important staple commodities increased substantially during the colonial period. Sugar hogsheads from the West Indies, for example, approximately doubled in weight,[1] and barrels of rice exported from the lower south increased in weight from about 350 pounds on the average in 1717 to about 525 pounds in the 1770s.[2] Also, it was stated in Chapter 4 that the average volume of the tobacco hogshead increased by approximately 68 per cent from 1675–1775. Because peacetime freight rates per hogshead remained unchanged, and because volume rather than weight was the constraint on shipping capacity, it was concluded that shipping productivity on the tobacco route increased by about 68 per cent over this period.

Besides affecting our productivity measure of shipping, it is also possible to indicate advances in packaging productivity by analyzing changing container sizes. In the case of tobacco, two reasons were important. First, as larger average sizes of hogsheads were adopted, and additional inputs, such as labor, larger staves, and bigger hoops and headings, were required for the production of larger hogsheads, the output, or service rendered by the larger hogshead, increased more than

---

If externalities prevented individuals from taking action, the query still remains of why the government did not systematically police the western Atlantic and the Caribbean earlier than the mid-eighteenth century. The answer is found by comparing the costs and gains of naval protection. The social gains of adopting vessels like the flyboat and reducing transportation costs grew as trade expanded. In the early periods of colonization when trade was limited these gains were slight, but as commercial and marketing activity increased the potential gains from lower transportation costs increased. Also, as Barbour has stated, where settlement was thin, it was difficult and costly to completely eliminate piracy, but as the population of the Caribbean and North Atlantic seaboard increased, safe hiding places became more and more scarce and evasion of the law more difficult. It appears that somewhere in the early eighteenth century the growth of ocean traffic raised the social gains of reduced transportation costs above the costs of naval action. The inevitable result was government intervention, the elimination of piracy, and the diffusion of low-cost shipping techniques like those used in the Baltic centuries earlier.

[1] Davis, p. 282.

[2] Lewis C. Gray, *History of Agriculture in the Southern United States to 1860* (Washington, D.C.: Carnegie Institution of Washington, 1933), II, p. 1020; and *Historical Statistics*, pp. 750–1.

proportionately to the additional inputs. This is because the volume, and thus the weight carried, of a container such as a barrel increases proportionately more than the surface area as the container increases in size.[1] Thus there was an incentive to adopt larger containers, which would only be offset at some large size when the difficulties of handling the larger container offset the economies gained from using it. This same economy based upon the use of a large container applied to many commodities, as is apparent from the growth in size of rice barrels and sugar hogsheads as well as those of tobacco. Secondly, in the case of tobacco, the hogshead not only increased by about 68 per cent in volume, but was approximately twice as heavy in 1775 as it had been in 1675. Consequently, 32 per cent of the increase in weight came from tighter compression of the tobacco in packing; thus 32 per cent more tobacco was shipped with probably little or no additional inputs expended.[2]

Another improvement in the marketing of colonial commodities came through reductions of inventory costs. In the early eighteenth century vessels typically were held up in port for long periods. The search for freight was extremely time-consuming, and purchases and deliveries were generally made in small lots, thus requiring many transactions before a vessel became filled. For instance, in the Chesapeake, ships plying from farmsite to farmsite to gather cargoes of tobacco were nearly a hundred days in port on the average near the turn of the century. By 1770 port times in the Chesapeake had been reduced to below fifty days. In this case, the main reason for the reduction of port times was the increased use of specialized facilities for the storing and inventorying of tobacco.[3] Ships arriving in the Chesapeake had shorter turn-around times because cargoes had already

[1] Output can be defined as weight carried, which increased at least as much as volume. The inputs of wood would have increased in proportion to the surface area, but labor time to assemble and construct the container would not have changed significantly as it grew in size. Consequently, output per unit of inputs increased as hogsheads and barrels increased in size.

[2] It should also be noted that standardization and improvements in quality of tobacco occurred in the mid-eighteenth century. Inspection systems were developed in Virginia and Maryland to standardize packaged tobacco and eliminate the 'tending and curing of seconds, suckers, and ground leaves, and the packing of trashey tobacco.' (Gray, I, p. 228). Tobacco came to be stored in public warehouses, and even private warehouses were open to inspection. Because tobacco certificates were issued on stored tobacco and circulated as a medium of exchange, it was imperative to specify the quality as well as the quantity of stored tobacco. An important effect of this inspection system was quality control and reduction of uncertainties associated with tobacco exchanges. (See Baxter, *The House of Hancock* (Cambridge, Mass.: Harvard University Press, 1945), pp. 193–4, for examples of the risks and difficulties imposed because of the variable quality of goods.)

[3] For evidence on the development of warehousing and inventorying in the Chesapeake, see Jacob M. Price, 'The rise of Glasgow in the Chesapeake tobacco trade, 1707–1775,' *The William and Mary Quarterly*, XI, 2 (April 1954), pp. 179–99. On pages 189–90 and 195–6, Price discusses the establishment of factors, 'who are always buying against the arrival of their ships,' (p. 189) and the improvements from the use of factors over the old pre-1740 method of 'bartering goods for tobacco' (p. 195). Also see Gray, pp. 225–31.

been assembled in several convenient locations. The result was that shorter periods were needed to search for freight and to make transactions.

Port times in the colonies reflected more than simply the time in which ships lay idle in port. Changing port times in the colonies also reflected changing inventory times on colonial exports. Of course, colonial port times were shorter than total inventory time in the colonies, which would include the period between the harvest and the ship's arrival, but reductions in the former suggest declines in the latter. Inventories are one form of capital, and, for any given value of inventory, the costs (alternative costs of capital) incurred vary directly with the length of time inventories are held. Reductions in port times in the colonies directly reduced inventory times on outbound cargoes.[1] In the Chesapeake inventory times were reduced by àt least fifty days, and reductions also occurred elsewhere. The reduction in the time during which the alternative costs of capital were imposed was one aspect of the overall reduction in inventory costs. Another aspect was the alternative costs of capital (market interest rates being the lower limit), which declined during the eighteenth century and further reduced inventory costs (see p. 77, note 7). At any rate, the combined effects of these changes do suggest that inventory costs were being reduced in the colonies.[2]

Perhaps one of the most important improvements to affect the costs of distribution in the eighteenth century was the decline of risks associated with trade. One aspect of this improvement is seen in insurance rates on goods shipped overseas. Rates varied greatly between war and peacetime, or even depending on the time of the year in the Caribbean because of the hurricane season, but between 1675 and 1775 average insurance costs fell significantly.

Although cargoes were not always formally insured (a common practice, for example, was for colonial merchants to insure one-half the cargo and bear the remainder of the risk personally), the practice of insuring goods in shipment was common by the eighteenth century. The decline in risks of shipment is reflected by the overall decline in insurance rates over the century. London was the financial hub of the Empire and most insurance on the trade to Great Britain was purchased there. Premiums could be purchased in the colonies, however, and most goods (if formally insured) were insured in the colonies on the inter-

---

[1] They probably had some favorable effects on the inventory costs of inward cargoes as well, but it is not possible to reach any firm conclusions on this point given only the evidence of port times.

[2] It is possible that the gains from reduced inventory times were offset by increased costs for warehouses and storage facilities. However, it is also possible that the replacement of numerous tobacco sheds by centralized storage facilities lowered inventory costs because of economies of scale in building. At present, there is no evidence to suggest which of these two possibilities occurred.

coastal routes or in the West Indies or southern European trades. London insurers generally refused to insure goods shipped on vessels that were unavailable for their inspection; thus loosely knit organizations of colonial merchants came to provide coverage on the trades other than to Great Britain.

As stated above, during the period the effective charge on insurance was lowered by approximately 10 to 20 per cent, because in the seventeenth century the customary payment in case of loss varied between 75 per cent and 90 per cent of the sum insured. This coverage increased to within 1 or 2 per cent of the loss by the mid-eighteenth century (see p. 77, note 2) thus lowering the effective charge. Second, rates on most trans-Atlantic routes had fallen to a common peacetime rate of 2 per cent (one way) by the 1720s. As noted above, however, routes into Jamaican waters were exceptional and rates there remained well above normal peacetime rates seen elsewhere (see p. 77, notes 3, 4, and 5). But substantial declines were seen on most other routes from New England to the West Indies (for example, to Nevis and St Thomas, where peacetime rates fell roughly by one-half between 1700 and 1770 – see p. 77, note 5).

The decline in insurance costs was caused by the same factors that contributed to the decline of insurance rates on ships and the decline of crew sizes. Risks associated with piracy and privateering decreased over the period. The decline in risks and uncertainties resulted from growing security in trade and commerce. The probability that a cargo would reach its destination safely was increasing.

Another factor affecting price differences between the colonies and overseas areas was the cost of credit. For instance, in the trade from Great Britain short-term credit was frequently used by colonists for the purchase of European goods. The normal procedure was for the English merchant to include a twelve-month interest charge in the price of the goods shipped (see Chapter 6 and Appendix IV). The fact that this was normally done suggests that short-term credit was extensively used. The credit charge was reimbursed (partially or completely) if payment was made before the twelve months elapsed. The general reduction in interest rates throughout the eighteenth century lowered the prices on colonial imports, and, to the extent that credit was used in trade to other areas, it lowered the total differential there as well. Also affected were discounts on bills of exchange.

The combination of the improvements stated above had favorable effects on the development of an Atlantic trading community. It is likely that other types of improvements were also taking place. For instance, the increased flow of vessels among areas probably reduced the cost of information about prices and market conditions. It is also likely that commission charges declined on an average over time, but scarcity of data prevents any definite conclusions regarding these costs. The general analysis of inventorying, packaging, and other costs permits only statements about the direction of change. This was downward, but precise magnitudes are difficult to pinpoint because of the scarcity and fragmentary nature of the data.

The apparent reductions in these distribution costs were essentially caused by the same sources which lowered shipping costs. Economies of scale were a more important source of improvement than in shipping, but technological change appears to have played little part. The reductions of insurance costs on cargoes were caused by the decline of piracy and privateering, which similarly reduced insurance rates on vessels. Productivity advances in packaging resulted from learning-by-doing. For instance, with tobacco, it took time and experience to find that size of hogshead which minimized packaging costs but still permitted easy handling. Economies of scale in inventorying probably lowered inventory costs. Changes in business organization towards more efficient and specialized facilities took place as production grew. The gains from specialized storage facilities required some minimum level of production and market use to offset the costs of organization. It should be noted that the reductions in port times in shipping were not independent of these changes. Lastly, the growth of trade and development of credit institutions in Europe lowered interest rates. The effect of increased trade was to lower risks, thus reinforcing commercial expansion.

CHAPTER 6

OVERSEAS COMMODITY TRADE, 1768–72

The lack of statistical evidence is a perennial complaint of economic historians, and the further into the past one treads, the greater the dearth seems to be. For those who deal in the 'dark ages' of American economic history prior to 1800, such a paucity is particularly acute. Most quantitative evidence pertaining to eighteenth-century economic activity is scarce and of a fragmentary nature. With respect to overseas trade, however, a fortunate product of British mercantilistic concern over their colonies and their activities is a record of all legal trade for a five-year period, 1768 through 1772. This source, the American Inspector-General's Ledgers,[1] records the quantities of commodities entering into all the legal overseas trade of the colonies for this period. The existence of this evidence has provided the basis for an intensive balance-of-payments study for these five years in this and the following two chapters, and accounts for the attention paid to this particular five-year period. Such a study permits us to examine the magnitude, patterns, and composition of overseas trade, and other factors which entered into the external economic relations of the colonies. Most of the statistical information and computations relating to commodity trade and to the estimation of export and import values have been placed in Appendix IV.

At this point a conspicuous and important warning must again be made to the reader about the reliability of eighteenth-century trade statistics. First of all, the statistics may not be completely accurate, even for the legal trade of the colonies. At the very least, however, they allow one to obtain an approximate picture of the magnitudes and patterns of legal trade. Another qualification of the estimates results from smuggling and illegal trade. The extent of smuggling certainly varied from trade to trade and from commodity to commodity, depending upon the duties levied and how severely the restrictions were applied. In general, we argue that the picture of the export trade is reasonably accurate, and that it is the estimates of import values (particularly in the West Indian trade) and the resulting balances of

---

[1] These records are deposited in the Public Record Office in London and cataloged there as Customs 16/1. They pertain to the period January 5, 1768, to January 5, 1773. See the description of these records in Appendix IV.

trade that must be qualified because of this unknown factor (a more detailed discussion of smuggling and these qualifications is found in Appendix IV). We wish to stress that usually the use of numbers adds an aura of precision that may not be deserved, but it is difficult to approach quantitative questions without using quantitative data. Our estimates are admittedly of a rough-hewn nature, but they reflect our best efforts to provide an accurate quantitative picture of colonial trade.

COMMODITY EXPORTS

Commodities exported from the British North American colonies were numerous and varied, but fortunately for the purpose of estimation a relatively few staple commodities, mostly foodstuffs and other primary products, comprised a large proportion of the total value of exports. These commodities tended to be reasonably standard and homogeneous, and their prices were published regularly in colonial newspapers, upon which price histories have been based.[1] Various sources of quantity data also exist, but as stated above, the only complete source of commodity trade for any years in the colonial period is the American Inspector-General's Ledgers. Using the quantity data from this source, and those prices which could be obtained from the price histories or from other sources (see Appendix IV), values for the major commodities[2] traded have been calculated and presented in Appendix IV (Tables 2 through 6, presenting the trade to Great Britain, Ireland, southern Europe, the West Indies, and Africa respectively). Also available are contemporary estimates[3] of the total value of commodities exported from the British North American colonies in 1768 and 1770.

To arrive at estimates of total exports (by major region) for the years 1768–72 we have combined the information from the contemporary estimates with the computed values of the major commodities traded (Tables 2 through 6, Appendix IV). The estimation procedure can be

[1] Anne Bezanson, *et al.*, *Prices in Colonial Pennsylvania* (Philadelphia: University of Pennsylvania Press, 1935); Anne Bezanson, *et al.*, *Prices and Inflation during the American Revolution, Pennsylvania, 1770–1790* (Philadelphia: University of Pennsylvania Press, 1951); Arthur H. Cole, *Wholesale Commodity Prices in the United States, 1700–1861: Statistical Supplement* (Cambridge, Mass.: Harvard University Press, 1938).

[2] The commodities for which values have been computed in Tables 2 through 6, Appendix IV, are those for which prices could be obtained. It turns out that they comprised the major part of the value of all exports (see below).

[3] The estimate for 1768 comes from a manuscript in the British Museum (Additional Mss 15485), which contains estimates of all export values and the value of imports from the West Indies, southern Europe and the Wine Islands, and Africa. The estimate for 1770, which gives export values only, comes from David Macpherson, *Annals of Commerce, Manufactures, Fisheries and Navigation* (London, 1805), III, pp. 572–3, and is reprinted in the U.S. Bureau of the Census, *Historical Statistics of the United States, Colonial Times to 1957* (Washington, D.C.: U.S. Government Printing Office, 1960), p. 761 (hereafter cited as *Historical Statistics*), with corrections made from the American Inspector-General's Ledgers (which undoubtedly was Macpherson's source). Abstracts from these sources are presented in Tables 9 and 10, Appendix IV.

described as follows: to estimate the value of total commodity exports from each colonial region to each of the five overseas areas of trade, the value of those commodities exported for which prices exist were assumed to have been the same proportion of the total value of exports from each region as they were of the total value of exports from all colonies,[1] as given in the contemporary estimates. For example, it was assumed that the computed values of those commodities in Table 2, Appendix IV, formed 86.24 per cent of the total value of exports to Great Britain from each colonial region in 1770 (the total computed value of exports to Great Britain from each colonial region is divided by 0.8624 to arrive at an estimated total value of all exports from each colonial region to Great Britain in 1770). The same procedure was followed for each region's trade with the other overseas areas for 1768 and 1770, using the percentages computed from the contemporary estimates.[2] Since there were no contemporary estimates for 1769, 1771, and 1772, a simple average of the percentages for 1768 and 1770 was used to estimate total exports for these other three years.[3] Finally,

[1] If the estimates of total exports are to be broken down by colonial region, this assumption must be made, because the contemporary estimates do not give commodity breakdowns by colony. By giving the computed value of certain commodities before proceeding to estimate total values of exports by region on the basis of the contemporary estimates, it is hoped to enable the interested reader to assess for himself any errors or biases that may be incorporated into the totals because of this assumption.

[2] There are certain problems of comparison between the contemporary estimates and the computed totals of selected commodities. Macpherson's totals do include commodities re-exported from the colonies, but they are not listed separately by commodity. Therefore there is no way of accounting for them when obtaining the percentages from the contemporary estimates of those commodities for which values have been computed. Because some re-exports (such as wine re-exported to the West Indies, West Indian rum re-exported to other overseas areas, and cotton re-exported to Great Britain) have been included in the computed value totals (from Tables 2 through 6, Appendix IV,) but not in the percentages derived from the 1770 contemporary estimate, the 1770 percentages will be lower than they should be, and the resulting total estimates thus will be higher. The magnitudes involved, however, will be slight. Cotton was 0.26 per cent of total exports to Great Britain in the 1768 contemporary estimate and wine re-exported to the West Indies was 1.31 per cent of total exports to the West Indies in the 1768 estimate. The 1768 estimate does not give colonial-produced rum separately from West Indian rum, so we cannot tell what proportion West Indian rum formed of total exports to the other overseas areas, but it probably was not very significant. There are also some differences in the category of pine boards. Values in Tables 2 through 5, Appendix IV, were computed only for pine boards. The 1770 contemporary estimates, however, included oak and cedar boards, and the 1768 contemporary estimate included pine timber and plank as well as boards. Because of the small difference involved, the problem of comparison between the contemporary estimates and the computed values has been ignored.

[3] The exception is Africa, which was not given separately in the 1768 contemporary estimate. The 1770 percentage for Africa has been used for all five years. The simple averages used for the other overseas areas for 1769, 1771 and 1772 are:

Great Britain	87.55	Southern Europe	96.87
Ireland	93.07	West Indies	89.34

The percentage for Great Britain was computed using a 1768 percentage which included deerskins, since values of deerskins were computed in Table 2, Appendix IV, for 1769 through 1772.

because these estimates are intended to represent the earnings of foreign exchange by the colonists in their commodity trade, an allowance for losses and spoilage during shipment has been made based on the prevailing insurance rates in each route (see note *a* to Table 6.1). The estimated values of total exports are presented in Table 6.1.

TABLE 6.I.   *Estimated values of total commodity exports from the British North American colonies (by colonial region) to overseas areas of trade, 1768–72* (thousands of pounds sterling)[a]

Overseas area of destination and colonial region of origin	1768	1769	1770	1771	1772
To Great Britain					
Northern colonies	17	25	38	66	38
New England	89	87	95	87	76
Middle colonies	101	73	71	78	52
Upper south	773	962	890	1,045	987
Lower south	379	378	338	444	636
Florida, Bahama and Bermuda Is.	1	15	17	41	39
Total to Great Britain	1,360	1,540	1,449	1,761	1,828
To Ireland					
Northern colonies	3	1	1	17	2
New England	b	3	1	1	2
Middle colonies	54	47	68	49	53
Upper south	11	28	61	36	16
Lower south	1	1	2	2	1
Florida, Bahama and Bermuda Is.	0	0	0	0	0
Total to Ireland	69	80	133	105	74
To southern Europe and the Wine Islands					
Northern colonies	68	87	106	236	168
New England	62	70	62	78	59
Middle colonies	103	225	214	146	237
Upper south	72	153	116	65	96
Lower south	73	69	67	32	32
Florida, Bahama and Bermuda Is.	0	0	0	0	0
Total to southern Europe and the Wine Islands	378	604	565	557	592
To the West Indies					
Northern colonies	8	9	10	13	21
New England	252	281	318	319	347
Middle colonies	162	207	255	253	344
Upper south	73	95	102	110	120
Lower south	85	103	127	115	129
Florida, Bahama and Bermuda Is.	3	4	3	3	3
Total to West Indies	583	699	815	813	964

[a] All estimates have been rounded to the nearest thousand pounds sterling. Estimates of total exports to Great Britain, Ireland, and southern Europe have been reduced by 2 per cent, exports to the West Indies by 2½ per cent, and exports to Africa by 4 per cent, to allow for losses and spoilage. These percentages were the prevailing insurance rates on these routes. See p. 120, note 2 for the sources of these rates.

[b] Less than £500.

TABLE 6.1. *Estimated values of total commodity exports from the British North American colonies (by colonial region) to overseas areas of trade, 1768–72* (thousands of pounds sterling)[a] – *continued*

Overseas area of destination and colonial region of origin	1768	1769	1770	1771	1772
To Africa					
Northern colonies	0	0	0	0	0
New England	13	23	20	15	25
Middle colonies	b	1	1	1	2
Upper south	0	0	0	0	0
Lower south	0	b	0	b	2
Florida, Bahama and Bermuda Is.	0	0	0	0	0
Total to Africa	13	24	21	16	29
To all destinations					
Northern colonies	96	122	155	332	229
New England	416	464	496	500	509
Middle colonies	420	553	609	527	688
Upper south	929	1,238	1,169	1,256	1,219
Lower south	538	551	534	593	800
Florida, Bahama and Bermuda Is.	4	19	20	44	42
Total to all destinations	2,403	2,947	2,983	3,252	3,487

The above procedure is equivalent to revaluing the contemporary estimates of exports by two price indexes that could have been constructed, one for 1768 and one for 1770, from the market prices used in the calculation of values of the individual commodities. For several reasons, however, the above procedure was followed instead of computing price indexes. For one thing, if export values are to be estimated by colonial region, the above (or some similar) procedure was necessary to make the regional breakdowns. Second, it may be of interest to some readers to provide approximate actual values for some of the more important commodity exports from the colonies. In case any doubt arises about the validity of the total estimates, this procedure makes it possible for the interested reader to make whatever adjustments he feels are appropriate, and to determine what effects such adjustments would have on the totals. Third, it was felt that the quantity data from the American Inspector-General's Ledgers were likely to be more accurate. These data have been tallied from the individual port district data, and the addition required to aggregate these districts to colonial regions has been thoroughly checked. The accuracy of the addition in the contemporary estimates probably suffered from a lack of modern adding machines. Several errors in addition were found in the values given in British Museum Additional Mss 15485, for instance. Finally, computation of price indexes for 1768 and 1770 would have resulted in estimates of total exports for these two years only. The procedure actually followed resulted in estimates of total exports for the entire five-year period.

It should be stressed that the estimates in Table 6.1 (and in Tables 2 through 6, Appendix IV, as well) are F.O.B. values. This follows from the use of colonial prices in the value computations. These are values that represent the earnings of foreign exchange by colonists from the sale of these commodities to buyers in overseas areas. Additional earnings were made by the colonists in carrying and selling these commodities to buyers in overseas areas. Such earnings were due to the sale of services, such as freight and insurance, and these invisible earnings for this period have been estimated in the following chapter.

The sale of ships to buyers in overseas areas was not recorded in the customs records, and the foreign exchange earnings from such sales are therefore not included in the above estimates of commodity exports. Earnings from ship sales were probably a small, but consistent, credit in the colonial balance of payments over much of the colonial period. By the late colonial period probably a sizable number of tons were built for sale to overseas buyers. In the absence of a statistical series of ship sales, reliance must be placed on fragmentary evidence in order to obtain some idea about the magnitude of these earnings. This fragmentary evidence is examined in Appendix VI, and we conclude that these earnings most likely ranged from £45,000 to £106,000 annually, but that £75,000 would be a reasonable estimate of average earnings from this source. Such earnings were therefore small relative to total commodity exports.

COMPOSITION, MAGNITUDES AND THE GROWTH OF EXPORTS

The estimates from the previous section permit the examination of the patterns and composition of colonial overseas trade. The annual average values of exports to the major overseas areas over this five-year period were:

Great Britain	£1,588,000
Ireland	92,000
Southern Europe and the Wine Islands	539,000
The West Indies	775,000
Africa	21,000
Total	£3,015,000

Great Britain was the largest overseas customer for colonial products. Exports to Great Britain were valued at more than those from all other regions combined; and, as historians have usually observed, it was the southern colonies which dominated this trade by furnishing 86 per cent of the total value of commodities exported to Britain. In terms of value, the West Indies was second with 26 per cent and southern Europe third with 18 per cent over this five-year period. The export trade to southern Europe was distributed more evenly among the various colonial regions (except for Florida, and the Bahama and Bermuda Islands, which had no recorded exports to that region), with the middle colonies having the largest share followed by the northern colonies (whose exports were primarily fish from Newfoundland). The thirteen colonies held the bulk of the export trade to the West Indies, with New England accounting for 39 per cent, the middle colonies 32 per cent, the upper south 13 per cent, and the lower south 14 per cent over this five-year period. Exports to Ireland were relatively small, with only 3 per cent of total exports for the five years going there.

For the most part, the description of the colonial export trade usually given by historians seems consistent with the above estimates. It is the African trade, however, which usually has not been put in proper perspective. Over this period, exports to Africa averaged less than 1 per cent of the total value of exports. One might suspect that the emphasis placed on the African trade by historians has been due to the immoral and inhumane aspects of this trade. Very probably this is true, but one can also find rather specific contentions made about the economic importance to the colonies of this export trade that are not supported by the above evidence, or by the evidence collected on colonial shipping. Consider, for example, the following statement by Nettels:

> Newport, Boston, New York, and other towns sent forth vessels laden with rum to purchase slaves in Africa, then to make the famous middle passage to the West Indies and there to dispose of their cargoes, chiefly for commodities marketable in England, and partly for molasses to be returned to the northern colonies as raw material for more rum. So important was this heady beverage in the trade that rum distilleries sprang up rapidly in New England (there were 63 of them in Massachusetts in 1750 and about 30 in Rhode Island). By 1771 the colonial slave traders employed between 60 and 70 vessels, each capable of transporting 65 Negroes – an investment equal to about a fourth of England's stake in the traffic.[1]

The above estimates of colonial exports to Africa would suggest that considerably more New England rum was drunk in America than in Africa. Nor do annual average ship clearances to Africa from the colonies of 1,291 tons[2] for this period suggest anything like the figure of sixty to seventy ships of colonial ownership trading with Africa. The value of Negro slaves brought in from Africa was significant (see Chapter 8), but the importance of the trade for earnings of foreign exchange by northern slave-traders has not been substantiated.

[1] Nettels, *The Roots of American Civilization: A History of American Colonial Life* (2nd ed.; New York: Appleton-Century-Crofts, 1963), pp. 435–6. Nettels gives no source for his statement concerning the number of vessels trading with Africa.
[2] See Chapter 7, Table 7.2.

The average annual values of the five highest-valued commodities exported over this five-year period were:

Tobacco	£766,000
Bread and flour	412,000
Rice	312,000
Dried fish	287,000
Indigo	117,000

These five commodities comprised over 60 per cent of the total value of exports. The importance of the southern staples of tobacco, rice, and indigo should come as no surprise if one has read the standard textbook description of the colonial export trade. Perhaps only the exports of bread and flour, primarily from the middle colonies and to a lesser extent from the upper south, have not been given proper emphasis by historians. Considering that they were second only to tobacco during this period, and comprised nearly 14 per cent of total exports (compared with 25 per cent for tobacco and 10 per cent for rice), they do deserve greater emphasis. From Tables 2 through 6, Appendix IV, it is also possible to assess the relative importance (in terms of value) of some of the other commodities that entered into trade with the various overseas areas, and which were important to various colonies or regions, yet were not of such magnitude to be included in the above top five commodities. Worthy of some mention here are deerskins, naval stores, whale oil, bar and pig iron, and potash that went to Great Britain. Significant exports of foodstuffs (especially bread, flour, and wheat) to Great Britain took place in 1768 and to a lesser extent in 1769 due to the poor British crops of the 1760s. The same was true with respect to Ireland and southern Europe. The variations in exports to those areas were related to the success of their crops. Flaxseed was the single most important commodity sent to Ireland over this period. Cotton, despite its later importance, was not a significant export from the colonies at this time.[1] Indian corn, spermaceti candles, beef and pork, livestock and wood products were consistent and moderately important exports to the West Indies. Indian corn was also exported in significant amounts to southern Europe, although wheat exports to that area were more important. It might be noted that, in the trade with the West Indies, wheat was an export of negligible importance, despite the exports of numerous other foodstuffs. Apparently it was a more efficient use of West Indian resources to devote them to the production of sugar and other tropical and semi-tropical produce than to engage in the manufacture of flour and bread from imported wheat. The export of wood products to the British Isles and to the West Indies was almost certainly more important than one might gather from the tables in Appendix IV.

---

[1] This cotton had been produced almost entirely in the West Indies and was being re-exported from the colonies. See the discussion below for the actual amounts involved.

The problem is that most wood products could not be valued because prices could not be found.

The increase in total export values from £2,403,000 in 1768 to £3,487,000 in 1772 was substantial to say the least, and deserves some comment at this point. It was due to a combination of increased prices paid for colonial exports and of increased quantities of commodities exported. Clearly, this five-year period was a time of increasing demand for colonial goods.[1] Bezanson makes the following statement with regard to prices in Philadelphia, which were reasonably typical of prices in the other colonies:

> prices in Philadelphia dropped more than 17 per cent in a comparatively unbroken recession from November, 1766, to April, 1769, and an advance from the low point then established had not progressed far when, in the spring of 1769, the merchants of Philadelphia joined with those of Boston and New York in an agreement to refrain from importing British goods. This measure, in force for the first nine months of 1770, did not prevent a selective advance in prices of domestic staples, salt, and a few other commodities, which gained momentum as the force of the European demand for grain made itself felt. As a result, prices of domestic staples not only reached the highest peak of colonial years in 1772 but held at relatively high levels until 1774.[2]

The increase in export values was not due to higher exports of any single commodity or increased trade with any one area. Exports to Great Britain increased the most over this five-year period (43 per cent of the increase in total exports went there). The West Indies accounted for 35 per cent of the increase, and southern Europe for 20 per cent.

The same commodities that are listed above as being the most valuable can be singled out as making up a large part of the increase. The value of bread and flour exported to the West Indies and southern Europe increased by the largest absolute amount (from £198,000 in 1768 to £522,000 in 1772). This increased value of bread and flour exports was due to a 69 per cent increase in the quantities exported

---

[1] The terms of trade were in all likelihood improving for the colonies during this period. This cannot be fully substantiated because of the scarcity of price data for British imports, but during this period we find some evidence of price decreases of British goods. See, for example, the testimony in 'Report from the Committee Appointed to Enquire into the State of the Linen Trade in Great Britain and Ireland' (Great Britain, Parliamentary Papers, *Reports from Committees from the House of Commons*, III, May 25, 1773, pp. 99–133), which claimed that linens were selling for 10 to 12 per cent less than they had been at the end of the Seven Years' War. There would also have been some downward pressure on the prices of British imports during the periods of the non-importation agreements. Providing the prices of imports fell, were stable, or rose less than prices of colonial exports, then the terms of trade would have improved for the colonies.

[2] Bezanson, *et al.*, *Prices and Inflation during the American Revolution*, p. 12. The important exception was tobacco prices in Maryland and Virginia, which rose from 1768 to 1770, then fell below their 1768 level in 1771 (See Table 1, Appendix IV).

and a 31 per cent increase in prices paid for these commodities. Tobacco exports to Great Britain rose from £589,000 in 1768 to £837,000 in 1772. The increased value of tobacco exported was due entirely to the fact that larger quantities of tobacco were shipped to Great Britain, since prices paid for tobacco in Maryland and Virginia declined by 45 per cent between 1768 and 1772. The value of rice exported to Great Britain rose from £216,000 in 1768 to £289,000 in 1772, while rice exported to the West Indies increased from £38,000 to £66,000 over this five-year period. Most of the rise in the value of rice exports was due to increased prices; the quantities of rice exported to these two overseas areas grew by only 27 per cent over this period. Exports of indigo rose from £79,000 to £209,000 between 1768 and 1772 (33 per cent of the increase in value was due to increased quantities exported and 67 per cent was due to higher prices). Finally, exports of dried fish to the West Indies increased from £82,000 in 1768 to £147,000 in 1772 (88 per cent was due to increased quantities exported and only 12 per cent to increased prices). Together these commodities exported to the specified overseas areas accounted for over 80 per cent of the total increase in export values between 1768 and 1772. The remainder came from increases in the values of the various other commodities exported to Great Britain, the West Indies, and southern Europe and the Wine Islands. Exports to southern Europe jumped to a peak in 1769 following a year of poor crops there, then fell and stabilized for the remaining three years above the 1768 level. Exports to Ireland increased until 1770, but then fell back to about the 1768 level by 1772. Exports to Africa fluctuated, and then rose in 1772, but they were not a significant part of the total value of exports.

No single commodity or trade showed as steady an increase as did the value of total exports. It so happened that the increase in value of the more important commodities alternated in such a way as to produce this smoother pattern of growth in the value of total exports. The rapid rate of growth in exports for this period (a compound rate of approximately 6 per cent per year) cannot be extrapolated backward over the colonial period. If this rate were projected back, the predicted export values would be far lower than the evidence suggests they actually were.[1] Therefore, this five-year period was one of unusually rapid growth in colonial exports. It is probably safe to say that the value of colonial exports had never before been as high as it was in 1772. It is not possible to say how long this trend continued after 1772 (in the few years remaining before the Revolution), but the official value of exports to Great Britain from the colonies reached a peak in 1775.[2]

---

[1] See the magnitudes of eighteenth-century overseas trade estimated in Chapter 3.
[2] *Historical Statistics*, p. 757.

Since we have estimates of population for the thirteen colonies for 1770, it is possible to calculate the per capita value of exports for this year. The estimated population[1] and the resulting per capita values of exports from the major regions of the thirteen colonies (calculated from Table 6.1) were:

	Population	*1770 per capita exports* (pounds sterling)
New England	581,038	£0.85
Middle colonies	555,904	1.10
Upper south	649,615	1.80
Lower south	344,819	1.55
Thirteen colonies	2,131,376	1.32

The meaning of these per capita export values already has been discussed in Chapter 3, where it was argued that these values represented a significant part of colonial economic activity. With regard to overseas trade in later years, if a comparison based on current prices is made with per capita exports for the United States in 1790, then the 1770 estimate for the thirteen colonies is slightly higher; but if an adjustment is made for changes in the price level, 1770 per capita exports appear to have been significantly higher than per capita exports in 1790.[2] The apparent interpretation is that the overseas trade was more important to the colonists in 1770 than to Americans in 1790. The 1770 figure, however, is below per capita export values attained in some years during the period of more prosperous foreign trade, 1793–1807.[3] If invisible earnings[4] are added to the per capita value of exports, then the

[1] *Ibid.*, p. 756. The estimated population of Kentucky and Tennessee has been deducted from the total.

[2] Commodity exports from the United States in 1790 have been estimated at $20,205,000 (Douglass C. North, 'The United States balance of payments, 1790–1860,' *Trends in the American Economy in the Nineteenth Century, Studies in Income and Wealth*, Vol. 24. N.B.E.R., (Princeton, N.J.: Princeton University Press, 1960), p. 590). This would mean per capita exports (based on current prices) of $5.14 in 1790 compared with the 1770 estimate of $5.86 (using the exchange rate of $4.44=£1). If these values are adjusted by the Warren and Pearson price index (*Historical Statistics*, p. 115), then the differential between the two years is substantially increased.

	Warren and Pearson price index (*1910–14=100*)	*Adjusted per capita values of exports*
1770	77	$7.61
1790	90	5.71

[3] Per capita exports in 1800 were $13.40, and $16.31 in 1807 when exports hit a peak just before the Embargo was imposed. Again these values are based on current prices. If these values of per capita exports for these years are adjusted by the Warren and Pearson price index, the differential between 1770 and 1800 and 1807 is narrowed, and per capita exports become:

	Warren and Pearson price index (*1910–14=100*)	*Adjusted per capita values of exports*
1800	129	$10.39
1807	130	12.55

[4] From Chapter 7.

value of overseas trade to each colonist, of course, is higher:

*1770 per capita values of commodity
exports plus invisible earnings*
(pounds sterling)

New England	£1.56
Middle colonies	1.57
Southern colonies	1.85
Thirteen colonies	1.70

The differentials between the various regions narrow considerably, indicating the importance of invisible earnings to the middle colonies and especially to New England.

THE ESTIMATION OF COMMODITY IMPORTS

Practical considerations have dictated the use of several different sets of data, and consequently of different procedures, for estimating the values of imports into the colonies from the various major overseas trading areas. Imports from the West Indies and southern Europe and the Wine Islands were primarily tropical, semi-tropical, or other commodities which could not be produced cheaply, if at all, in the colonies. Like exports from the colonies, these were fairly standard commodities, such as foodstuffs or raw materials, for the more important of which prices have been compiled in the price histories[1] from colonial sources. The value of imports from these areas thus could be estimated by the same procedures used above to estimate the value of exports.

Unlike the staple-type exports from the colonies and the imports from the West Indies and southern Europe, imports from the British Isles were composed of a large number of commodities of widely varying grades or qualities. The American Inspector-General's Ledgers listed the quantities of these exports for the three years, 1769, 1770, and 1771; and in 1770, for example, some 241 different commodities of British and Irish manufacture were listed as having been imported into the colonies, and 242 different commodities of foreign manufacture were listed that had first been imported into Britain, and then re-exported to the colonies. British re-exports tended to be substantial because most goods of foreign origin were required by the Navigation Acts to first pass through Great Britain.[2] Given the almost

---

[1] Cited on p. 92, note 1.

[2] The exceptions were commodities like wine and salt from southern Europe and the Wine Islands, and the various commodities imported from the West Indies. See Lawrence A. Harper, *The English Navigation Acts: A Seventeenth-Century Experiment in Social Engineering* (New York: Columbia University Press, 1939), pp. 400–4, for a summary of the restrictions on colonial imports imposed by the Navigation Acts, and the exceptions made to these restrictions. The colonies were not allowed to trade directly with continental Europe north of Cape Finisterre, which is on the northwestern coast of Spain. The drawback (or refund) of import duties was allowed on the re-export of most goods. This meant that commodities like German linens could be competitive with British and Irish linens in colonial markets.

insurmountable problem of finding accurate average annual prices for such a large number of commodities of varying qualities, the British and Irish customs records[1] (which recorded the official values of imports, and exports, unlike the American records which recorded only quantities) were used to estimate values of imports from the British Isles.

COMMODITY IMPORTS FROM SOUTHERN EUROPE AND THE WEST INDIES

Like exports, values for a relatively few staple commodities comprised a large proportion of the total value of imports from these two overseas areas. These values were computed using quantity data from the American Inspector-General's Ledgers and price data from the price histories. The computed values of salt and wine imported from southern Europe[2] are listed in Table 7, Appendix IV, and the computed values of seven commodities (coffee, cotton, molasses, rum, salt, muscovado sugar, and wine) imported from the West Indies are listed in Table 8, Appendix IV. As stated above, salt and wine were the only commodities which could be legally imported from southern Europe; therefore, they presumably comprised 100 per cent of commodity imports from there.[3] Estimates of these imports are given in the first part of Table 6.2, and were taken directly from Table 7, Appendix IV. According to the contemporary estimate (Table 10, Appendix IV) of the value of imports from the West Indies in 1768, the seven commodities for which values could be computed (Table 8, Appendix IV) comprised 86.86 per cent of the total value of imports in that year. Therefore, as was done above in estimating total export values, it was assumed that the computed values of the seven commodities (in Table 8, Appendix IV)

[1] London, Public Record Office, Customs 3 (England and Wales), Customs 14 (Scotland), and Customs 15 (Ireland). These are the English, Scottish, and Irish Inspector-General's Ledgers, respectively.

[2] The term 'southern Europe' will be used to include the Wine Islands (which consisted of the Azores, and the Madeira, Canary, and Cape Verde Islands) whenever mentioned in this chapter.

[3] There is some question whether salt and wine were the only products being imported directly from southern Europe into the colonies at this time, despite the prohibitions of the Navigation Acts. See, for example, James G. Lydon, 'Fish and flour for gold: southern Europe and the colonial American balance of payments', *Business History Review*, XXXIX, 2 (Summer 1965), p. 172, who states that imports from southern Europe in the eighteenth century also included oranges, limes, currants, raisins, olives, anchovies, Leghorn hats, Barcelona handkerchiefs and other luxury goods. The American Inspector-General's Ledgers list no such imports from southern Europe for this period (although a small number of hides, some logwood, and small values of unspecified goods were recorded for 1772). Whether such goods were imported at all and, if they were, whether the values were significant, are open questions. If they were imported, then presumably they were either smuggled or else the customs officers were not strictly enforcing the Navigation Acts. The latter may well have been the case, because small amounts of salt were being imported directly into the southern colonies even though permission to do this had never been given by a subsequent amendment to the Navigation Acts (see Harper, p. 401, and Lydon, p. 177).

TABLE 6.2. *Estimated values of total commodity imports into the British North American colonies (by colonial region) from southern Europe and the Wine Islands, and the West Indies, 1768–72* (thousands of pounds sterling)a

Overseas area of origin and colonial region of destination	1768	1769	1770	1771	1772
From southern Europe and the Wine Islands					
Northern colonies	6	4	6	12	12
New England	15	26	14	15	20
Middle colonies	35	30	43	22	32
Upper south	15	14	5	10	10
Lower south	6	5	7	7	9
Florida, Bahama and Bermuda Is.	1	2	1	1	1
Total from southern Europe and the Wine Islands	78	81	76	67	84
From the West Indies					
Northern colonies	10	4	10	10	11
New England	258	362	350	322	403
Middle colonies	169	290	307	185	321
Upper south	82	104	112	115	134
Lower south	47	64	94	53	83
Florida, Bahama and Bermuda Is.	8	10	4	6	12
Total from West Indies	574	834	877	691	964

a All estimates have been rounded to the nearest thousand pounds sterling.

were 86.86 per cent of the total value of imports into each of the major colonial regions from the West Indies in each year of the period, 1768–72. The values of total commodity imports from the West Indies thus estimated are also presented in Table 6.2.[1]

The values of imports estimated in this manner with colonial prices are C.I.F. values (i.e. values that include the cost of insurance, freight to the colonies, mercantile profits, and so forth). These are, of course, unlike the F.O.B. values of exports estimated above. To the extent that these imports were purchased from foreigners in the colonies, they reflect the proper debit in the colonial balance of payments. The West Indian and southern European trades, however, were largely in the hands of colonial merchants and shippers. These estimates thus over-state the amount of foreign exchange spent on imports from these areas. In Chapter 7, when the values of services which were sold abroad are estimated, the value of that part of those services which was actually purchased by colonists from other colonists will enter the current account as a credit. Thus, to the extent that the estimates are reliable,

[1] This procedure for estimating southern European and West Indian imports, like that for estimating exports, is equivalent to revaluing the contemporary estimate of imports for 1768 by a price index. For the reasons stated on p. 95, however, the above procedure was followed instead. The estimates have the same advantages, and are subject to the same reservations, elaborated above and in Appendix IV.

the net balance on current account with these areas will reflect the proper debit.

The value of imports of salt and wine from southern Europe was not large relative to the total value of trade of the colonies. The annual average values for the period 1768–72 (by major region and rounded to the nearest thousand pounds sterling) were:

Northern colonies	£8,000
New England	18,000
Middle colonies	32,000
Upper south	11,000
Lower south	7,000
Florida, Bahama and Bermuda Is.	1,000
Total	£77,000

A total of £77,000 is not large when compared with average annual exports to all overseas areas of £3,015,000 (it is about 2½ per cent). As would be expected, the middle colonies, which led in exports to southern Europe, also imported the most from there. As has often been stated by historians in their accounts of colonial trade,[1] the colonies reaped a tidy surplus in this trade, which, of course, was very helpful in paying part of the deficit which they incurred in their trade with Britain. It seems likely that a sizable surplus would have existed in this trade even had the Navigation Acts not prohibited the direct import of all commodities except salt and wine. Some other southern European goods, such as raisins and other fruits, did reach the colonies via England; but the values of such commodities were small, and it seems unlikely that colonial demand for them was sufficiently elastic for imports to have been significantly higher if they had been imported directly.[2] Of the two commodities which were imported, salt comprised less than 40 per cent of the total, and wine a little over 60 per cent. Imports from southern Europe fluctuated mildly over this period, but like exports to the same region, showed no noticeable rising or falling trend.

Imports from the West Indies, on the other hand, were more numerous and of considerably greater magnitude. The average annual imports for the five years 1768–72 (on a regional basis and rounded to the nearest thousand pounds sterling) were:

Northern colonies	£9,000
New England	339,000
Middle colonies	254,000
Upper south	109,000
Lower south	68,000
Florida, Bahama and Bermuda Is.	8,000
Total	£788,000[3]

[1] See, for example, Lydon, *op. cit.*
[2] This statement is subject to the qualifications discussed on p. 103, note 3.
[3] The regional figures do not add up to the total due to rounding.

The value of such imports was over ten times that of imports from southern Europe, and over one-quarter of the value of imports for this period. West Indian imports fluctuated considerably, showing a substantial decline in 1771 due largely to lower molasses, rum, and sugar imports into the middle colonies; but, like exports to the West Indies, they appear to have been on a rising trend over this five-year period. On the basis of the estimates of commodity trade alone (and before invisible earnings are taken into account in Chapter 7), the colonies appear to have incurred on the average a small deficit in their trade with the West Indies for the period. Three commodities – molasses, rum, and muscovado (brown, or semi-refined) sugar – accounted for a large share (over three-quarters) of the estimated value of West Indian imports. The average annual values of the seven commodities for which values were computed (rounded to the nearest thousand pounds sterling) were:

Coffee	£16,000
Cotton	19,000
Molasses	201,000
Rum	285,000
Salt	31,000
Sugar	132,000
Wine	1,000

Most of the molasses (over 90 per cent) went to New England and the middle colonies – 70 per cent went to New England alone, presumably to be used as the chief raw material for that region's numerous rum distilleries.[1] Rum and sugar imports were more evenly divided among the various colonial regions although the middle colonies took larger proportions (36 per cent of the rum and 46 per cent of the sugar) than any of the other regions. This perhaps indicated the middle colonists' preference for West Indian rum over the lower-quality rum that was produced in the colonies. Almost ten times as much cotton was imported into the colonies as was re-exported to Great Britain (2,116,607 lb. were imported over this five-year period and 218,340 lb. were exported to Britain over the period). Most of the cotton (about 96 per cent) went to New England and the middle colonies, with New England taking over 70 per cent of the total. Cotton together with coffee and salt accounted for about 8 per cent of the value of West Indian imports over the five years 1768–72. Judging from the contemporary estimate of imports for 1768 (Table 10, Appendix IV), the other commodities of significant value imported from the West Indies were cocoa, logwood, mahogany, and sarsaparilla (together they comprised about 7 per cent of the contemporary estimate). Small amounts of other commodities, such as various dyewoods and pimento, entered the colonies from the West Indies, but the values of such commodities were relatively small.

[1] See the quotation from Nettels on p. 97 concerning the large number of rum distilleries in New England.

COMMODITY IMPORTS FROM AFRICA

The notorious slave trade, of course, furnished the most important import from Africa. The numbers of slaves that were brought into the colonies, and the impact of this trade on the colonial balance of payments, will be discussed in Chapter 8. There were, however, a few commodities imported into the colonies from Africa that were recorded in the American customs records. The quantities of all such commodities are given in Table 11, Appendix IV, for purposes of illustration. It appears that ivory, beeswax, and various types of wood, such as ebony, were the principal commodities entering the colonies from Africa. In 1770, the year in which the largest quantities of beeswax were imported, the value of this beeswax was less than £1,000. No prices could be found with which to value any of the other commodities, and for this reason commodity imports from Africa will not be incorporated into the estimates of commodity imports made in this chapter. It seems highly unlikely, however, that the values of these imports were of significant magnitudes relative to total imports into the colonies.

COMMODITY IMPORTS FROM GREAT BRITAIN AND IRELAND

The most important types of goods of British and Irish manufacture (in terms of value) were the linens and woolens of various sorts, and the various metals, primarily brass, copper, and iron, that were wrought or cast into finished wares, such as nails, pots and pans, and tools. But the number of less important goods abounded, and included such items as articles of wearing apparel, for example hats and haberdashery; other sorts of household goods, such as glass-, earthen-, and chinaware and pewter utensils; gunpowder and shot; paper; glass; silk; leather and leather goods; drugs; and so on. The more important commodities re-exported from Great Britain to the colonies included goods like tea, hemp, German and Russian linens, and various spices and drugs. Again, a whole host of numerous but less valuable commodities were included in this list of re-exports. Perhaps the best short description of this trade in imports from Britain and Ireland has been given by a Philadelphia merchant, who wrote that British imports included:

> all kinds of British manufactories in great abundance and India goods, etc. In the last of the winter or early in the spring [we] choose to import our linens and other things fit for summer, the latter end of which we should have our woolen goods of all kinds ready for the fall sale to use in winter. The spring is the best time for iron mongery, cutleryware, furniture for furnishing houses, and all other brass and iron work. Our imports of those articles are very large, the people being much employed in

agriculture, husbandry, clearing and improving lands, but slow progress is made in the manufactories here.[1]

For the purposes of a balance-of-payments study, knowing the quantities of British and Irish imports from the American Inspector-General's Ledgers does little good unless prices of all, or at least some of the more important, commodities are also known. Bezanson lists wholesale prices for a few goods imported from Great Britain (specifically tea, pepper, gunpowder, London loaf sugar, Liverpool salt, hemp, and ginger), but 'the bulk of the trade consisted of manufactured articles.'[2] The difficulties[3] in obtaining prices for such goods, and thus the reasons why they are not included in Bezanson's price series, were stated as follows:

[1] Letter from Thomas Clifford, Philadelphia, to Abel Chapman, Whitby, England, July 25, 1767, quoted from Bezanson *et al.*, *Prices in Colonial Pennsylvania*, p. 263.

[2] *Ibid.*

[3] To illustrate the problem that can be encountered from varying grades of a single commodity, one might also cite any number of invoices for textiles that were received by colonial merchants. In one such invoice (Harvard University, Baker Library, Reynell and Coates Collection, Vol. 1, 1744–85), received by the Philadelphia firm of Reynell and Coates for 2,541 yards of Irish linen, the price per yard ranged from 11½d. to 2s., and in some instances even wider price variations were found. The average price per yard in this particular invoice was slightly over 15½d. per yard. In the American customs records, quantities of Irish linen were put into one of two categories – 'linen, Irish free' and 'linen, Irish bounty.' Bounties given to the export of linens from England in 1743 were applied as well to Irish linens re-exported from England. These bounties lapsed in 1753, but were renewed for certain types of linens from time to time until 1830 (see Conrad Gill, *The Rise of the Irish Linen Industry* (Oxford: The Clarendon Press, 1925), p. 71). Linens of considerably different qualities would be put into these two categories. Not only were different qualities of a commodity put into one category, but some categories included many different items that could hardly be called the same commodity. The categories in the American customs records for metals, for example, were listed as 'wrought iron,' 'wrought brass,' and 'wrought copper.' Quantities are given simply in terms of weight rather than by descriptions of the hundreds of items that were probably included in these general classifications. W. A. Cole, speaking about the category of 'wrought iron,' states that he believes it refers 'to all kinds of finished goods, and...it probably included a good many castings' (letter from W. A. Cole, Cambridge, England, to T. S. Ashton, London, May 20, 1959). (This correspondence is deposited together with Elizabeth B. Schumpeter's worksheets of eighteenth-century British overseas trade at the British Library of Political and Economic Science, The London School of Economics, London. Cole and Ashton were discussing the category as it appeared in the English Inspector-General's Ledgers rather than the American records, but the category was the same in both. This has to be the case, for there are no other categories that would have included all the various items of hardware that were imported into the colonies from England.) To illustrate the diversity of these goods, another invoice from the Reynell and Coates Collection can be cited. This was from Welch, Wilkinson & Startin, Birmingham, to William Seede, Bristol, August 5, 1770, with orders to ship on board the first vessel bound for Philadelphia to Reynell and Coates in that city, and it listed 'buttons, vests, buckles, boxes, brass buckles, oval buckles, chapes, shovels & tongs, 5 small br'ad screw gimblett, saws – whet & sett, sash pullies, brass ink potts, hand saw files, inch shoe rasps, smiths vices, stone wyre, dead stock locks, padlocks, sheep shears, boucles, candlesticks, dotted awl blades, shoe tacks, steel buckles, pen knives, pistol cap'd pocket knives, sham buck table knives, flatt rough files, chest locks, cloth colour'd and blew thread, money scales, common snuffers, steel knees, shapper bellows, hunters whips, window cords', and so the list went on. This was received in Philadelphia by Reynell and Coates on April 7, 1771, after the shipment had been delayed while the non-importation agreements were in force.

The varying specifications of the grades of these goods have prevented the determination of a consecutive series of prices. The
changes in the grades and in the description of the grades was only
one reason why these commodities were not quoted in the prices
current lists of the newspapers. An even more pertinent reason was
that they were imported by Philadelphia merchants from British
houses who granted credit terms or were sent on consignment to
the Philadelphians. In either case the local merchants usually
disposed of these goods at retail.[1]

These problems were thus serious obstacles to the estimation of
values of British and Irish imports into the colonies. Fortunately, an
alternative is open to us at this point. This is to use the British and
Irish customs records. These exist for England (including Wales)
beginning in 1696, for Ireland beginning in 1698, and for Scotland
beginning in 1755.[2] Unlike the American records, which listed only
quantities, the English, Scottish, and Irish customs records gave the
value as well as the quantity of each commodity exported. These values
were not declared values, however; rather they were the notorious
'official values' of the British and Irish eighteenth-century trade
statistics. Discussion of the derivation and meaning of the English
official values (which are given in Table 12, Appendix IV), and the
evidence pertaining to the actual or market values of imports from
England (which were used in Chapter 3) is presented in Appendix II.
The evidence suggests that for exports of English manufacture the
average English market values overstated the official values in England
by probably not more than 5 per cent, and that to convert these values
to C.I.F. values in the colonies they must be increased by an additional
8 per cent. The English official values of goods of English manufacture
thus have been multiplied by 1.13 to obtain estimates that approximate
the actual expenditures of the colonists on these commodities.[3] Unlike

---

[1] Bezanson, *et al.*, *Prices in Colonial Pennsylvania*, p. 263. While it is true that the local merchants
who specialized in importing British goods often sold at retail, it is also true that they often
would act as wholesalers to other merchants – either smaller local retailers, or ones located
outside the urban areas who operated country stores, or to peddlers. Since most of the
population lived in rural areas this may not have been an unimportant part of the market for
British imports. See the description of James Beekman's trade in New York in Philip L.
White, *The Beekmans of New York in Politics and Commerce, 1647-1877* (New York: New-York
Historical Society, 1956), pp. 335-530.

[2] Cited on p. 103, note 1. These will be referred to as the English, Scottish, and Irish customs
records, respectively.

[3] Let OV=official value of such exports,
  MV_e=average market value in England, and
  MV_c=average market value in the colonies.
Then $OV+0.05\ OV=MV_e$,
  $MV_e+0.08\ MV_e=1.08\ MV_e=MV_c$,
  $MV_c=1.08\ (1.05\ OV)=1.1340\ OV$.
This factor has been rounded to 1.13 in view of the rough nature of this approximation.

the goods of English manufacture, re-exports from England to the colonies were generally over-valued by the official rates. Apparently the prices of these re-exports fell over the course of the eighteenth century. The official values have been adjusted by the price index given in Table 5, Appendix II.

Because similar official values exist in the Scottish Inspector-General's Ledgers (which are given in Table 13, Appendix IV), it is possible to make the same re-valuation of exports from Scotland to the colonies. Different rates were used in the English and Scottish customs records to value many of the commodities exported, but the differences in most cases were small.[1] Because of the small differences, and the fact that the value of Scottish exports to the colonies was only about 10 per cent of the value of English exports,[2] the same adjustments have been applied to the Scottish official values, both for exports of British manufacture and for re-exports from Scotland to the colonies.[3]

Statistics of Irish exports to the colonies cannot be obtained directly for this period. The Irish Inspector-General's Ledgers gave the destination of Irish exports to America as 'exports to the plantations,' which included the British West Indies as well as the continental colonies. These records listed the following as 'exports to the plantations for the year ended 25th March, 1770:'[4]

Beef	74,929 barrels	£93,661
Butter	34,636 hundredweight	69,272
Linen cloth	826,513 yards	61,988
Pork	27,188 barrels	40,783
Other commodities		15,300
Total		£281,004

These values were computed using Irish 'official rates' in the same way as were the English and Scottish official values, but the rates were different from either the English or the Scottish rates[5]. It should be

---

[1] See Phyllis Deane and W. A. Cole, *British Economic Growth, 1688–1959* (London: Cambridge University Press, 1964), p. 316.

[2] The total official value of Scottish exports to the colonies for the period 1768–72 was 10.62 per cent of the total English official values for this same period.

[3] The Scottish Inspector-General's Ledger for 1769 was not in the Public Record Office and is apparently lost. The total official values of Scottish exports to the colonies in 1769 were taken from Macpherson (*Annals of Commerce*, III, p. 495), but he did not give the breakdown between exports of British manufacture and re-exports. In estimating the actual value of Scottish exports to the colonies for 1769, the average proportion of re-exports to total exports for the years 1768 and 1770–2 was assumed to be appropriate for 1769. One additional difference between the English and Scottish records was that exports of Irish linen were included in the English official values of exports of British manufacture, and in the Scottish records they were included in the official values of re-exports. No adjustment was made for this discrepancy because it would have made no significant difference in the estimated actual values given in Table 6.3.

[4] Re-exports were also listed, but no commodity breakdown was given. The value given of re-exports from Ireland 'to the plantations' for this year was only £11,349.

[5] The rate used to value linen in the Irish ledgers was 18d. per yard, for example. This is higher than the 12d. per yard rate used in the English ledgers, but two things must be

possible to calculate exports from Ireland to the colonies by comparing the English and Scottish records with the American records, which gave imports from Great Britain and Ireland together for three years, 1769–71. The difference between the American records and the British records should represent exports from Ireland. Such severe problems of comparison exist, however, that this result cannot be obtained.[1]

Despite the lack of any direct estimates of Irish exports to the colonies, we can say with certainty that such exports were relatively small when compared with exports from England and Scotland. The above quoted official value of exports from Ireland of £281,004 for the year ended March 25, 1770, was less than 9 per cent of the annual

---

remembered. First, 18d. in Irish currency was equivalent to about 16.6d. in English sterling; and, secondly, the 12d. per yard rate in the English ledgers applied only to linen worth from 6d. to 18d. per yard, whereas the Irish single rate of 18d. per yard was used to value all linens, which included the more expensive, higher quality linens exported, as well as those worth under 18d. per yard. The Irish rates were called 'a medium of the current prices,' and unlike the English and Scottish rates they supposedly were revised occasionally in an attempt to keep them in line with current average market prices in Ireland.

[1] The problems of comparison pertain mainly to linen cloth, which was certainly the most important export of Ireland to the continental colonies. These problems are three. First, discrepancies probably arise due to the shipping lag which would have caused different recording dates in the British and American records. One shipment entered in 1768 in the British records may have reached the colonies and been recorded in the American records in 1769. The great variations in British imports in these years due to the non-importation agreements served to accentuate such discrepancies. Second, the categories in the English, Scottish, and American records all differed in some respect from one another. The American records used four major categories – 'British bounty,' 'British free,' 'Irish bounty' and 'Irish free.' The English records used three major categories – 'British bounty,' 'Irish bounty' and 'above bounty.' The Scottish records used two categories – 'plain linen' and 'Irish linen.' Finally, different units were used in the English and American records for what, in some instances, must have been the same linen. One unit used in the English category, 'linen above bounty,' was 'pieces' of linen, while the American records used both 'yards' and 'pieces' to measure what was probably the same linen. Pieces of Irish linen averaged about 25 yards in invoices that were sent to colonial merchants (and that were examined by the authors and cited in the sources to Table 3, Appendix II), but 'official rates' used in the English records to value the 'above bounty' linen exported from London (35s. per piece) and from the outports (18d. per ell – one ell being 27 inches), suggested an average length of 17½ yards (this is the average length for which the two official rates are equated at 24d. per yard). The average quantity of British and Irish linen imported into the thirteen colonies and recorded in the American records for the three years 1769–71, was approximately 5,875,000 yards if it is assumed pieces of linen averaged 25 yards (it was about 5,676,000 yards if it is assumed pieces averaged 17½ yards). For the same years, the English and Scottish records show average exports to the thirteen colonies of 7,290,000 yards (assuming pieces averaged 25 yards) or 6,799,000 yards (assuming pieces averaged 17½ yards). In either case, the records show that more was shipped from Great Britain than was received in the colonies. The most probable explanation is that exports rose sharply after the non-importation agreements were lifted in 1770, but that this increase did not begin to be recorded in America until 1771. If annual average linen exports to the thirteen colonies for the years 1768–70 are computed from the English and Scottish records, they are 5,944,000 (assuming average pieces of 25 yards), or 5,558,000 yards (assuming average pieces of 17½ yards). This more nearly agrees with the American records, but it suggests that most of the linen entering the colonies came from Great Britain, and very little directly from Ireland (see the quotation from Gill below).

average official value of all exports from England and Scotland for the five years 1768–72; and part – probably the largest part – of the Irish exports went to the West Indies. Although some of the foodstuffs exported from Ireland did find their way to the colonies, most of these provisions were destined for the West Indies.[1] Of these major exports, only Irish linen would have gone to the continental colonies in significant amounts, and in describing the eighteenth-century Irish export trade of linen, Gill states: 'The most striking point in regard to the export trade in Irish linen is its domination by English merchants. Not only were English people themselves by far the largest consumers, but even the cloth that was sent abroad went for the most part by way of London, Liverpool, or Bristol.'[2]

Nevertheless, for the purposes of this chapter, it is desirable to make explicit estimates of direct imports from Ireland, and it is possible to construct such estimates since we already have a rough notion of what the upper limit to such imports might have been. If we assume that 10 per cent of the butter, beef, and pork, and 80 per cent of the linen cloth exported from Ireland 'to the plantations' went to the continental colonies, then imports from Ireland would have amounted to about £70,000 annually. It is highly unlikely that direct imports from Ireland were significantly more than this during this period. If we distribute this amount among the colonial regions on the basis of the percentage of tonnage entering each colonial region directly from Ireland for the entire five-year period (these percentages are shown below in parentheses), the estimates of imports from Ireland are:

Northern colonies (18%)	£13,000
New England (3%)	2,000
Middle colonies (42%)	29,000
Upper south (27%)	19,000
Lower south (9%)	6,000
Florida, Bahama and Bermuda Is. (1%)	1,000
Total	£70,000

These estimated values of Irish exports to the colonies are added to the estimated actual values of English and Scottish exports, which have been derived in the manner outlined in this section, and the totals are presented in Table 6.3.

From Table 6.3 it is clear that the import trade from Great Britain and Ireland dwarfed imports from all the other overseas areas. During this period British and Irish imports were over four times the value of commodity imports from all other areas combined: 90 per cent of

[1] The American records show average annual imports of 3,347 hundredweight of butter and 9,668 barrels of beef and pork for the three years 1769–71. This was less than 10 per cent of the exports of these commodities from Ireland 'to the plantations' according to the Irish customs records for the year ended March 25, 1770. Most of these foodstuffs that did enter the continental colonies were imported into the northern colonies.

[2] Gill, p. 177.

TABLE 6.3. *Estimated value of imports into the British North American colonies from Great Britain and Ireland, 1768–72* (thousand pounds sterling)[a]

Destination	1768	1769	1770	1771	1772
Northern colonies	208	288	423	353	394
New England	441	228	457	1,446	912
Middle colonies	1,005	325	717	1,551	979
Upper south	728	774	1,117	1,339	1,100
Lower south	399	429	261	572	635
Florida, Bahama and Bermuda Is.	56	55	63	85	60
Total, British North American colonies	2,837	2,099	3,038	5,346	4,080

[a] All estimates have been rounded to the nearest thousand pounds sterling.

these goods came from England, about 9.5 per cent from Scotland, and less than 0.5 per cent from Ireland. Clearly England held the dominant position in supplying imports to the colonies, and most of these (about 80 per cent of English exports to the colonies) were goods of English manufacture. Textiles were the most important group of commodities exported from England to the colonies. Judging from the official values in the English customs records woolens comprised about 40 per cent of the value of all goods of British manufacture, and linens about 25 per cent (including Irish linens that were re-exported from England). Hardware and metal goods of all shapes and descriptions comprised another 15 per cent. German linens, for which import duties in England were rebated upon re-export to the colonies, were a popular item and formed about 16 per cent of the value of re-exports to the colonies from England. Tea comprised more than 12 per cent, with the rest coming from a wide variety of foodstuffs, spices, drugs, textiles and other miscellaneous goods. London, of course, was the most important port in English trade with the colonies, exporting four times the value of goods that went from the outports to the continental colonies (78 per cent of the commodities of English manufacture and 88 per cent of re-exports were exported from London).

It is also quite clear from Table 6.3 that the non-importation agreements had a considerable impact upon British imports during these five years. The timing of the impact upon imports from Britain varied in each colony, as did its magnitude. From the estimates in Table 6.3, it appears that the agreements had far more impact upon the trade of the New England colonies, the middle colonies, and the lower south than upon Maryland and Virginia. The estimates also substantiate contemporary comments about the flood of imports that came into the colonies beginning in 1771 from Britain after the non-importation restrictions were lifted.

CHAPTER 7

THE BALANCE OF TRADE AND INVISIBLE EARNINGS IN OVERSEAS TRADE, 1768–72

THE BALANCE OF TRADE

There is widespread agreement among historians of the colonial period, as there was among contemporary observers, that a significant deficit existed in the American colonies' balance of trade with Great Britain.[1] That a large deficit did exist in the late colonial period is shown by estimates of commodity trade given in Table 7.1 for the period 1768 through 1772. It is clear from this table that the overall deficit in the commodity trade with the British Isles was due mainly to the deficits incurred by New England and the middle colonies.[2] Similarly, it appears that on the average for this five-year period, the southern colonies, as well, incurred a deficit – although a relatively small one – in their commodity trade with Great Britain.

There were various ways in which this deficit with Great Britain could have been paid. Part was paid by surpluses earned in commodity trade with southern Europe. Any remaining deficit in the balance of commodity trade would have been paid by earnings from the sale of services to overseas residents (invisible earnings), and/or financed by capital inflows (in the balance-of-payments sense of indebtedness incurred to foreign residents) from the overseas areas. One contemporary observer, Benjamin Franklin, gave the following reply to a Parliamentary committee in 1766 when asked the question of how Pennsylvania paid for its trade deficit with Britain:

> The balance is paid by our produce carried to the West Indies, and sold in our own islands, or to the French, Spaniards, Danes and Dutch; by the same carried to other colonies in North-America, as to New-England, Nova-Scotia, Newfoundland, Carolina and

---

[1] See, for examples, Curtis P. Nettels, *The Roots of American Civilization* (New York: Appleton-Century-Crofts, 1938), p. 264; and Douglass C. North, *Growth and Welfare in the American Past* (Englewood Cliffs, N.J.: Prentice-Hall, Inc., 1966), p. 40.

[2] A word of caution should be given at this point regarding the regional breakdown of the estimated balances of commodity trade. The balances represent the trade of each colonial region with each overseas trading area. There was undoubtedly some modification of these balances brought about by the trade that took place among the colonies themselves (as suggested in the statement of Benjamin Franklin quoted below). No attempt has been made to account for the effects of trade between the colonies in these balances.

North American colonies, 1768–72 (thousand pounds sterling)

Overseas area of trade and major colonial region	1768			1769			1770			1771			1772		
	Exports	Imports	Balance	Exports	Imports	Balance	Exports	Imports	Balance	Exports	Imports	Balance	Exports	Imports	Balance
Great Britain and Ireland															
Northern colonies	20	208	−188	26	288	−262	39	423	−384	83	353	−270	40	394	−354
New England	89	441	−352	90	228	−138	96	457	−361	88	1,446	−1,358	78	912	−834
Middle colonies	155	1,005	−850	120	325	−205	139	717	−578	127	1,551	−1,424	105	979	−874
Upper south	784	728	56	990	774	216	951	1,117	−166	1,081	1,339	−258	1,003	1,100	−97
Lower south	380	399	−19	379	429	−50	340	261	79	446	572	−126	637	635	2
Florida, Bahama and Bermuda Is.	1	56	−55	15	55	−40	17	63	−46	41	85	−44	39	60	−21
Total	1,429	2,837	−1,408	1,620	2,099	−479	1,582	3,038	−1,456	1,866	5,346	−3,480	1,902	4,080	−2,178
Southern Europe and Wine Islands															
Northern colonies	68	6	62	87	4	83	106	6	100	236	12	224	168	12	156
New England	62	15	47	70	26	44	62	14	48	78	15	63	59	20	39
Middle colonies	103	35	68	225	30	195	214	43	171	146	22	124	237	32	205
Upper south	72	15	57	153	14	139	116	5	111	65	10	55	96	10	86
Lower south	73	6	67	69	5	64	67	7	60	32	7	25	32	9	23
Florida, Bahama and Bermuda Is.	0	1	−1	0	2	−2	0	1	−1	0	1	−1	0	1	−1
Total	378	78	300	604	81	523	565	76	489	557	67	490	592	84	508
West Indies															
Northern colonies	8	10	−2	9	4	5	10	10	0	13	10	3	21	11	10
New England	252	258	−6	281	362	−81	318	350	−32	319	322	−3	347	403	−56
Middle colonies	162	169	−7	207	290	−83	255	307	−52	253	185	68	344	321	23
Upper south	73	82	−9	95	104	−9	102	112	−10	110	115	−5	120	134	−14
Lower south	85	47	38	103	64	39	127	94	33	115	53	62	129	83	46
Florida, Bahama and Bermuda Is.	3	8	−5	4	10	−6	3	4	−1	3	6	−3	3	12	−9
Total	583	574	9	699	834	−135	815	877	−62	813	691	122	964	964	0
Africa															
Northern colonies	0	0	0	0	0	0	0	0	0	0	0	0	0	0	0
New England	13	0	13	23	0	23	20	0	20	15	0	15	25	0	25
Middle colonies	†	0	†	0	0	0	1	0	1	1	0	1	2	0	2
Upper south	0	0	0	†	0	†	0	0	0	†	0	†	†	0	†
Lower south	0	0	0	†	0	†	0	0	0	0	0	0	2	0	2
Florida, Bahama and Bermuda Is.	0	0	0	0	0	0	0	0	0	0	0	0	0	0	0
Total	13	0	13	24	0	24	21	0	21	16	0	16	29	0	29
Totals															
Northern colonies	96	224	−128	122	296	−174	155	439	−284	332	375	−43	229	417	−188
New England	416	714	−298	464	616	−152	496	821	−325	500	1,783	−1,283	509	1,335	−826
Middle colonies	420	1,209	−789	553	645	−92	609	1,067	−458	527	1,758	−1,231	688	1,332	−644
Upper south	929	825	104	1,238	892	346	1,169	1,234	−65	1,256	1,404	−208	1,219	1,244	−25
Lower south	538	452	86	551	498	53	534	362	172	593	632	−39	800	727	73
Florida, Bahama and Bermuda Is.	4	65	−61	19	67	−48	20	68	−48	44	92	−48	42	73	−31
Total	2,403	3,489	−1,086	2,947	3,014	−67	2,983	3,991	−1,008	3,252	6,104	−2,852	3,487	5,128	−1,641

Source: Chapter 6.

* The table reads as follows: goods valued at an estimated £89,000 were exported from New England to Great Britain and Ireland in 1768; goods valued at an estimated £441,000 were imported into New England from Great Britain and Ireland in 1768; New England's balance of trade with Great Britain and Ireland was −£352,000 (a deficit) in 1768; and so forth. The balance of trade equals exports minus imports.

† Less than £500.

Georgia, by the same carried to different parts of Europe, as Spain, Portugal and Italy: In all which places we receive either money, bills of exchange, or commodities that suit for remittance to Britain; which together with all the profits on the industry of our merchants and mariners, arising in those circuitous voyages, and the freights made by their ships, center finally in Britain, to discharge the balance, and pay for British manufactures continually used in the province, or sold to foreigners by our traders.[1]

Historians have generally recognized that invisible earnings were probably important in paying for the deficits in the British trade. Some have also stated that colonial deficits were partly settled by an increasing indebtedness to British merchants.[2] Nevertheless, there are no available estimates of the magnitude of colonial invisible earnings or of capital inflows.

The central purpose of this chapter is to indicate the importance of invisible earnings in settling the overall deficit of commodity trade. We propose to do this by estimating the earnings from the sale of services to overseas areas. For the period 1768–72, at least, the resulting estimates strongly suggest that earnings from invisibles were very important as a source of sterling to the colonies. For the North American colonies, the average annual deficit remaining on the balance of commodity trade for this five-year period was £1,331,000. Estimates of their annual average shipping earnings for this period were £610,000 and estimates of other invisible earnings were £222,000. Thus, an estimated 62 per cent of the deficit from commodity trade was paid by these invisible earnings.[3]

A secondary objective of our estimates is to place more clearly in perspective the importance of colonial shipping compared with other market-oriented activities. Of course, value-added measures for various industries are not available, but the export values of particular commodities serve as a reasonable means of comparison. Our estimates reveal that shipping earnings were larger than the value of any commodity export with the one exception of tobacco.

---

[1] Quoted from Harold U. Faulkner, *American Economic History* (8th ed.; New York: Harper & Brothers, Publishers, 1960), p. 81.

[2] Nettels, *The Roots*, p. 256; and Guy S. Callender, 'The early transportation and banking enterprises of the states in relation to the growth of the corporation,' *Quarterly Journal of Economics*, XVII, 1 (November 1902), p. 137.

[3] It should be noted that the remaining annual average deficit of £500,000 was not entirely financed by capital inflows. Sterling was also earned from expenditures made by the British government in the colonies for defense and civil administration and our estimates of these expenditures, which are given in Chapter 8, suggest that they gave rise to foreign exchange of probably at least £400,000 annually. There was an additional credit due to the sale of ships to overseas buyers, and there were additional debits due to the immigration of slaves and indentured servants.

SHIPPING EARNINGS

Shipping earnings were unquestionably the largest source of earnings from the sale of services for the colonies. An estimate of shipping earnings should consist of the following components:

(a) shipping earnings on exports carried on colonial-owned ships;
(b) plus earnings of colonial-owned ships on imports when imports were valued C.I.F. (as they are in Table 7.1);
(c) plus shipping earnings of colonial-owned ships between foreign ports;
(d) minus port costs of colonial-owned ships abroad;
(e) plus port costs of foreign ships in colonial ports.[1]

The estimates made below will include (a) and (b), and suggest what a lower limit to (c) may have been. Shipping earnings between foreign ports (c) may have been significant if the description given by historians of the triangular trade routes has been accurate.[2] However, as stated in Chapter 4, there is serious doubt that colonial ships did follow such trade routes to any significant extent. It seems more likely that shuttle trades were the rule throughout most of the colonial period, and that triangular patterns were the exception. Some fragmentary evidence about such earnings does exist, however, and from this we will suggest what a lower limit to such earnings may have been in the late colonial period. The evidence needed to estimate port costs is too incomplete, and it will therefore be assumed that (d) and (e) roughly offset each other.[3]

The basis for estimating shipping earnings will be the aggregate tonnage of ships that entered and cleared each colonial port. These data are given in the American Inspector-General's Ledgers, and are presented in Table 7.2. These are registered tons, and they are the so-called 'tons burden' or 'dead-weight tons,' which reflected the carrying capacity of the vessels.[4] These data on tonnage flows serve as the

---

[1] See Douglass C. North and Alan Heston, 'The estimation of shipping earnings in historical studies of the balance of payments,' *Canadian Journal of Economics and Political Science*, XXVI, 2 (May 1960), pp. 266–7.

[2] See p. 49, n. 1 and the accompanying text.

[3] Some support is given to this assumption by the fact that for the five years taken together, 53 per cent of the tonnage entering the colonies was colonial-owned. The remaining 47 per cent was owned in the West Indies or in Great Britain (or Ireland). As a result, colonial tonnage in foreign ports was approximately equal to foreign tonnage in colonial ports. Although we have no information on port times for colonial-owned vessels in foreign waters and foreign-owned vessels in colonial waters, if they were about the same, then these port costs would very nearly offset each other.

[4] See the statement by Lawrence A. Harper in U.S. Bureau of the Census, *Historical Statistics of the United States, Colonial Times to 1957* (Washington, D.C.: Government Printing Office, 1960), p. 745; and Ralph Davis, *The Rise of the English Shipping Industry* (London: Macmillan & Co., Ltd, 1962), p. 7. For a discussion of the different definitions of tonnage, see Frederic C. Lane, 'Tonnages, medieval and modern,' *Economic History Review*, 2nd Series, XVII, 2 (December 1964), pp. 213–33, and footnotes 1 and 2, p. 237.

TABLE 7.2. *Tonnage entering and clearing the North American colonies (by major region) from and to the major areas of overseas trade, 1768–72*[a]

Overseas origin or destination and colonial destination or origin	1768 tons entered	1768 tons cleared	1769 tons entered	1769 tons cleared	1770 tons entered	1770 tons cleared	1771 tons entered	1771 tons cleared	1772 tons entered	1772 tons cleared
Great Britain and Ireland										
Northern colonies	9,019	6,995	13,212	7,752	12,171	6,232	14,731	7,559	16,641	6,348
New England	12,160	14,109	15,820	17,054	15,726	17,069	12,375	12,418	13,925	15,172
Middle colonies	18,029	15,357	14,529	13,689	13,639	15,356	19,268	14,028	16,999	11,504
Upper south	35,435	36,487	36,138	40,710	34,929	43,090	42,222	49,022	42,786	48,959
Lower south	26,873	28,056	24,219	26,735	18,640	23,310	20,384	28,881	21,213	25,987
Florida, Bahama and Bermuda Is.	1,170	1,350	1,552	450	815	1,294	1,190	935	1,055	1,362
North American colonies	102,686	102,354	105,470	106,390	95,920	106,351	110,170	112,843	112,619	109,332
Southern Europe and the Wine Islands										
Northern colonies	2,484	6,129	2,340	7,349	3,467	8,693	5,629	17,837	6,719	13,439
New England	10,136	5,849	7,370	5,117	6,278	5,301	5,016	6,411	5,615	4,443
Middle colonies	7,561	9,640	13,470	15,318	18,274	14,315	8,649	9,512	11,515	11,054
Upper south	4,527	8,619	9,175	13,710	8,585	9,019	4,828	5,241	5,222	6,345
Lower south	3,233	6,706	2,270	6,938	3,001	7,266	3,421	3,659	3,610	2,344
Florida, Bahama and Bermuda Is.	645	100	130	0	135	0	40	0	0	0
North American colonies	28,586	37,043	34,755	48,432	39,740	44,594	27,583	42,660	32,681	37,625
West Indies										
Northern colonies	1,015	900	995	1,145	735	1,180	378	1,235	947	1,305
New England	43,711	49,234	41,146	45,453	46,045	50,078	48,993	52,565	47,935	55,150
Middle colonies	18,758	19,690	19,742	17,980	24,943	22,492	22,975	22,598	22,668	25,451
Upper south	16,102	14,618	16,345	14,755	14,640	15,214	17,100	16,760	15,606	17,675
Lower south	18,375	18,778	17,883	17,976	20,836	20,265	19,347	18,253	16,604	19,315
Florida, Bahama and Bermuda Is.	3,354	4,510	1,771	280	1,674	3,318	2,485	3,304	2,519	4,611
North American colonies	101,315	107,730	97,882	97,589	108,873	112,547	111,278	114,715	106,279	123,507

Overseas origin or destination and colonial destination or origin	1768		1769		1770		1771		1772	
	tons entered	tons cleared	tons entered	tons cleared	tons entered	tons cleared	tons entered	tons cleared	tons entered	tons cleared
Africa										
Northern colonies	0	0	0	0	0	0	0	0	0	0
New England	0	704	36	1,218	36	1,240	0	727	0	1,225
Middle colonies	130	35	30	235	230	98	0	205	0	280
Upper south	305	0	270	0	823	0	110	0	702	0
Lower south	613	0	2,536	20	490	30	1,363	30	2,196	410
Florida, Bahama and Bermuda Is.	50	0	82	0	152	0	0	0	0	0
North American colonies	1,098	739	2,954	1,473	1,731	1,368	1,473	962	2,898	1,915
All overseas areas										
Northern colonies	12,518	14,024	16,547	16,246	16,373	16,105	20,738	26,631	24,307	21,092
New England	66,007	69,896	64,372	68,842	68,085	73,688	66,384	72,121	67,475	75,990
Middle colonies	44,478	44,722	47,771	47,222	57,086	52,261	50,892	46,343	51,182	48,289
Upper south	56,369	59,724	61,928	69,175	58,977	67,323	64,260	71,023	64,316	72,979
Lower south	49,094	53,540	46,908	51,669	42,967	50,871	44,515	50,823	43,623	48,056
Florida, Bahama and Bermuda Is.	5,219	5,960	3,535	730	2,776	4,612	3,715	4,239	3,574	5,973
North American colonies	233,685	247,866	241,061	253,884	246,264	264,860	250,504	271,180	254,477	272,379

Source: London, Public Record Office, Customs 16/1.

[a] This table reads as follows: 9,019 tons entered northern colonial ports from Great Britain and Ireland in 1768; 6,995 tons cleared from northern colonial ports destined for Great Britain and Ireland in 1768; and so forth.

quantity data in our procedure of estimating shipping earnings. To estimate colonial earnings, the tonnage engaged on each route that was owned by persons living elsewhere in the British Empire, and that which was lost en route, must be deducted from the totals.[1] The percentages of tonnage engaged on each route that were owned in each of the various colonial regions are given in Table 7.3. The percentage of clearances that was lost en route is estimated by insurance rates, which were typically 2 to $2\frac{1}{2}$ per cent per crossing each way.[2]

What might be called the price data can be obtained by estimating average earnings per ton of shipping. These estimated average earnings per ton are the product of (1) the average freight rates per registered ton prevailing on a particular trade route, and (2) the actual proportion of this tonnage utilized, on the average, on that route. The product of the quantity and price data (colonial tonnage times average earnings per ton) for each route will be an estimate of components (a) and (b) in colonial shipping earnings.[3]

[1] The tonnage figures in Table 7.2 include all vessels legally entering and clearing colonial ports. The Navigation Acts excluded foreign ships from colonial ports, but ships owned in the colonies had the same privileges as those owned by residents of Great Britain. For the present purposes, then, we must know what porportion of the tonnage entering and clearing colonial ports was owned by residents of the American colonies as opposed to residents of other parts of the Empire. The clearances, of course, are an ex-ante figure; not all vessels successfully completed their voyages. To obtain an estimated export figure we rely on insurance rates for the required reduction.

[2] See William Walton's Insurance Book, New York Chamber of Commerce Library, New York; Ezekiel Price's Policy Books, Boston Athenaeum, Boston, Mass.; John Hancock Collection, Vol. 28, Manuscripts Division, Baker Library, Harvard University; and Rough Journals of the London Assurance Company, London, England. Losses on the African route were higher, but this makes no significant difference for these calculations.

[3] More formally, if no vessels were lost en route, shipping earnings for any year accruing to a particular colonial region d in its trade on a particular route between colonial region r and overseas area a would be:

$$S^d = T^c \cdot O^{dc} \cdot F^c \cdot U^c + T^e \cdot O^{de} \cdot F^e \cdot U^e$$

where S^d is shipping earnings of colonial region d in its trade between colonial region r and overseas area a; T^c and T^e are total tonnages that cleared colonial region r for overseas area a and entered colonial region r from overseas area a, respectively, in tons; O^{dc} and O^{de} are the percentages of colonial-owned vessels from region d which cleared and entered, respectively, in the trade route between r and a; F^c and F^e are the average freight rates charged by ships travelling from region r to area a and from area a to region r, respectively, in pounds sterling per ton; and U^c and U^e are the percentages of shipping capacity (tonnage) utilized in the trade route between r and a, and a and r, respectively.

Total shipping earnings (of components a and b) of the colonies for any year would be:

$$\sum_{d=1}^{5} \cdot \sum_{r=1}^{6} \cdot \sum_{a=1}^{4} S^d_{ra}.$$

If freight rates were available for every commodity on every route it would be a simple task to estimate shipping earnings directly by the price charged multiplied by the quantity shipped. Lacking complete rates, however, the quantities of commodities have to be converted to a standard unit of shipping tonnage, the quantity for which we have been able to construct average freight rates.

In contrast to the quantity data, sound and reliable price data are less easily acquired. The structure of average freight rates given in Table 7.4 is based primarily on pre-Revolutionary peacetime rates, some of which have been collected and presented in Chapter 4 and Appendix III.[1] Unfortunately, rates are not available for every route, and some of the rates given in Table 7.4 have had to be assumed. In such cases, direct evidence has been replaced by indirect evidence. This, however, is not likely to be a serious defect. Given the competitive structure of the industry in colonial waters, routes with similar long-run cost conditions would have reflected similar rates.[2] For example, rates to Great Britain from the lower south in all likelihood approximated those from the upper south to Great Britain. Since the costs of shipping over these two routes were similar, the rates observed for the tobacco route can be used to approximate the route from the lower south. Note that this is not an argument for rates to be the same in both directions on the same trade route. Because of differences in utilization on outward- and inward-bound ships on a route, rates were different. In general, capacity was more fully utilized on outward-bound ships from the colonies because of the nature of the bulk, staple-type goods that comprised the major share of colonial exports.[3]

Rates that were charged for shipping tobacco raise another problem, concerning nominal rates (the charges customarily quoted) versus effective rates (the rates actually charged per registered ton). Peacetime tobacco rates from the upper south to Great Britain were consistently £7 to £8 per 'ton.' But this was not the effective rate for the late colonial period for the registered tons which are presented in Table 7.2. Both the size and density of an average tobacco hogshead increased over the eighteenth century. Throughout most of the seventeenth

[1] Some of the rates given in Chapter 4 and Appendix III have previously appeared in published form, for example, John M. Hemphill II, 'Freight rates in the Maryland tobacco trade, 1705–62,' *Maryland Historical Magazine*, LIV, 1 and 2 (March and June 1959), pp. 36–58 and 153–87; Davis, p. 283; Herbert C. Bell, 'The West India trade before the American Revolution,' *American Historical Review*, XXII, 2 (January 1917), p. 274; Lawrence A. Harper, *The English Navigation Laws* (New York: Columbia Press, 1939), p. 268; William B. Weeden, *Economic and Social History of New England, 1620–1789*, Vol. 1 (New York: Hillary House Publishers, Ltd, 1963), pp. 126, 261, and 369.

[2] The existence of economies of scale might be one reason for rates on similar routes to differ and for the long-run supply curve not to be horizontal. But shipping was probably of sufficient volume in most of the trans-Atlantic routes that whatever economies of scale existed were captured on all routes. One might ask whether or not freight rates fluctuated so substantially that cost conditions are irrelevant in the short run. The series on tobacco rates suggests a significant degree of short-run stability, remaining at about £7 to £8 per 'ton' (of four hogsheads) during peacetime. This stability of tobacco rates supports the use of the same rate per route for each year in this period (as given in Table 7.4).

[3] See North and Heston, p. 269; Davis, pp. 185–8; Douglass C. North, 'Ocean freight rates and economic development, 1750–1913,' *Journal of Economic History*, XVIII, 4 (December 1958), p. 539; and Bell, p. 278. The African trade was an exception, of course, to this pattern of utilization.

TABLE 7.3. *Percentages of shipping tonnage entering and clearing colonial ports owned by colonial residents, by trade route and colonial region of residence*[a]

Overseas area of origin or destination and colonial region of destination or origin	Northern colonies Entries	Northern colonies Clearance	New England Entries	New England Clearance	Middle colonies Entries	Middle colonies Clearance	Southern colonies Entries	Southern colonies Clearance	Florida, etc. Entries	Florida, etc. Clearance	colonial-owned[b] Entries	colonial-owned[b] Clearance
Great Britain and Ireland												
Northern colonies	4	10	14	13	9	0	0	0	0	0		
New England	0	0	66	85	0	0	2	0	0	0	63	72
Middle colonies	0	0	3	6	1	0	5	6	0	0		
Upper south	0	0	0	6	2	2	8	15	0	0		
Lower south	0	0	0	20	0	0	0	0	0	0		
Florida, Bahama and Bermuda Is.	*	*	*	*	*	*	*	*	*	*		
Southern Europe and the Wine Islands												
Northern colonies	8	14	30	37	15	0	0	0	0	0		
New England	0	0	84	93	0	0	0	0	0	0		
Middle colonies	0	0	2	0	0	0	0	0	0	0		
Upper south	0	0	12	0	0	0	31	88	0	0	76	75
Lower south	0	0	0	0	0	0	8	0	0	0		
Florida, Bahama and Bermuda Is.	*	*	*	*	*	*	*	*	*	*		
West Indies												
Northern colonies	49	30	5	0	14	3	0	0	0	0		
New England	0	0	95	95	1	1	0	0	0	0	84	80
Middle colonies	0	0	4	6	0	0	0	0	0	0		
Upper south	0	0	6	11	6	10	57	79	0	0		
Lower south	0	0	2	0	4	0	18	30	0	0		
Florida, Bahama and Bermuda Is.	6	1	*	*	4	0	7	6	66	81		
Africa												
Northern colonies	*	*	*	*	*	*	*	*	*	*		
New England	*	0	*	100	*	0	*	0	*	0	100	100
Middle colonies	0	*	53	*	0	*	0	*	0	*		
Upper south	*	*	*	*	*	*	*	*	*	*		
Lower south	0	*	0	*	0	*	0	*	0	*		
Florida, Bahama and Bermuda Is.	0	*	0	*	0	*	0	*	0	*		

* No vessels were observed in the samples on these routes.

Source: The sources for the ownership percentages are taken from the recorded entries and clearances of ships taken from a sample of the Naval Office Lists of certain colonial ports. The ports included in the sample and the dates of the recordings are: Charleston, South Carolina (January 5, 1767 to September 29, 1767); the ports of Upper James River (full year, 1754); York, South Potomac, and Rappahanock in Virginia (March 1754 to March 1755); Annapolis, Maryland (full year, 1764); New York (two separate samples of 5 per cent and 6 per cent taken from the years 1715–43, 1751–5, 1763–5 although some years were incomplete); Boston, Massachusetts (July 5, 1764 to July 5, 1765); Salem and Marblehead, Massachusetts (January 5 to October 10, 1765); and Piscataqua, New Hampshire (April 5, 1768 to April 5, 1769); Halifax, Nova Scotia (full years 1750 and 1765); and New Providence, Bahamas (1726, 1728–31, and 1733–8 for entries of ships; 1727–38, except for 1732, for clearances of ships).

Ownership was explicitly given in most cases, but registration was used instead of ownership when the latter was not given. Registration was substituted for ownership for the following ports: Upper James River, Annapolis, Boston, Salem and Marblehead and Piscataqua. Registration is not necessarily the same as ownership, but it is a close substitute and is likely to add little error to the estimates.

In an attempt to test the hypothesis that registration was a close proxy for ownership, a comparison between ownership and registration was made for the two separate samples of New York shipping, for which both the place of registration and ownership were known. Four classifications were set up in order to test for discrepancies between ownership and registration: (1) both colonial-owned and -registered; (2) neither colonial-owned nor -registered; (3) not colonial-owned, but colonial-registered; and (4) colonial-owned but not colonial-registered.

The 6 per cent sample showed the following respective percentages for the four classifications: (1) 69.5 per cent; (2) 22.8 per cent; (3) 4.0 per cent; and (4) 3.5 per cent. Likewise, the second sample showed: (1) 82.5 per cent; (2) 15.5 per cent; (3) 1.4 per cent; and (4) 0.4 per cent. Thus only a small percentage of the total showed any difference between ownership and registration, and this small difference (classifications 3 and 4) was roughly balanced. This tended to cancel out the error. Hence, it is unlikely that the substitution of registration for ownership in the several cases above adds any significant error to our estimates of colonial-owned shipping entering and clearing colonial ports.

a This table reads as follows: 4 per cent of all ships entering the northern colonies from Great Britain and Ireland observed in the samples were owned in the northern colonies, 14 per cent were owned in New England, 9 per cent in the middle colonies, and none from the other continental colonies. The remainder of the ships entering the northern colonies observed in the samples (73 per cent), which are not specified in the table, were owned elsewhere in the British Empire.

b In the case of ships entering and clearing the middle colonies we have been unable to give a breakdown of colonial ownership by region. We therefore have assumed that all colonial-owned ships entering and clearing middle colonial ports were owned in the middle colonies. The likely result is an overstatement of the shipping earnings of the middle colonies and an understatement of New England's earnings.

TABLE 7.4. *Average freight rates per registered ton by route, 1768–72*[a]

Overseas origin or destination	Great Britain and Ireland		Southern Europe and Wine Islands		West Indies		Africa	
	Enter	Clear	Enter	Clear	Enter	Clear	Enter	Clear
Northern colonies	3.0	3.0	3.0	3.5	2.5	3.0	—	—
New England	3.0	3.0	3.0	3.5	2.5	3.0	4.0	3.0
Middle colonies	3.0	3.0	3.0	3.5	2.0	2.5	4.0	3.0
Upper south	3.0	3.5	3.0	3.5	1.5	2.0	4.0	—
Lower south	3.0	3.5	3.0	3.5	1.5	1.5	—	—
Florida, Bahama and Bermuda Is.	3.0	3.5	3.0	3.5	1.0	1.0	—	—

Sources: see text and p. 121, note 1.

[a] These rates are expressed in pounds sterling per registered ton, or ton burden. This rate is interpreted as the price charged for shipping capacity of approximately 60 cubic feet, or 2,240 lb.

century, four hogsheads occupied roughly one registered ton, but by the end of the colonial period four hogsheads occupied an average of two registered tons.[1] The effective rate was therefore £3.5 to £4 per registered ton. The rates given in Table 7.4 have been taken from various published and primary sources and adjusted in the way suggested by the various sources as most likely to reflect the effective charge per registered ton.

As mentioned above, with the exception of the African trade, vessels tended to be more fully loaded, on the average, on the outward voyage from the colonies than on the inward voyage. Despite many qualitative statements which support this claim (see p. 121, note 3), no quantative estimates of utilization have ever been made for colonial shipping. Our estimates of utilization are presented in Table 7.5. The evidence used to make these estimates of utilization is cited in Appendix v and the method of derivation of the percentages is discussed in detail there. In general, we have attempted to estimate the shipping capacity that the various commodities exported or imported (which are given in the American Inspector-General's Ledgers) and immigrants to the colonies occupied on each route. In most cases conversion factors (based on either weight or volume) can be found. The only case in which they cannot be determined is the route from Great Britain to America. This trade was characterized by shipments of high-value goods relative to their weight (mainly woolen and linen textiles, various items of hardware, and British re-exports, such as tea) and immigrants traveling to the colonies. It is difficult to determine with any accuracy what proportion of shipping capacity was occupied by such British exports. The problems associated with this route and the basis for the assumptions made are also discussed in Appendix v.

Total shipping earnings should include freight earnings of colonial ships travelling between overseas areas. As stated above, our findings strongly suggest that triangular or multilateral patterns of physical shipping movements involving the colonies and two or more overseas areas were far less prevalent than has been implied in the traditional descriptions of colonial trade.[2] If this is true, then earnings of colonial shipowners from voyages between overseas areas are not likely to have been significant. This tentative conclusion is amply supported by the evidence we have gathered on shipping between overseas areas and by the rough estimates of earnings based on this evidence made below.

[1] See Lewis C. Gray, *History of Agriculture in the Southern United States to 1860* (Washington, D.C.: Carnegie Institution of Washington, 1933), 1, pp. 220–1; and Davis, p. 282. See also the discussion in Chapter 4.

[2] We do not mean to imply that ships engaged in trade between the colonies and the West Indies typically may not have gone to several islands, or in the southern European trade, to several southern European ports. We do mean that routes involving two or more overseas areas, such as from the colonies to the West Indies to Great Britain and back to the colonies, were not typical.

TABLE 7.5.   *Estimated percentage utilization by route, 1768–72*[a]

Overseas area and colonial regions	1768		1769		1770		1771		1772	
	Enter	Clear	Enter	Clear	Enter	Clear	Enter	Clear	Enter	Clear
Great Britain and Ireland										
Northern colonies	40	31	40	26	40	34	40	69	40	42
New England	45	75	45	68	45	77	45	84	45	68
Middle colonies	85	85	85	100	85	100	85	100	85	95
Upper south	40	100	40	100	40	100	40	100	40	100
Lower south	30	100	30	100	30	100	30	100	30	100
Florida, Bahama and Bermuda Is.	40	7	40	16	40	7	40	16	40	12
Southern Europe and Wine Islands										
Northern colonies	81	100	61	100	68	100	85	100	70	100
New England	40	100	100	100	73	100	51	100	80	100
Middle colonies	72	100	35	100	29	100	45	100	32	100
Upper south	30	100	9	100	2	100	7	100	3	100
Lower south	7	100	13	100	5	100	5	100	8	100
Florida, Bahama and Bermuda Is.	3	0	39	—	13	—	35	—	—	—
West Indies										
Northern colonies	44	100	37	100	69	100	100	100	63	100
New England	45	100	61	100	51	100	60	100	63	100
Middle colonies	56	100	68	100	57	100	47	100	69	100
Upper south	25	100	28	100	32	100	31	100	41	100
Lower south	22	100	23	100	26	100	20	100	33	100
Florida, Bahama and Bermuda Is.	29	10	60	100	26	19	36	16	26	16
Africa										
Northern colonies	—	—	—	—	—	—	—	—	—	—
New England	—	100	8	100	0	88	—	100	—	100
Middle colonies	6	77	0	23	15	58	—	39	—	34
Upper south	62	—	77	—	70	—	95	—	97	—
Lower south	80	—	91	45	89	0	93	33	100	13
Florida, Bahama and Bermuda Is.	82	—	73	—	58	—	—	—	—	—

Source: see Appendix v.

[a] A dash (—) signifies that no tonnage was observed.

There were twelve potential shipping routes between the four major overseas areas in which colonial ships could possibly have been engaged (for example, southern Europe to the British Isles, the West Indies to Africa, the backhauls on these routes and so forth). Only three of these twelve routes have ever been singled out by historians as having been of possible importance in employing colonial ships. These routes were (1) Africa to the West Indies, (2) the West Indies to Great Britain, and (3) southern Europe to Great Britain. On the basis of evidence from the Naval Office Lists, a fourth could be added for consideration, and that is the one from southern Europe to the West Indies. We have not found any evidence indicating significant engagement of colonial ships on the other possible routes.

Some clue about the possible magnitudes of shipping tonnage on these routes can be obtained from Table 7.2. For example, more tonnage usually cleared New England (and, to a lesser extent, the middle colonies) for Africa than returned from there. Part of this difference undoubtedly returned by way of the southern colonies, as the tonnage flows into the southern colonies from Africa suggest. The estimated earnings from this shipping (that returned via the southern colonies) would be included in components (*a*) and (*b*) of shipping earnings. Over the five-year period a total of 6,457 tons cleared the colonies for Africa, mostly from New England and the middle colonies. Most of this tonnage – probably almost all of it – was owned in New England and the middle colonies. And for the entire period 10,154 tons entered the colonies, mainly the southern colonies. The data on ownership (see Table 7.3) indicate that about half of this tonnage – about 5,000 tons – was owned in the colonies. This leaves about 1,000 to 1,500 tons unaccounted for, which probably either returned via the West Indies, or were lost en route. Given the hazards of this route perhaps as much as 500 tons were lost. This would suggest that between 500 and 1,000 tons of colonial shipping completed the voyage on the Africa–West Indies route on the average during these five years. Assuming full utilization (which was typical for slave ships) and a rate of £4 per ton, a range of average earnings on this route would have been between £2,000 and £4,000, or an annual average of £400 to £800, most of which was earned by New England. The minor importance of this route to colonial shipping earnings is also supported by independent evidence from the Naval Office Lists of Jamaica for 1764 and Barbados for 1773. Of all entries into these islands from Africa, 184 colonial-owned tons came into Barbados in 1773, and 60 tons owned in New England came into Jamaica in 1764.[1] This would suggest annual

---

[1] The sources are C.O. 133–17 and C.O. 142–18, Public Record Office, London. We are indebted to Professor Lawrence A. Harper who kindly permitted us to use his copies of the Barbados Naval Office Lists for 1773.

average earnings of about £1,000: we accept this figure and assign it to New England.

With regard to the West Indies–Great Britain route, an average of about 6,000 more tons cleared annually for the West Indies than returned. Annual losses of probably 5 per cent (judging from insurance

TABLE 7.6.   *Estimated shipping earnings, 1768–72* (thousand pounds sterling)[a]

Overseas area and Colonial region	1768	1769	1770	1771	1772
Great Britain and Ireland					
Northern colonies	1	1	1	2	2
New England	55	62	66	60	60
Middle colonies	61	57	59	66	55
Southern colonies	27	27	25	30	28
Florida, Bahama and Bermuda Is.	0	0	0	0	0
Total	144	147	151	158	145
Southern Europe and Wine Islands					
Northern colonies	3	4	5	10	8
New England	39	46	42	55	48
Middle colonies	39	52	51	36	40
Southern colonies	28	43	28	16	20
Florida, Bahama and Bermuda Is.	0	0	0	0	0
Total	109	145	126	117	116
West Indies					
Northern colonies	1	2	2	2	2
New England	193	195	205	225	235
Middle colonies	62	64	75	69	83
Southern colonies	36	37	39	40	44
Florida, Bahama and Bermuda Is.	1	1	1	1	1
Total	293	299	322	337	365
Africa					
Northern colonies	0	0	0	0	0
New England	3	4	4	2	5
Middle colonies	0	0	0	0	0
Southern colonies	0	0	0	0	0
Florida, Bahama and Bermuda Is.	0	0	0	0	0
Total	3	4	4	2	5
Total, Overseas areas[a]					
Northern colonies	5	7	8	14	12
New England	296	313	323	348	354
Middle colonies	165	176	188	174	181
Southern colonies	94	110	95	89	95
Florida, Bahama and Bermuda Is.	1	1	1	1	1
Total, North American colonies	561	607	615	626	643

Source: Tables 7.2 through 7.5.

[a]The total estimates for each year include component *c*, the earnings between overseas areas, as well as components *a* and *b*. Component *c*, totaling £13,000, is allocated by region as follows: New England £6,000, middle colonies £3,000, and the upper and lower south £3,000 (the remainder is lost in rounding).

rates) accounted for perhaps 5,000 of these tons. Sales of ships in the West Indies and tonnage not owned by colonial residents were included in the remaining 1,000 tons. The direct evidence from the Naval Office Lists of Jamaica in 1764 shows the following colonial-owned tonnages clearing for Great Britain: 655 tons owned in New England, 230 tons owned in the middle colonies, and 70 tons owned in the lower south for a total of 955 colonial-owned tons. Only 120 tons (Georgia-owned) were observed leaving Barbados for the British Isles in 1773. If two-thirds[1] of the colonial vessels going from the West Indies to the British Isles left from Jamaica and Barbados, and the two years observed were representative of the late colonial period, possibly 1,500 tons of colonial-owned shipping on the average were engaged in this route yearly. Average freight rates were about £3.5 per ton, and depending upon utilization (which was probably high), earnings would have averaged about £5,000 annually. If this estimate is close to the mark, the regional allocation based on the above tonnages clearing Jamaica and Barbados would be:

Northern colonies	£ 0
New England	3,100
Middle colonies	1,100
Upper south	0
Lower south	800
Florida, etc.	0

The biggest discrepancies between tonnage that cleared the colonies and tonnage that entered for any particular route are for the colonies–southern-European route. An annual average of about 9,500 more tons cleared from the colonies to southern Europe than returned from there. Insurance rates suggest annual losses of about 4 per cent, or about 1,700 tons. Table 7.3 suggests that about 75 to 80 per cent of the remaining 7,800 was owned in the colonies, indicating that about 6,000 colonial-owned tons may have annually gone to Great Britain from southern Europe, some vessels having then been sold and some returning from Great Britain to the colonies. Freight rates on wine from southern Europe to Great Britain were about £2 per 'ton.'

Probably utilization was not too high. If we assume 50 per cent utilization, earnings would have been around £6,000. Distributing this by regional tonnage clearances to southern Europe (1768) times ownership, gives the following regional allocation:

Northern colonies	£ 400
New England	2,000
Middle colonies	2,000
Upper south	1,600
Lower south	0
Florida etc.	0

[1] This was roughly the proportion of exports going to Great Britain from Barbados and Jamaica relative to total exports from all the West Indies. See Davis, p. 298.

For the years 1764 and 1773, seven colonial-owned vessels totaling 530 tons entered Jamaica and Barbados from southern Europe. Out of these, 270 tons were in ballast, but the rest were nearly filled. The ownership of the remaining 260 tons was: 120, middle colonies, 100, upper south and 40, Bermuda. Assuming a freight charge of £3 per ton, earnings of £360, £300 and £120, respectively, would have accrued to these regions.

Total shipping earnings between overseas areas may thus have been about £13,000. These estimates admittedly are very rough, but it is not likely that actual shipping earnings between overseas areas were significantly larger than this. In any case, such earnings were not an important source of foreign exchange for the colonies relative to colonial earnings in direct trades, especially trade with the West Indies.

The final total estimates of shipping earnings (for components (*a*), (*b*), and (*c*)) are presented in Table 7.6. These estimates should be looked upon as rough magnitudes, for they are subject to some margin of error. Nevertheless, in our opinion, they are the best estimates that can be made at this time, and we believe they do give a reasonable idea of the magnitude of shipping earnings and of the relative importance of the shipping industry to the colonial economy.

INTEREST, INSURANCE, AND MERCANTILE PROFITS

When colonial merchants traded with overseas areas, not only did they earn foreign exchange by selling shipping services (i.e. providing that the ship was colonial-owned), but the C.I.F. prices charged for the goods included other costs of shipment and distribution, including a return for the services of the merchants who were organizing and carrying out this trade. Very often these services, including shipping, furnished to overseas buyers were not separately distinguished. As Nettels states, 'the freighting and marketing of goods in those days were simply aspects of a single operation, and freights and profits were frequently indistinguishable.'[1] If we knew the F.O.B. and C.I.F. prices for the colonial regions and various overseas areas, it would be a simple task to compute the 'invisible' earnings as a whole. Lacking overseas price data, however, it is necessary to examine each of the major components of these services separately for the major trade routes. Of these costs other than shipping, the most important were insurance purchased from colonial underwriters or borne by the colonial merchant personally; interest, if the goods were sold on some sort of credit terms, as they may have been; and the return to the merchant for his services, or what will be called 'mercantile profits.'

[1] Curtis P. Nettels, *The Money Supply of the American Colonies before 1720* (Madison, Wis.: University of Wisconsin Press, 1934), p. 70.

Though London underwriters seldom insured colonists in the West Indies and coastal trades, insurance in the trade with Great Britain and Ireland was usually purchased in London, even for colonial-owned ships. It is probable that some portion of the goods shipped between the colonies and the British Isles was not insured formally, and thus such goods were transported with the owner personally bearing the risk. A customary practice in peacetime, for example, was to insure one-half the value of a shipment of goods to the colonies. To the extent that colonial merchants were not insured formally and were the owners of goods in transit, the insurance costs included in the estimated values of goods imported from Great Britain and Ireland as given in Table 7.1 should be reduced. We have assumed that colonial merchants purchased insurance in Great Britain on all their imports and one-half their exports on this route. This leaves 1 per cent (half of 2 per cent) of the value of exports that was personally borne by colonial risk-takers or insured in the colonies.

Interest, if it was of any significance in this trade, was probably a debit rather than a credit item in the colonial balance of payments, since it was usually the colonial merchant who needed credit. Widely observed credit terms were for the colonial merchant to make payment for orders twelve months after they had been received. If payment was made in advance, the buyer was to receive a credit equal to 5 per cent of the amount so paid.[1] Also, many tobacco planters were said to have been in debt to the London merchant who handled their tobacco. In fact, Americans were said to have owed English merchants £2 m. to £6 m. at the outbreak of the Revolution.[2] Because these estimates

---

[1] Philip L. White, *The Beekmans of New York in Politics and Commerce, 1647–1877* (New York: The New-York Historical Society, 1956), p. 348.

[2] See Richard B. Sheridan, 'The British credit crisis of 1772 and the American colonies,' *Journal of Economic History*, xx, 2 (June 1960), pp. 166–7. Callender (*op. cit.*, p. 137) has said the debt was $28 million, which would have meant about £6 million. Thomas Jefferson said that Virginians 'certainly owed two millions sterling to Great Britain at the conclusion of the war' (Julian P. Boyd, *et al.* (eds.), *The Papers of Thomas Jefferson* (Princeton, N.J.: Princeton University Press, 1954), x, p. 27). Benjamin Franklin in 1765 stated: 'It is said here [London] among the merchants that North America owes them no less than four millions sterling. Think what a sum the interest of this debt amounts to, and thence how necessary it is for us to practice every point of frugality and industry, that we may be able to pay them honestly' (letter from Benjamin Franklin, London, to John Ross, Philadelphia, February 14, 1765; Read Manuscripts, 1716–1872, Historical Society of Pennsylvania, Philadelphia). A statement of the debts submitted to the British government in February 1791 by British merchants claimed a total of £4,984,655 was owed them by Americans (London, Public Record Office (Chatham Papers) 30/8/343/167, 'List of Debts due by Citizens of the United States of America to the Merchants and Traders of Great Britain contracted previous to the year 1776 with interest on the same to January 1, 1790'). Since these claims (column 1) included 14 years' interest (which the documents states that 'as near as can at present be computed amounts to two millions and upwards') some adjustment must be made if they are to approximate the amounts alleged by the British merchants to be the indebtedness at the beginning of 1776. Assuming that this interest was calculated at a rate of 5 per cent (according to Sheridan, 'The British credit crisis of

may have overstated the actual indebtedness, and because under the usual credit terms interest would not have been paid on that part of the debt less than one year old, interest paid by Americans to their British creditors probably was not of a significant magnitude in the present context.

Estimates of the magnitude of mercantile profits in the British and Irish trade also suffer from lack of evidence. Commissions charged on flaxseed sent to Ireland by colonial merchants were from 5 to $7\frac{1}{2}$ per cent in New York.[1] This, however, did not include any assumption of

---

1772,' pp. 166–7, this was the rate used) compounded annually, the 1776 debts would have been the amounts shown in column 2 (rounded to the nearest thousand pounds sterling):

	(1)	(2)
Virginia	£2,305,409	£1,164,000
Maryland	571,455	289,000
South Carolina	687,954	347,000
North Carolina	379,344	192,000
Georgia	247,782	125,000
Pennsylvania	229,452	116,000
New York	175,095	88,000
Rhode Island	49,208	25,000
Massachusetts	287,983	145,000
Connecticut	28,653	14,000
New Hampshire	21,796	11,000
New Jersey	524	—
Totals	£4,984,655	£2,516,000

This, of course, assumes that none of the debts had been paid between 1776 and 1790; but some surely were. Those that had been collected by this time were in general from the large commercial towns in the northern colonies, thus explaining why the bulk of the alleged debt left in 1790 was owed by the southern colonies. The different system of distribution in the South probably was the reason more debts had not been collected there. British goods in the South were typically sold by partners or agents of British firms who had come to America and who left when the war broke out. Typically they extended credit to numerous planters – most debts were of moderate amounts and there were a large number of them outstanding. Typically the planter paid by produce which the merchant shipped to England (or elsewhere, perhaps) (Rufus King, United States representative to Great Britain, *American State Papers*, Class I, *Foreign Relations*, II, p. 400). Had the principal, however, been in the neighborhood of £2,500,000 in 1776, interest (if paid) would have been about £125,000 to £200,000 annually if the average rate of interest charged was from 5 to 8 per cent. Lawrence H. Gipson ('Virginia planter debts before the American Revolution,' *The Virginia Magazine of History and Biography*, LXIX (July 1961), p. 260), quotes one source which said Virginia planters were paying 8 per cent on their debts. Curtis P. Nettels says planters 'were obliged to pay an interest charge of 6 per cent or more,' (*The Roots of American Civilization*, p. 256). There are two reasons, however, why interest paid to British merchants was probably much less than this. First, it is very likely that the amounts claimed by British merchants were exaggerated (see Aubrey C. Land, 'Economic behavior in a planting society: the eighteenth-century Chesapeake,' *Journal of Southern History*, XXXIII, 4 (November 1967), pp. 482–3). Second, explicit interest payments would not have been made on part – probably the largest part – of this debt since it was outstanding short-term trade credit granted by British merchants. The point is that the prices charged included normal interest costs under the usual credit terms (as stated above), and the values of imports estimated in Table 7.1 have been based upon the prices charged.

[1] White, p. 254.

risk on the shipment. Sufficient information does not exist to determine the average rate of return to those who sent flaxseed on their own account, but it must have been something more than commissions over the long run. Probably 10 per cent or more could be defended, but a conservative estimate of $7\frac{1}{2}$ per cent will be accepted. These earnings, however, must be based only on exports. The method of estimating imports from Great Britain was to mark up British exports to the colonies by insurance, freight and British commission charges (see Appendix II). Because this was a different procedure from valuing imports at C.I.F. prices in the colonies (as was done with imports from all other areas), no return should be credited for the services rendered by colonial merchants in their import trade with Great Britain.

In the West Indian and southern Europe trades, colonial traders generally purchased insurance in the colonies or bore the risk of shipment personally. The average rate for insurance was $2\frac{1}{2}$ to 3 per cent on the West Indies routes and 2 per cent on the southern European route for one-way voyages during peacetime. These insurance earnings, however, must be based only on colonial exports to these areas (the export figures in Table 7.1 have been reduced by the appropriate insurance percentages, and they should be interpreted as the value of goods which safely reached their destination). No account has been taken of the value of goods purchased by colonists in southern Europe or in the West Indies that were ultimately lost or spoiled in transit to the colonies. This loss of foreign exchange is made good by colonial insurance earnings on imports, but having failed to include the one, we also must delete the other.

Interest is again a doubtful charge for the southern European route, but credit terms were sometimes given in the West Indies. Nevertheless, we have found few specific references to credit terms and the extent of indebtedness in this trade[1] and will, therefore, not include it in the estimates at this point.

As with the trade to Great Britain, we do not have estimates of the average rates of return on traded goods to the West Indies or southern Europe. A lower bound, however, can be obtained by using percentage markups by commission agents. Pares reports that 5 per cent was a normal commission on exports to the West Indies, and $2\frac{1}{2}$ per cent on return cargoes, but he gives accounts of charges up to 15 per cent.[2]

---

[1] Edward Edelman states that balances running beyond six months or a year were charged interest of 6 per cent by mainland colonists in the West Indies. We have no indication, however, of the yearly principal outstanding. See Edward Edelman, 'Thomas Hancock, colonial merchant,' *Journal of Economic and Business History*, 1 (1928–9), pp. 77–104; reprinted in Ross M. Robertson and James L. Pate (eds.), *Readings in United States Economic and Business History* (Boston: Houghton Mifflin Co., 1966), p. 157.

[2] Richard Pares, *Yankees and Creoles* (Cambridge, Mass.: Harvard University Press, 1956), pp. 81–2.

Also, Bell gives evidence that commission charges in the West Indies were often 10 per cent (and sometimes more) of the value of goods traded, and return cargoes from the West Indies to Philadelphia also bore a charge of 10 per cent.[1] It is likely that 10 per cent was less than the average return in the long-run since we have not accounted for risk. Nevertheless, to be on the conservative side once more, a rate of 10 per cent is chosen for both the West Indian and southern European trades.

Other invisible earnings on the trades from Africa and between overseas areas undoubtedly accrued to colonial merchants who engaged in them. For example, insurance was sold by colonial underwriters for rates varying from 8 to 11 per cent, in peacetime, for routes from the

TABLE 7.7. *Estimated invisible earnings other than shipping, 1768–72* (thousand pounds sterling)

Overseas area and colonial region	1768	1769	1770	1771	1772
Great Britain and Ireland					
Northern colonies	0	0	0	1	0
New England	15	16	16	18	17
Middle colonies	11	9	10	9	8
Southern colonies	9	10	9	11	13
Florida, Bahama and Bermuda Is.	0	0	0	0	0
Total	35	35	35	39	38
Southern Europe and Wine Islands					
Northern colonies	1	2	2	4	3
New England	12	14	13	21	16
Middle colonies	12	23	23	15	24
Southern colonies	8	17	12	7	11
Florida, Bahama and Bermuda Is.	0	0	0	0	0
Total	33	56	50	47	54
West Indies					
Northern colonies	1	1	1	1	1
New England	55	67	71	70	80
Middle colonies	30	44	51	41	60
Southern colonies	16	20	21	24	27
Florida, Bahama and Bermuda Is.	1	1	1	1	1
Total	103	133	145	137	169
Total, overseas areas					
Northern colonies	2	3	3	6	4
New England	82	97	100	109	113
Middle colonies	53	76	84	65	92
Southern colonies	33	47	42	42	51
Florida, Bahama and Bermuda Is.	1	1	1	1	1
Total, North American colonies	171	224	230	223	261

Source: see text.

[1] Bell, pp. 273, 283, and 285.

colonies to Africa and return to the West Indies.[1] Profits of colonial merchants engaging in the slave trade are discussed in Chapter 8. Earnings of other types would have been small, and hence can safely be ignored.

The percentages that will be used to estimate the value of other invisible earnings thus will be:

	Great Britain and Ireland		West Indies		Southern Europe	
	Exports	*Imports*	*Exports*	*Imports*	*Exports*	*Imports*
Interest	—	—	—	—	—	—
Insurance	1.0	—	2.5	—	2.0	—
Mercantile profits	7.5	—	10.0	10.0	10.0	10.0
Total	8.5	0.0	12.5	10.0	12.0	10.0

We must also know what proportion of total commodity trade was handled by colonial merchants before the estimates of invisible earnings (other than shipping) can be made. It is assumed that the percentages of each trade handled by colonial merchants were the same as the percentage of colonial-owned tonnage entering and clearing colonial ports in each trade (as given in Table 7.3). The estimated values of services (other than shipping) sold abroad can thus be estimated by the product of the above percentages, ownership percentages, and the value of goods traded. These estimates are presented in Table 7.7.

THE IMPORTANCE OF INVISIBLE EARNINGS

It is difficult to overemphasize the importance of invisible earnings, especially shipping earnings. When compared with the average annual values of the five most important commodities exported from 1768 through 1772, shipping earnings rank second only to tobacco:

Tobacco	£766,000
Shipping earnings	610,000
Bread and flour	412,000
Rice	312,000
Fish	287,000
Indigo	117,000

The sale of shipping services to overseas buyers was a major source of foreign exchange and comprised a major part of colonial market activity. This is particularly true of New England, which earned 54 per cent of all colonial shipping earnings. The importance of shipping earnings has frequently been overlooked, or at least not properly stressed, by economic historians. One American economic history textbook,[2]

---

[1] Elizabeth Donnan (ed.), *Documents Illustrative of the History of the Slave Trade to America* (Washington, D.C.; Carnegie Institution of Washington, 1933), III, pp. 215–16.

[2] Ross M. Robertson, *The History of the American Economy* (2nd ed.; New York: Harcourt, Brace & World, Inc., 1964).

for example, makes no mention of the major importance of shipping services although considerable attention is given to the various staple crops of the different regions, and to shipbuilding. In fact, the evidence given in Chapter 6 (Appendix VI) suggests that shipbuilding was a much smaller source of income and foreign exchange to colonists than the sale of shipping services, even for New England.

Lastly, it should be stressed that total invisible earnings were relatively large and offset 62 per cent of the overall deficit of commodity trade.[1] These earnings substantially reduced the deficits of New England and the middle colonies and raised to a surplus position the balances of the southern colonies. It should be noted also that for all the colonies taken together, the West Indies trade produced small deficits on the average if one considers only the commodity trade, but when the invisible earnings are included, the surpluses earned there approach those earned in southern Europe.

---

[1] We feel that the method of estimation and assumptions used were generally conservative. Consequently, the actual earnings may have been higher than our estimates.

CHAPTER 8

THE BALANCE OF PAYMENTS, 1768–72

THE CURRENT ACCOUNT: A PRELIMINARY VIEW

From the estimates of commodity trade and invisible earnings presented in the preceding two chapters, we now can begin to draw some conclusions about the magnitudes of the deficits or surpluses on current account incurred by each colonial region with each overseas area. Table 7.1 in Chapter 7 summarizes the estimates of commodity exports and imports and the resulting balances from commodity trade. As briefly mentioned in Chapter 7, the colonies did indeed incur very large deficits in their commodity trade with Great Britain. An average annual deficit of £1,800,000 was estimated from the colonies' trade with Great Britain and Ireland. The greatest part of this deficit (almost 94 per cent) was due to the northern colonies, New England, and the middle colonies. Only relatively small deficits were incurred by the southern colonies in their trade with Britain. Florida, the Bahamas and the Bermuda Islands incurred an average annual deficit of £41,000, which was large relative to the total trade of these areas. This relatively large deficit in all likelihood reflected the efforts of the British to settle and develop East Florida, and the fact that this settlement and development was being financed by British capital. The trade with southern Europe was the only one in which a large surplus was earned from commodity trade alone. This surplus averaged £462,000 annually, and all the regions except Florida, the Bahamas and the Bermuda Islands shared in it. The colonies exported about as much as they imported in their commodity trade with the West Indies (one should recall that the estimates of export values were based on F.O.B. prices and the estimates of import values on C.I.F. prices). There was a small average annual deficit of about £13,000 in this Caribbean commodity trade. All regions incurred small deficits, on the average, except the lower south which consistently earned a surplus in its commodity trade with the West Indies. Commodity exports to Africa probably exceeded commodity imports from there, but when the importation of slaves is taken into account sizable deficits resulted from the colonies' African trade.

Table 8.1 summarizes the balances on current account after the invisible earnings estimated in Chapter 7 have been added to the balances resulting from commodity trade (Table 7.1). Invisible earn-

TABLE 8.1. *Estimated balances on current account in the balance of payments of the British North American colonies, 1768–72ᵃ* (thousand pounds sterling)

Overseas area and colonial region	1768	1769	1770	1771	1772
Great Britain and Ireland					
Northern colonies	−187	−261	−383	−267	−352
New England	−282	−60	−279	−1,280	−757
Middle colonies	−778	−139	−509	−1,349	−811
Southern colonies	73	203	−53	−343	−54
Florida, Bahama and Bermuda Is.	−55	−40	−46	−44	−21
North American colonies	−1,229	−297	−1,270	−3,283	−1,995
Southern Europe and Wine Islands					
Northern colonies	66	89	107	238	167
New England	98	104	103	139	103
Middle colonies	119	270	245	175	269
Southern colonies	160	263	211	103	140
Florida, Bahama and Bermuda Is.	−1	−2	−1	−1	−1
North American colonies	442	724	665	654	678
West Indies					
Northern colonies	0	8	3	6	13
New England	242	181	244	292	259
Middle colonies	85	25	74	178	166
Southern colonies	81	87	83	121	103
Florida, Bahama and Bermuda Is.	−3	−4	1	−1	−7
North American colonies	405	297	405	596	534
Africa					
Northern colonies	0	0	0	0	0
New England	16	27	24	17	30
Middle colonies	0	1	1	1	2
Southern colonies	0	0	0	0	2
Florida, Bahama and Bermuda Is.	0	0	0	0	0
North American colonies	16	28	25	18	34
Total, Overseas areasᵇ					
Northern colonies	−121	−164	−273	−23	−172
New England	80	258	98	−826	−359
Middle colonies	−571	160	−186	−992	−371
Southern colonies	317	556	244	−116	194
Florida, Bahama and Bermuda Is	−59	−46	−46	−46	−29
Total, North American colonies	−354	764	−163	−2,003	−737

Source: computed by adding the balances of trade from Table 7.1 to the estimated invisible earnings from Tables 7.6 and 7.7.

ᵃ These balances do not include estimated earnings from the sale of ships to overseas areas or from British civil and defense expenditures in the colonies, or debits due to the immigration of slaves and indentured servants. They do include the balances of commodity trade plus estimated shipping and other invisible earnings from Chapter 7.

ᵇ The totals for all overseas areas include estimated shipping earnings between overseas areas of £12,000 (£6,000 for New England, £3,000 for the middle colonies, and £3,000 for the southern colonies).

ings of the colonies from their direct trade with the British Isles slightly reduced the estimated deficit from the British trade (these earnings averaged £185,000 annually during this period), but it was essentially earnings from trade and shipping with southern Europe and the West Indies that contributed toward paying the deficit incurred in the British trade. When shipping and other invisible earnings are considered, not only does the surplus earned in the southern European trade increase to an average of £633,000 annually, but the balance from the West Indian trade is transformed from a small average deficit to a relatively large annual average surplus of £447,000. Given these surpluses of over one million pounds sterling from the southern European and West Indian trades, the deficit remaining after considering commodity and invisible earnings with all overseas areas is £499,000, which is composed of regional average deficits of £151,000 for the northern colonies; £150,000 for New England; £392,000 for the middle colonies; £45,000 for Florida, the Bahama and the Bermuda Islands; and an average surplus of £239,000 for the southern colonies.[1] It is very likely that trade between the colonies brought a redistribution of these deficits and of the southern colonies' surplus. Probably part of the latter was earned by the middle colonies and New England in trade with the southern colonies. Two of the colonial regions, the northern colonies and Florida, the Bahama and the Bermuda Islands, together incurred a deficit of about £200,000, which was large relative to their population. As stated above, this relatively large deficit probably reflects the fact that the development of these regions was being subsidized by British residents or by the British government.

The remaining deficit of roughly one-half million pounds sterling was not the final balance on the current account of the colonies for this period 1768–72. Several other items, some relatively large, remain to be taken into account. In Chapter 6 it was suggested that the sale of ships to overseas buyers probably averaged about £75,000 annually during this period (see Appendix VI). There were also the debits in the colonies' balance of payments due to the immigration of slaves and indentured servants, which were discussed in Chapter 3, and which are estimated below explicitly for this period. Finally, the probable magnitude of a large source of foreign exchange earnings, the civil and defense expenditures made by the British government in the colonies, is also discussed below.

IMMIGRATION AND THE COLONIAL BALANCE OF PAYMENTS

There are several ways in which immigration may affect the balance of payments. Free immigration, i.e. migration of people (who paid their

[1] See p. 114, note 2, regarding caution in interpreting the regional balances.

own costs of transportation) to the colonies on a voluntary basis, would result in a credit if these immigrants traveled on colonial-owned ships. These people would not yet be residents of the colonies and presumably would be paying for their passage with sterling. The colonial shipowner would thus be earning foreign exchange when selling them passage. These credits are accounted for in the estimates of shipping earnings given in Chapter 7.

Any sterling or other foreign funds brought by the immigrants with them to the colonies should be a credit in the balance of payments. Although there were some immigrants who were well enough off to be able to bring funds with them,[1] there is no evidence that many of the immigrants were in a position to do so. This was true not only for the colonial period, but also for the earlier part of the nineteenth century.[2] Because of the lack of evidence, and the likelihood that this item was of doubtful significance, no attempt has been made to estimate it.

Once these immigrants became residents, family ties may have induced them to remit money to relatives in their home country. Immigrants' remittances were indeed significant in the nineteenth-century U.S. balance of payments.[3] But again it is doubtful that this item was significant during colonial times. First, we know of few instances of any such remittance from contemporary sources. Second, the colonial economy was based to a smaller degree on monetary exchange than was that of the nineteenth century. The nineteenth-century immigrant often came and worked for money wages. The colonial immigrant more often went into agriculture, where he engaged in a combination of self-sufficient production and production for the market. With the money earned from market sales he had to buy such necessities as gunpowder, hardware, textiles, and so forth. It is doubtful that he would have been able to save much to send abroad. Furthermore, much of his market produce was not exchanged for money, but was bartered directly for these goods. Third, due to the lack of banking facilities the typical colonist did not have ready access to foreign exchange markets. These markets, though well developed in the eighteenth century, existed only in the major commercial centers; and evidence suggests that they were used only by the merchants in these centers. Finally, it appears that family ties, with the exception of a few merchant families, did not remain strong in the world of the eighteenth century. The Atlantic

[1] See Mildred Campbell, 'English emigration on the eve of the American Revolution,' *American Historical Review*, LXI, 1 (October 1955), p. 9; and Ian C. C. Graham, *Colonists from Scotland: Emigration to North America, 1707–1783* (Ithaca, N.Y.; Cornell University Press, 1956), p. 41 (see p. 147, note 6 below).

[2] See Douglass C. North, 'The United States balance of payments, 1790–1860,' *Trends in the American Economy in the Nineteenth Century*, Studies in Income and Wealth, National Bureau of Economic Research, Vol. 24 (Princeton, N.J.: Princeton University Press, 1960), pp. 611–15.

[3] *Ibid.*, pp. 616–18.

ocean presented a tremendous barrier in terms of direct costs and risks of travel,[1] and few families expected to see again those members who migrated to the new world. For these reasons, then, it is assumed that this item of immigrants' remittances was not significant during this period.

There were, however, several obvious ways in which immigration did affect the colonial balance of payments. Not all immigration to the colonies was of a free and voluntary nature. As mentioned earlier, two institutions arose which operated to furnish more labor than could be obtained from free immigration alone. These institutions, of course, were slavery and indentured servitude.

IMPORTS OF SLAVES

Payments for Negro slaves, which were made mainly by southern plantation owners, entered the current account as a debit. The American Inspector-General's Ledgers list the number of slaves imported from Africa and the West Indies. These figures are presented in Table 8.2.

Providing that these figures are reasonably accurate, all that needs to be done to establish the magnitude of this debit, is to obtain some idea about the average prices that were paid for these slaves. No price series exist for slaves sold during the colonial period. Reliance must be placed on prices mentioned in colonial correspondence, or statements by historians who have examined these sources. The secular trend of slave prices was upwards over the colonial period.[2] A contemporary source estimating the value of imports and exports of the colonies for 1768 used an average price of £35 to value slaves imported.[3] Twenty years later in 1788 another writer used the rate of £50 to compute the value of 450,000 slaves in the British West Indies, demonstrating that slave prices continued upward.[4]

Fortunately a large number of documents concerning the slave trade

---

[1] It is for similar and rather obvious reasons that tourist expenditures are not considered to have been a significant item. They did not become important in the U.S. until after 1850. See *ibid.*, pp. 614–15 and 618–19.

[2] See Curtis P. Nettels, *The Roots of American Civilization* (2nd ed.; New York: Appleton-Century-Crofts, 1963), p. 419, who states that slave prices took roughly the following course over the colonial period (prices in pounds sterling):

1650	£20
1700	25
1741	30
1750	40–60
1770s	50–80

[3] London, British Museum, Add. Mss 15485, 'The Exports and Imports of North America, 1768–1769,' (January 5, 1768 to January 5, 1769).

[4] London, British Museum, Stowe Mss 921.

TABLE 8.2.   *Number of slaves imported into the British North American colonies, 1768–72*

Area of origin and place of importation	Years				
	1768[a]	1769	1770[b]	1771	1772
Africa					
Northern colonies	—	0	0	0	0
New England	—	6	0	0	0
Middle colonies	—	0	67	0	19
Upper south	—	414	1,148	207	1,357
Lower south	—	4,622	875	2,547	5,262
Florida, Bahama and Bermuda Is.	—	119	176	0	0
North American colonies	—	5,161	2,266	2,754	6,638
West Indies					
Northern colonies	—	0	0	0	0
New England	—	4	0	7	6
Middle colonies	—	10	2	8	4
Upper south	—	281	277	771	876
Lower south	—	851	327	1,214	2,241
Florida, Bahama and Bermuda Is.	—	84	3	108	25
North American colonies	—	1,230	609	2,108	3,152
Total overseas areas					
Northern colonies	0	0	0	0	0
New England	85	10	0	7	6
Middle colonies	19	10	69	8	23
Upper south	642	695	1,425	978	2,233
Lower south	1,328	5,473	1,202	3,761	7,503
Florida, Bahama and Bermuda Is.	143	203	179	108	25
Total, North American colonies	2,217	6,391	2,875	4,862	9,790

Source: London, Public Record Office, Customs 16/1.

[a] The source does not distinguish the origin of slaves imported for 1768.

[b] It might be noted that the non-importation agreements undoubtedly affected slave imports as well as imports of British manufacture for 1770. The reason was that many (probably a substantial majority) of the slaves were purchased from British slave dealers. Both the non-importation agreements of Virginia and South Carolina, the largest slave importing colonies, specifically mentioned slaves. See Elizabeth Donnan (ed.), *Documents Illustrative of the History of the Slave Trade to America* (Washington, D.C.: Carnegie Institution of Washington, 1935), IV, p. 433; and W. E. Burghardt DuBois, *The Suppression of the African Slave Trade to the United States of America, 1638–1870* (New York: Russell & Russell, 1965), p. 42.

has been published,[1] so we may rely on a substantial number of observations of prices taken from these documents. Many of these observations refer to the average selling price of entire cargoes of slaves, or even to the average price for larger numbers imported over some particular period. Averages of these observed prices (weighted where possible with the number of slaves sold at this price) are given in Table 8.3.

[1] Elizabeth Donnan (ed.), *Documents Illustrative of the History of the Slave Trade to America* (Washington, D.C.: The Carnegie Institution of Washington, 1930–5), I–IV.

TABLE 8.3.   *Average prices (in pounds sterling) of slaves sold in the thirteen colonies and the West Indies, 1768–72*[a]

Place of sale	1768	1769	1770	1771	1772
Upper south	38	35	b	36	b
Lower south	34	38	b	38	45
West Indies	28	b	33	36	36

Source: computed from prices quoted in sources printed in Elizabeth Donnan (ed.), *Documents Illustrative of the History of the Slave Trade to America* (Washington, D.C.: The Carnegie Institution of Washington, 1930–5), II–IV.

a No prices were found for sales taking place in New England or the middle colonies.

b No prices were found for this area in this year.

Clearly, from the trend of prices given by the documents reprinted in Donnan, an average price of over £35 per slave existed during this period, and in 1772 there was clearly a sharp jump in slave prices (although perhaps not as sharp as Table 8.3 might indicate). By using

TABLE 8.4.   *Value of slaves (pounds sterling) imported into the British North American colonies, 1768–72*

Area of origin and place of importation	Years				
	1768	1769	1770	1771	1772
Africa					
Northern colonies	—	0	0	0	0
New England	—	225	0	0	0
Middle colonies	—	0	2,512	0	760
Upper south	—	15,525	43,050	7,762	54,280
Lower south	—	173,325	32,812	95,512	210,480
Florida, Bahama and Bermuda Is	—	4,463	6,600	0	0
North American colonies	—	193,538	84,974	103,274	265,520
West Indies					
Northern colonies	—	0	0	0	0
New England	—	150	0	262	240
Middle colonies	—	375	75	300	160
Upper south	—	10,537	10,387	28,912	35,040
Lower south	—	31,912	12,262	45,525	89,640
Florida, Bahama and Bermuda Is.	—	3,150	113	4,050	1,000
North American colonies	—	46,124	22,837	79,049	126,080
Total, overseas areas					
Northern colonies	0	0	0	0	0
New England	3,187	375	0	262	240
Middle colonies	712	375	2,587	300	920
Upper south	24,074	26,062	53,437	36,674	89,320
Lower south	49,799	205,237	45,074	141,037	300,120
Florida, Bahama and Bermuda Is.	5,362	7,613	6,713	4,050	1,000
Total, North American colonies	83,183	239,662	107,811	182,323	391,600

Source: computed from Tables 8.2 and 8.3.

the average prices of £37½ per slave for the first four years and £40 in 1772, a fairly close approximation of the amounts spent on slaves can be made. From the quantities and these average prices, then, the values of slaves imported from Africa and from the West Indies into the British North American colonies can be estimated. These figures are presented in Table 8.4.

The entire amount of the above estimates did not accrue to foreigners. Some part was earned by the slave traders of New England, especially those of Rhode Island. The average tonnage leaving for Africa during the period 1768–72 was slightly over 1,000 tons per year. This amount of tonnage returned with possibly as many as 2,000 slaves either directly from Africa or via the West Indies. The value of such slaves may have been as high as £80,000 per year on the average. The actual debit incurred annually by the colonies due to the importation of slaves should be reduced by some portion of this amount of £80,000 – specifically, that portion which remained after deducting whatever sterling was spent for slaves by the colonists in Africa. An upper estimate of the average amount spent for slaves in Africa is £60,000;[1] thus the reduction to the estimated debit due to the importation of slaves is £20,000.[2] This essentially represents a lower limit to colonial merchants' earnings in the slave trade.

IMMIGRATION OF INDENTURED SERVANTS

The other class of immigrants which affected the colonial balance of payments was that group 'variously known as indentured servants, redemptioners, or, in order to distinguish them from the Negroes, as Christian or white servants.'[3] These people ranged from convicts, to French, German, and Swiss Protestants fleeing from religious persecution, to poor Irish, Scottish, and English farmers or artisans who were unable to pay their own way to the colonies.[4] This institution of indentured servitude came into existence fairly early in the seventeenth century.[5] Its usual form was that of a legal contract, where the servant bound himself to serve a colonial master in some form of

---

[1] Donnan (*ibid.*, ii, p. 547) gives prices of prime male slaves on the Gold Coast at £20 in 1772. The steady upward movement of prices and the above-average quality of prime male slaves makes £20 an upper bound price. We have assumed that 3,000 slaves were purchased in Africa, 1,000 dying in transit.

[2] The annual average colonial shipping earnings between Africa and the West Indies for the period 1768–72 were estimated to have been £1,000. In principle, this should be deducted from this figure, leaving £19,000.

[3] Abbot E. Smith, *Colonists in Bondage: White Servitude and Convict Labor in America, 1607–1776* (Chapel Hill, N.C.: University of North Carolina Press, 1947), p. 3.

[4] *Ibid.*

[5] 'By the year 1636 one could procure printed indentures, with blank spaces left for the names of the servant and master and for any special provisions desired.' *Ibid.*, p. 17.

employment (either agreed upon beforehand, or assigned afterward by the master) for some specified period of years, most often four. The servant was to be furnished board and room, and in most cases was given a reward, his 'freedom dues', at the end of the service.[1] 'Re-demptioners,' a term which came to apply to a particular group of immigrants in the eighteenth century, referred to persons who, seeking passage to the colonies, found that their resources were insufficient to pay for the total costs of passage. A merchant or ship captain accord-ingly might take what money the person had, put him and his family aboard the ship, and contract to deliver them to some destination in the colonies. After arrival the person was allowed a specified period of time to raise the balance owing for his passage. If he could not obtain it within this time, commonly fourteen days, then he was to be sold into indentured servitude by the captain of the ship.[2]

There would appear to be some implications for the balance of payments in these different ways by which people became indentured servants. It was customary to supply the person with food, clothing, and shelter from the time he signed his indenture. For the indentured servant who signed in Europe, costs of delivering him to a colonial master would be higher than for the redemptioner who signed in the colonies and perhaps had contributed something towards his own passage. It would be expected that the former would have to enter into a longer period of servitude than the latter. Evidence of this was not found, however. The explanation probably rests in the fact that the servant who signed his indenture in Europe was almost invariably required to be unmarried, without dependants, and no one's ap-prentice; whereas the redemptionist system applied generally to married men who brought their families and worldly goods with them.[3] Possibly the additional costs incurred from equipping and maintaining an indentured servant over a longer period of time were largely offset by the higher cost of transporting the redemptioner and his family.

As was stated in Chapter 3, there are no complete statistics for immigration during the colonial period, and the data pertaining to indentured servants are among the most incomplete. One traveler in 1765 stated:

> It is Computed that there are at least ten thousand Convicts and passengers, or indented Servants, imported yearly into the Different Colonies, the first are Sent to Virginia and maryland only, and likewise Indented servants; But the Colonies to the Northward of maryland admit no Convicts, by Serv'ts as many as will Come. there has Come to philadel'ᵃ alone, 5000 in one year,

[1] *Ibid.*
[2] *Ibid.*, pp. 20–1.
[3] *Ibid.*, p. 22.

¾ of which were from Ireland, great numbers of Dutch and germans; . . .[1]

As discussed in Chapter 3, migration from the British Isles to the colonies almost certainly increased around 1768–70, and with it we might suppose the number of indentured servants. It follows that debits in the colonial balance of payments for purchases of indentured servants probably rose to substantial levels during 1768–72.

Although the data are incomplete, fragmentary statistics do give us at least a rough notion of what was occurring. Concerning emigration from England and Scotland there exist weekly reports of departures compiled by customs officers from December 1773 to April 1776. The English returns have been discussed by Mildred Campbell and George R. Mellor, the latter having also examined the Scottish returns and the evidence for Ireland.[2] These returns indicate that close to 6,000 people left England and Wales for the new world,[3] most of whom were emigrants destined for the mainland colonies. These were years of relatively heavy English emigration, and it seems doubtful that the numbers leaving were as high during 1768–72 (Mellor suggests the annual average was 1,500 during these years).[4] The returns from Scotland show 2,952 emigrating during 1774 and 1775 (this includes 72 who were going to the West Indies)[5]. The Scottish returns are incomplete, however, and Mellor would put the actual average number leaving each year at 2,500 for the entire period 1765–75.[6] Estimates of emigration also were constructed for Scotland from various records and newspaper reportings by Graham, which roughly match Mellor's statements.[7] He suggests that emigration from Scotland increased around 1768–70,[8] and that from 1763 to 1773 20,000 Scots migrated to North America followed by 5,000 more during 1774 and 1775.[9]

Emigration from Ireland, mostly from Ulster,[10] was greater than from Britain at this time. It was said to have been 28,600 for the three

---

[1] 'Journal of a French traveller in the colonies. 1765,' *American Historical Review*, XXVI, p. 744; quoted from Smith, p. 331. The observation about great numbers of Dutch immigrants was obviously an error, but it was a common mistake of the time which mislabeled these immigrants as 'Pennsylvania Dutch.' They were actually Germans who traveled down the Rhine and departed for the colonies from the Netherlands.

[2] Campbell, pp. 1–20; and George R. Mellor, 'Emigration from the British Isles to the New World, 1765–1775,' *History*, New Ser., XL (February and June 1955), pp. 68–83. The authors are indebted to Herbert Heaton for calling attention to the latter source as well as to some of the other sources cited below in this section.

[3] Campbell, p. 4; and Mellor, p. 72. Mellor counts 5,811 persons, 521 of whom were going to the West Indies.

[4] Mellor, p. 80.

[5] *Ibid.*, p. 73.   [6] *Ibid.*, p. 81.

[7] Graham, Appendix, pp. 185–9.

[8] *Ibid.*, pp. 21 and 24.   [9] *Ibid.*, pp. 185–6.

[10] See R. J. Dickson, *Ulster Emigration to Colonial America, 1718–1775*. (London: Routledge & Kegan Paul, 1966), especially pp. 66–7, where he suggests that emigration from the south of Ireland was small during this period.

years 1771–73 alone.[1] Like that from Britain, emigration from Ireland picked up after 1770 and was relatively heavy during the period 1771–75.[2] Mellor puts it at about 6,000 annually from 1766 to 1770, and 10,000 from 1771 to 1775.[3] On the basis of emigrant shipping tonnage, Dickson states that 'about 7,700 emigrated in 1771, 9,300 in 1772, 12,300 in 1773, and 8,300 in 1774,' although he seems to suggest lower figures than Mellor for the 1760s.[4]

The following rough estimates of average annual immigration to the colonies from the British Isles during 1768–72 serve to summarize the above evidence and speculation:

from England and Wales	1,500 to 2,000
from Scotland	2,000 to 2,500
from Ireland	4,000 to 10,000
Total	7,500 to 14,500

To this must be added immigration from Germany, which, as stated in Chapter 3, reached a peak in the late 1740s and early 1750s, and, unlike that from the British Isles, did not increase during the 1770s. One estimate for the late colonial period puts it at 4,000 in 1765.[5] If it was in this neighborhood during 1768–72, then immigration of whites into the colonies ranged from about 11,000 to 19,000 per year, probably being toward the lower end of this range at the beginning of the period and increasing toward the upper end in 1772. If, as suggested by Abbot E. Smith, 'not less than one-half, nor more than two-thirds, of all white immigrants to the colonies were indentured servants or redemptioners or convicts,'[6] then the number of such persons entering the colonies each year in this period would have ranged from 5,000 to 10,000.

Prices for indentured servants ranged from £6 to £60 over the colonial period,[7] but judging from the costs of taking a servant to the colonies it seems likely that the average price would have been near the lower end of this range. The costs of a trans-Atlantic passage never exceeded £5 to £6 for adults during the colonial period, and half

[1] Smith, pp. 313–14.
[2] Dickson, p. 60.
[3] Mellor, p. 82.
[4] Dickson, p. 64. He cites a contemporary estimate of 4,000 for the 1760s, and suggests it was more than likely an exaggeration (p. 58).
[5] Smith, p. 315.
[6] *Ibid.*, p. 336. Campbell, p. 5, says 60 per cent (including convicts) of the English emigrants were indentured servants. Dickson suggests that a high proportion of Ulster emigrants went as indentured servants or redemptioners (p. 85), but that the proportion fluctuated and was lower in the later colonial period – 'those who were emigrating [in the 1770s] were paying passengers of the middle class' (p. 97). Graham, p. 41, with reference to Scottish emigration, states: 'It is probably safe to say that most of the emigrants of the 1770s were poor – so poor as to be obliged to obtain a passage to America by indenting themselves – but that a higher proportion than ever before possessed some money with which to establish themselves in the colonies.'
[7] Smith, pp. 38–40.

that for children under ten.[1] Total costs of procuring a servant, equipping him, and transporting him to the colonies ranged somewhere between £4 and £12, depending upon how long servants had to be fed before the departure, what clothing and necessities were furnished them, and what the scale of operations was.[2] An individual taking one servant along with him to the colonies would not have achieved the economies that a merchant or shipowner would, who was gathering together a larger cargo of servants to send. Prices in Philadelphia in the early 1770s were said to have averaged about £20 in Pennsylvania currency for adult males, or about £12 in sterling.[3] If the average price for all servants entering the colonies was £10, then the debit in the colonial balance of payments due to this immigration would have ranged from £50,000 to £100,000 annually during 1768–72.

Because by far the greatest number of servants went to Pennsylvania, Maryland, and Virginia, the distribution of this debit among the various colonial regions must be weighted in their favor.[4] The lower south received far fewer servants than did the middle colonies and the upper south, although the numbers were not insignificant.[5] The debit should be assigned to the trade with Great Britain, because British and colonial merchants and shipowners had exclusive control of the trade. The above estimates overstate the actual debit to the extent that payments for indentured servants went to other colonists. However, a credit for carrying indentured servants was included in the estimate of shipping earnings presented in Chapter 7. This offsets that part of the above debit which did not actually go to foreigners.

In view of the sparse evidence, it seems impossible to be any more precise about this item. We can conclude with some certainty, however, that the expenditure of sterling on indentured servants was significantly smaller than the amounts spent on the importation of slaves, and that it averaged more during the late 1760s and early 1770s than at any other time during the colonial period.

BRITISH GOVERNMENTAL EXPENDITURES IN THE COLONIES

Expenditures made by the British government probably went far towards eliminating the remaining deficits on the colonies' current

---

[1] *Ibid.*, p. 35; and Campbell, p. 17.

[2] Smith, pp. 35–8. An additional cost would have been due to the efforts of merchants, and the risks they bore, in organizing and carrying out the servant trade. A factor that would have produced a discrepancy between these average costs and prices of indentured servants was the 'freedom dues' (that is, goods and/or cash) required to be given to servants at the expiration of their terms of indenture. See *Ibid.*, pp. 238–40.

[3] *Ibid.*, p. 40.   [4] See *ibid.*, pp. 307–32.

[5] See Warren B. Smith, *White Servitude in Colonial South Carolina* (Columbia, S.C.: University of South Carolina Press, 1961), who argues that the descriptions by historians of the immigration of indentured servants to the colonies have given a false impression of a negligible immigration of such persons to South Carolina.

account with Great Britain. Expenditures for defense purposes were undoubtedly the most important in this category; and to these were added certain costs of civil administration and justice that were assumed by Great Britain, and the costs of maintaining the customs administration and enforcing customs regulations. Unfortunately, it is not clear exactly what the costs of defending and administering the colonies were to Great Britain, and even if they were known, they are not the relevant facts for this study. Rather, the concern is with that part of those costs which gave rise to purchases of goods and services by the British in the colonies. From these expenditures should be deducted the colonial revenues that accrued to the British government, primarily from customs duties. From what evidence is available, it seems almost certain that expenditures made for civil and customs administration were greater than the customs revenues, which averaged £39,000 per annum for the period 1768–72.[1]

In contrast to British expenditures in the colonies for civil and customs administration, the military and naval costs incurred by the British very likely resulted in significant earnings of sterling. The standing British army during this period consisted of sixteen regiments, which at full strength numbered 477 men each.[2] It is unlikely that the

[1] P.R.O. Customs 16/1. There are no estimates of the costs of the customs administration to Britain, but some have said the costs were greater than the customs revenues by sizable amounts. For example, John C. Miller, *Origins of the American Revolution* (Stanford, Cal.: Stanford University Press, 1959), p. 83, states: 'To collect two thousand pounds in customs duties in the colonies cost the British government eight thousand pounds.' There were also other costs of administering the colonies, some of which were borne by the British army. The army not only garrisoned the Indian country and enforced the boundary line, but it 'bore the expenses of the Indian department and the cost of the civil governments of such "infant" colonies as Nova Scotia, Georgia, and the Floridas' (Jack M. Sosin, *Whitehall and the Wilderness: The Middle West in British Colonial Policy, 1760–1775* (Lincoln, Neb.: University of Nebraska Press, 1961), p. 79). Amounts for subsidizing these 'infant' colonial governments and costs of 'general surveys of his Majesty's dominions in North America' were £19,068 in 1768 and £18,797 in 1769 (William Cobbett, *The Parliamentary History of England* (London, 1813; reprinted by the Johnson Reprint Corporation, 1966), XVI, pp. 413–18 and 621–6). (This source does not list the subsidies after 1769.) Salaries in the Northern Indian Department were said by General Gage in 1768 to be £3,299 (Clarence E. Carter (ed.), *The Correspondence of General Thomas Gage, 1763–1775* (New Haven, Conn.: Yale University Press, 1933), II, pp. 385–6). Earlier in the same year Gage had said that £3,000 should be provided for occasional presents to the Indians and for various other expenses (Carter, p. 63). If the Southern Indian Department's costs were roughly of this magnitude, then expenditures for the Indian departments would have been at least £12,000 per annum. (According to Sosin, p. 132, they were £20,000.) Given only this fragmentary evidence, it is difficult to place any precise estimate on such expenditures by the British government in the colonies; but it is probable that they were in the neighborhood of £30,000 to £40,000 or more per annum for this period.

[2] The number of regiments and the estimates below of regimental strength and pay and subsistence of a regiment are taken from Maclyn P. Burg, 'An estimation of the cost of defending and administering the colonies of British North America, 1763–1775' (unpublished paper, Department of Economics, University of Washington, 1966). His information was based upon statements of regiment size, number, location, and pay scales in Edward E. Curtis, *The Organization of the British Army in the American Revolution* (New Haven,

army was maintained at full strength due to desertions, illness, and casualties. General Gage's report of July 19, 1775 lists the strength of each regiment as varying from 333 to 457 men each. At full strength, the pay and subsistence for a regiment came to almost £18,000 per year, or over £230,000 per year for sixteen regiments at about 80 per cent of strength. It seems highly probable that most of this pay and subsistence was spent in the colonies.

The Royal Navy's North American squadron comprised around twenty-seven vessels of various sizes during this period, and if fully manned by the standard number of men and officers (probably over 4,000 men), the wages and subsistence would have been approximately £260,000.[1] It is likely that these vessels were not fully manned; and it may also have been the case that the naval men had less opportunity than soldiers to spend their wages in the colonies. Although it is impossible to say with any certainty what portion of this sum was spent in the colonies it would seem reasonable that at least from £150,000 to £200,000 per year was spent there. The Royal Navy in North America was based at Halifax, and we know that naval stores and provisions were purchased there as well as at other colonies visited during their cruising along the American coast.

In all, it seems unlikely that British defense expenditures were less

---

Conn.: Yale University Press, 1926), pp. 3–5 and 158; Carter, pp. 689–90; and Sir John Fortescue, *Correspondence of George the Third* (London: Macmillan & Co., 1928), III, p. 319. It is suggested that this estimated pay and subsistence of the army is only a lower bound to what British military expenditures in the colonies actually were. Note, for example, the statement by Sosin (*op. cit.*, p. 132): 'on February 18 [1767],...the Secretary-at-War brought in the extraordinary expenditures of the American army for the previous year. They came to over £300,000. Thus, the annual cost of the American defense establishment to Great Britain was over £700,000 [in 1767]. Only a relatively small portion of this sum, £20,000, went to the Indian departments. The difficulty in supplying the remote forts in the interior accounted for most of the added expense.' The expenses of the military establishment probably did not remain this high over the period 1768–72, however. 'Since the ministers were acutely aware of the need for a reduction of the financial burden on Great Britain, they carried out a gradual withdrawal of the forces from the interior in the years from 1768 to 1774. Indeed, the mounting tensions which increased the need for troops on the turbulent seacoast accelerated the process' (Sosin, p. 220).

[1] In 1763, there were 27 British naval vessels assigned to North American stations (*London Magazine*, XXXII (December 1763), p. 674). In December 1774, there were 24 ships manned by 2,835 men stationed in North America, and 30 ships and 3,435 men in June 1775 (G. R. Barnes and J. H. Owen (eds.), *The Private Papers of John, Earl of Sandwich, 1771–1782* (Greenwich, England: The Naval Records Society, 1932), I, p. 42). Also see William B. Clark (ed.), *Naval Documents of the American Revolution* (Washington, D.C.: U.S. Government Printing Office, 1964), I, p. 1351. This estimate of the number of ships in the five years 1768–72 assumes that the number between 1763 and 1775 was approximately constant. The estimated expenditures are taken from Burg, *op. cit.*, and are based on evidence about the type of vessels and naval manning characteristics and pay published in Allen French, *The First Year of the American Revolution* (Boston, Mass.: Houghton Mifflin Co., 1934), p. 345; J. G. Bullocke (ed.), *The Tomlinson Papers* (Greenwich, England; Naval Records Society, 1935), pp. 150–1; and Michael Lewis, *A Social History of the Navy, 1793–1815* (London: George Allen & Unwin, Ltd., 1960), pp. 294–5, 300, and 304.

than £400,000 per year in the colonies. They may well have been higher, but the available evidence does not allow a more precise estimate. If defense expenditures were in this neighborhood, then any deficits remaining in the current account of the colonies' balance of payments, especially the balance of payments of the thirteen colonies which were soon to revolt, were probably nonexistent for the southern colonies, and were relatively small for New England and the middle colonies.[1] The magnitudes of these balances do hold implications for capital and monetary flows, to the discussion of which we now turn.

CAPITAL AND MONETARY FLOWS

So far this and the previous two chapters have dealt with items in the current account of the colonies' balance of payments, which included all transactions which gave rise to or used up colonial income. There are, however, two additional categories in the usual balance-of-payments framework – the capital section and the monetary section – which should be examined.[2] Unfortunately, little direct evidence concerning capital and monetary flows exists. From descriptions by historians of colonial trade, from colonial correspondence and records and contemporary comments, and from the balances discussed in the previous section, we

---

[1] It may be worthwhile to recapitulate the specific conclusions of the above sections at this point. It will be recalled that an estimated deficit of about £500,000 existed from commodity trade and invisibles. It was suggested that the sale of ships to overseas buyers probably averaged around £75,000 annually, and that debits due to the immigration of slaves and indentured servants averaged at most about £230,000 to £280,000 annually during this period (slave imports averaged around £140,000 from Africa and about £60,000 from the West Indies, less estimated colonial merchants' profits from the slave trade of £20,000, and the debit due to expenditures on indentured servants, which was hazarded as having been in the neighborhood of £50,000 to £100,000 per year). This, together with a credit of £400,000 due to British defense expenditures, leaves an estimated average annual deficit of·roughly £250,000 to £300,000. If £200,000 of this deficit was incurred by the northern colonies and Florida (see the above discussion in the first section of this chapter), this makes the remaining deficit for the thirteen colonies look very small indeed. Admittedly, these calculations are very crude, and this remaining balance is very sensitive to the accuracy of the evidence and to various steps in making the foregoing estimates. Four steps, in particular, might be pointed out as being particularly crucial. These are (1) the average tobacco prices used (Table 1, Appendix IV), (2) the specific adjustments of the official values made to approximate amounts actually paid by the colonists for these goods (Appendix II), (3) the expenditures on indentured servants and (4) the British defense expenditures in the colonies. Due to lack of evidence, the margin of error is probably large. Because of this, an attempt was made to make the debit due to the immigration of indentured servants an upper bound, and the credit due to British defense expenditures a lower bound. Given this intended bias, it is probable that an even smaller deficit existed for the thirteen colonies for this particular five-year period, and possibly none at all.

[2] The capital account records changes in claims of residents of an area on residents of other areas, and changes in liabilities owed. To the extent that there was a positive or negative balance on the current account, there must have been either changes in these claims or liabilities, or off-setting monetary flows, or some combination of both. To the extent that capital flows did not exactly offset the balance on the current account, then the final settlement must have been made by movements of gold or silver bullion or specie.

know the probable directions in which capital and monetary movements occurred. This study, however, has been devoted to the question: How much? Although the evidence necessary to give a direct answer does not exist, the balances on current account (from Table 8.1 plus the additional modifications suggested in the preceding sections of this chapter) provide an indirect answer to what capital and monetary flows may have been. The average deficit balance of £250,000 to £300,000 for all the British North American colonies during the period 1768–72 suggests that, on the average, there were net capital inflows and/or exports of monetary bullion or specie.[1] Such a balance also suggests that these capital inflows were relatively small. If we look at the regional balances, they suggest that the tobacco-growing regions together with the lower south did not face a growing indebtedness to Great Britain, at least during this five-year period. If long-term investments had been made by the British during this period, it seems that the investment opportunities in the southern colonies would have been the more favored from the viewpoint of British investors, and it seems less likely that long-term British capital went to the middle colonies and New England. We therefore hazard the conclusion that whatever deficits were incurred by New England and the middle colonies, such deficits probably represented growing short-term mercantile debt that was needed to finance growing trade with Britain.[2] We suggest that such deficits for New England, at least, were relatively small, and that long-term foreign investments in the thirteen colonies were nil. Longer-term investments were undoubtedly made by the British in their effort to develop and settle East Florida, and such investments or unilateral transfers by the British government may well have been incurred in subsidizing the northern colonies as well.

If our conclusion that capital inflows into New England and the southern colonies were small is correct, it would mean that a growing capital stock in these colonies would have been due almost entirely to colonial saving and not to foreign investment. This does not belittle the importance of trade to the development of these colonies, but only the importance of foreign borrowing. The exceptions to this conclusion appear to be the northern colonies and the middle colonies, which were left with relatively large deficits on current account in their overseas trade. It may be that the typical stages of the international economic relations of a developing country (i.e. young debtor, mature debtor, young creditor, and mature creditor), if they are typical, were preceded by a long period of relative self-sufficiency with regard to

---

[1] See p. 151, note 1.

[2] For an excellent description of the nature of these debts see Aubrey C. Land, 'Economic behavior in a planting society: the eighteenth-century Chesapeake,' *Journal of Southern History*, xxxiii, 4 (November 1971), pp. 467–85.

capital accumulation. At any rate, these typical stages do not appear universally valid for the colonies.

The magnitude of monetary flows to and from the colonies also cannot be ascertained directly because of the lack of evidence. There are no records of monetary bullion or specie exports from the colonies, but contemporary accounts of trade are filled with complaints about the lack of 'hard' money, and about the tendency for all such money that did come into the colonies to be shipped out rapidly to pay British debts. The American Inspector-General's Ledgers do record imports of specie from the West Indies to Virginia,[1] which (valued in pounds sterling) were:

1768	£2,272	1771	5,561
1769	5,338	1772	2,508
1770	3,214		

These records are undoubtedly incomplete because merchants' records and correspondence from the middle colonies and New England do occasionally mention receipts of various foreign coins from the West Indies. How much more these unrecorded imports of specie or bullion might have been one cannot tell. It seems unlikely, however, that they were of any large magnitude. If they were not significant, then exports of specie or bullion would not have been large because the colonies had no domestic source of precious metals or specie other than trade. This does not, of course, mean that monetary flows were not large. Another form which these flows took was an inflow into the colonies of bills of exchange earned in the West Indies (and perhaps in southern Europe).[2] In any case, such imports of bills of exchange and specie from these areas where the colonies earned surpluses would not have been larger than the surpluses earned there. If these monetary earnings were then used to pay part of the deficits incurred in trade with Great Britain, the remaining deficits with Great Britain would necessarily have reflected increases in indebtedness to her. The average balances of the colonies with the surplus areas of southern Europe and the West Indies for 1768–72 (from Table 8.1 less average values of imports of slaves from the West Indies as estimated above) were:

Northern colonies	£139,000
New England	353,000
Middle colonies	321,000
Southern colonies	210,000
Florida, Bahama and Bermuda Is.	−6,000
Total	£1,017,000

[1] The only recorded destination for specie imported was Virginia. Southern Europe was included with the West Indies in the American Inspector-General's Ledgers for 1768, but since the other four years attribute these imports to the West Indies and none to southern Europe, it is likely that the West Indies was the only source in 1768.

[2] See J. Sperling, 'The international payments mechanism in the seventeenth and eighteenth centuries,' *Economic History Review*, 2nd Series, xiv, 3 (April 1962), pp. 446–68, for a discussion of bills of exchange and the nature of the international payments mechanism that had developed by the eighteenth century.

Providing that these surpluses earned in the southern European and West Indian trades were not offset significantly by increases in indebtedness of residents of these overseas areas to colonial merchants (it seems likely that colonial merchants would not have allowed such indebtedness to increase substantially) then monetary flows of various sorts which effected the transfer of these surpluses to the deficit areas would have been in the neighborhood of one million pounds sterling annually, on the average, for this period.

THE LONGER VIEW

How well can one generalize about the entire colonial period from these five years, 1768–72? These years were certainly unique because of the non-importation agreements, but the use of annual averages possibly corrects for these fluctuations. These were years of peace, and the question immediately arises whether 1768–72 would be representative of the longer peace-time period 1763–75. Any answer is highly problematical. The years 1768–72 appear to have been ones of increasing trade and included the upswing (and probably a peak) of a marked business cycle. A similar study based on the earlier years of the 1760s, for example, might have yielded substantially different results. Consequently, any generalizations about this longer period must be made with caution in view of the fluctuations that characterized economic activity over this period.

War years, of which there were many in the eighteenth century, are also another matter, and it may not be valid to extend our generalizations to them. As was seen in Chapter 3, if the official values of British exports and imports to and from the colonies[1] can be accepted as a rough guide, it appears that deficits to Britain substantially increased as a percentage of the value of trade during the Seven Years' War. It is likely, however, that these were offset by higher British defense expenditures in the colonies during that period. Also, it seems unlikely that British merchants and investors would have made either significant amounts of long-term investments or allowed short-term mercantile debt to rise substantially during periods of conflict. For the first half of the eighteenth century, the British standing army in the colonies was considerably smaller, and consequently sterling earned from British military expenditures would have been significantly lower. There is no indication, however, that naval protection was less in earlier years.[2] It may well have been that the sterling earned from British defense and civil expenditures were about the same percentage of total trade over

---

[1] *Historical Statistics*, p. 757.

[2] The evidence presented by Nettels suggests relatively large naval expenditures in the colonies for the period 1708–11; see Curtis P. Nettels, *The Money Supply of the American Colonies before 1720* (New York: Augustus M. Kelley, 1964), p. 195. These expenditures fell during Queen Anne's War, however.

most of the eighteenth century. Furthermore, the official values suggest relatively small deficits with England for earlier years.[1] As a result, the conclusions at which we have arrived regarding the importance of foreign investment in colonial development may well apply to most of the eighteenth century. This contention was earlier argued in Chapter 3, where long-term trends in trade were examined and the implications drawn for the colonial balance of payments. We conclude that this intensive study of the period 1768–72 supports the earlier contention.

[1] *Historical Statistics*, p. 757

CHAPTER 9

REINTERPRETATIONS OF ISSUES IN
COLONIAL HISTORY

Previous studies[1] of the British North American colonies, especially those related to shipping, trade, and commerce, have provided an important background and foundation to this study. We do, however, present new quantitative evidence that touches on a number of historical issues about the development of a market economy in colonial North America. Consequently, it is important to emphasize where our findings and interpretations depart from the traditional view[2] of colonial history.

One illustration of such differences is the subject of patterns of colonial commerce. The traditional view has been that New England and middle colonial shippers frequently switched among routes and extensively followed triangular or multilateral routes.[3] This is a misrepresentation of the shipping and commercial activities of New England and the middle colonies. When ship movements in the aggregate are considered, it is clear that shuttle voyages were the dominant form of vessel movements, and that triangular and multilateral voyages were the exception.[4] Of equal importance is the fact that regularity of route was common during the colonial period and that vessels did not frequently switch among several different routes.

The argument used in support of the traditional view is that these

---

[1] See the bibliography for a listing of the major contributions to American colonial economic history.

[2] As we state in Chapter 1 (p. 5, note 1), there is no single view or interpretation of colonial development, and we use the term 'traditional view' to refer to those interpretations which repeatedly appear in the literature.

[3] It is a curiosity how the treatment of colonial trade patterns and their description became so homogeneous in textbooks on American economic history (see p. 49, note 1, Chapter 4). Our belief (it is admittedly no more than this) is that the general descriptions given in most textbooks were originally derived from the few specific voyages and instances of trade portrayed by William B. Weeden, *Economic and Social History of New England, 1620–1739* (Boston: Houghton, Mifflin, & Company, 1891), II, pp. 449–72 and 553–4.

[4] We do not dispute the fact that some vessels took triangular or multilateral voyages, but our interest is to describe the dominant and more general characteristics of commerce, rather than exceptional cases. We do not mean to imply that ships engaged in trade between the colonies and the West Indies or southern Europe went to only one port in those areas. Certainly, there was search for trade among ports within these areas, although even this was limited to a very few ports where commercial contacts were secure. Our main argument is that trades involving two or more overseas areas such as from the West Indies to Great

activities increased ship utilization and raised freight earnings. The implicit hypotheses is that load-factor, and thus freight earnings, were increased by changing routes and seeking out new ports. The oversight in this argument has been that the attempt to increase load-factor by frequenting many ports also increased port times, an important form of vessel under-utilization. In general, shippers did not search for trade among overseas areas and ports with which they were unfamiliar, and there was a limit to the number of ports and areas that they knew well and in which they had reliable commercial contacts. Information costs and the risks associated with overseas trade were very high during the eighteenth century, and unfamiliarity raised these costs even higher, slowed the process of exchange and lengthened port times. In order to increase vessel utilization and lower costs, shippers attempted to shorten port times as well as increase load-factors. In fact, a complete analysis of commercial and shipping characteristics is much more than simply a problem of maximizing freight earnings. In colonial times, shipping services were not distinct and specialized services as they are today. Merchandizing, insurance, and shipping services were highly inter-related and it was often difficult to distinguish one service from another. Potentially higher freight earnings were sometimes sacrificed for increased profits in trade. Information costs and risks were an important aspect of the realization of profitable trading ventures and this, plus the interdependence of trade and shipping, strongly influenced the character of shipping activity.

Most general descriptions of the colonial economy emphasize the importance of commodity production. Activities associated with the distribution of these commodities and the importance of the commercial sector have often been neglected. In those instances where the importance of the commercial sector has been stressed, no explicit theoretical framework (such as that in Chapter 2) has been given to relate improvements in commercial activities to the process of economic development; nor have these improvements been quantified so that their importance could be assessed. In light of the new evidence on the importance of distribution costs (e.g. the total differential between the producers' and consumers' prices) and our estimates of shipping earnings, the stress and accuracy of previous descriptions are open to doubt. Descriptions of the staple commodities and trades have led to distortion in the descriptions of the relative importance of other

---

Britain and back to the colonies, were not typical. It is possible, of course, to describe the pattern of international settlements as triangular or multilateral (for example, the West Indies earned surpluses in their trade with Britain, the continental colonies earned surpluses in their West Indies trade, and Britain earned surpluses in its American trade). Such a description would be correct, but it adds nothing to the description of these settlements in Chapter 8. Furthermore, it is clear that the descriptions of triangular trades have specifically referred to shipping movements.

colonial economic activities. When activities such as shipping and other merchandizing activities are considered, the relative importance of commodity production is reduced.

Another reason to emphasize the importance of distribution costs in the colonies is that these costs were responsible for a very significant share of the retail (and even the wholesale) prices of goods. The evidence clearly shows that the distribution costs of commodities, even the relatively high-valued, low-bulk English wares, were often as important as production costs in determining their value. Consequently, if we are to increase our understanding of colonial economic welfare, especially that determined within the market sector, it is as important to analyze the costs of distribution as the costs of production.

Finally, the relative amounts of resources used in the commercial sector, in contrast to the agricultural or some other sector, are a poor reflection of the importance of activities associated with distribution. For instance, in the subsistence sector of the economy, no distribution costs are observed. This does not mean, however, that market forces were unimportant or did not influence decisions regarding production. Decisions at the margin were significantly affected by market forces. Distribution costs were an important factor in deciding what to produce, what scale of production should be undertaken, how much should be marketed and how much self-sufficiency should be maintained. An increased understanding of the importance of market forces and a fuller appreciation of the problems of distribution during the colonial period would broaden significantly our understanding of colonial development.[1]

The substantial amount of empirical evidence presented in Chapters 4 and 5 shows that significant improvements were occurring in shipping and other merchandizing activities. Many descriptions of the colonial economy suggest that little or no improvements occurred, except perhaps that the Atlantic fringe areas were relieved of frontier hardships as the frontier moved inland. These descriptions generally indicate that living standards and the general sophistication of the economy remained unchanged, or changed but little, during the period. The picture is one of a collection of frontier colonies that were continuously dependent on Great Britain for their economic well-being and accumulation of capital. Although this view is certainly correct for the early years of settlement, it would appear that by the beginning of the eighteenth century the colonies were almost entirely self-sufficient with regard to capital formation. From the few scattered early settlements that initially were dependent on England for provisions and aid, there

[1] For an enlightening article on the importance of commercial development in the overall process of growth, see John C. H. Fei and Gustav Ranis, 'Economic development in historical perspective,' *American Economic Review*, LIX, 2 (May 1969), pp. 386–400.

emerged a network of colonies that rivaled the mother country in commercial enterprise and material well-being. The growth of cities like Boston, New York, Philadelphia, and Charleston was an important reflection of this commercial development and it should be remembered that on the eve of the Revolution Philadelphia was the largest city in the British empire, excepting only London.[1] In short, the colonial period was one of significant change and development and the reduction of distribution costs and the growth of commercial activity were important aspects of this transition and development.

We are not suggesting that anything similar to an industrial revolution occurred. No sudden or dramatic changes within the economy are seen, nor can we pinpoint any periods of acceleration that might accompany a period of rapid technological change. Our findings, in fact, indicate that technological change was not an important source of productivity advance in the commercial sector. Other scholarly inquiries on the agricultural sector also suggest that little apparent technological change took place. Nevertheless, in our opinion the long view is one of gradual change and improvement.

In the commercial sector, and clearly in the shipping industry, the types of improvements seen came from a variety of sources associated with the reduction of risks, increased information about markets, increased knowledge about doing business in these markets and improvements in business organization. It is difficult to over-emphasize the importance of the growing security of trade. The mere growth of population had an important influence on the level of risks and possibilities due to the market. For instance, as settlement increased and trade expanded, the gains from better law enforcement, like that of removing pirates from the seas (and using international diplomacy to reduce privateering and the issues of letters of marque) came to exceed the costs of these actions and specialized naval facilities were ultimately used to eliminate piracy. Also, the growth of trade itself had important feedback effects, which lowered the costs of distribution and led to further expansion of trade. Information costs and the risks associated with trade were reduced as trade increased and commercial centers were established. Two examples may prove useful to describe the effects of these changes. First, in the Caribbean trade, colonial shippers had to undertake a great deal of search and undergo an immense amount of petty detail in the process of exchange. Colonial goods had to be sold

---

[1] This assertion was made by Carl and Jessica Bridenbaugh, *Rebels and Gentlemen: Philadelphia in the Age of Franklin* (New York: Reynal & Hitchcock, 1942), and again by Carl Bridenbaugh in *The Colonial Craftsman* (New York: New York University Press, 1950), p. 66. Somewhat later he qualifies this assertion and states that Edinburgh and Dublin may have exceeded Philadelphia in population; see his *Cities in Revolt* (New York: Knopf, 1955), p. 217n. The point is undecided, but clearly Philadelphia was one of the Empire's major urban centers in 1775, as well as New York, Boston, Charleston and Newport (*ibid.*, p. 216).

and return cargoes acquired at the best possible prices. To find the best markets (for delivery and purchase) required much search and then there were the problems of quality variation, credit, media of exchange, currencies of fluctuating value, etc., which had to be settled. The strengthening of commercial ties as trade developed reduced these problems. Second, in the Chesapeake trade, we have a fairly clear account of numerous changes that lowered the distribution costs of tobacco. As the production and trade of tobacco increased it became profitable to establish centrally-located warehouses for the storage of tobacco. This reduced the costs of search and lowered port times and inventory times. Also, certificates of tobacco deposits came to be used as a medium of exchange, and this led to inspection systems which permitted quality control of tobacco. These and other improvements, such as productivity advances in the packaging of tobacco, permitted a marked reduction in the difference between the price of tobacco in the colonies and in Europe. The price of Virginia leaf tobacco in Amsterdam was nearly four times the Philadelphia price in the early eighteenth century, but by 1770 it was only about twice as high as in Philadelphia. It was these and similar improvements that played such an important role in the commercial growth of the period. As stated above, technological change appears to have been an unimportant aspect of this development.

Improvements in transportation and distribution, together with a growing population, widened markets, increased possibilities for trade and strengthened ties between the colonies and their various overseas markets. The estimates of commodity trade clearly show the relative importance of each overseas area as a trading partner with each colonial region. Table 9.1 shows in percentage terms the importance of each overseas area as a market for each region's commodity exports. Table 9.2 shows the importance of each overseas area as a source of

TABLE 9.1.   *The share of each region's commodity exports to each overseas area, 1768–72* (in percentages)

	Great Britain and Ireland	Southern Europe	West Indies	Africa
Northern colonies	22	71	7	0
New England	18	14	64	4
Middle colonies	23	33	44	0
Upper south	83	9	8	0
Lower south	72	9	19	0
Florida, Bahama and Bermuda Is.	88	0	12	0
Total	56	18	26	1

Source: these percentages are an average of the five years, 1768–72, and are derived from Chapter 6. Where the sum of the percentages does not equal 100, it is due to rounding.

TABLE 9.2.   *The share of each region's commodity imports from each overseas area, 1768–72* (in percentages)

	Great Britain and Ireland	Southern Europe	West Indies	Africa
Northern colonies	95	2	3	0
New England	66	2	32	0
Middle colonies	76	3	21	0
Upper south	89	1	10	0
Lower south	86	1	13	0
Florida, Bahama and Bermuda Is.	87	2	11	0
Total	80	2	18	0

Source: see Table 9.1.

each region's commodity imports.[1] Southern Europe was the predominant export market of the northern colonies, rivaling the importance of
the West Indies as a market for New England exports. No single
overseas area greatly dominated the export trade of the middle
colonies, but for the regions south of Pennsylvania, Great Britain was by
far the most important market. However, a substantial proportion of
these southern exports were ultimately re-exported from Great Britain
to other European countries. For instance, over 90 per cent of the
tobacco imported into Great Britain was re-exported in 1768–72.[2] Of
the total value of commodity exports, 56 per cent went to Great
Britain and Ireland, 18 per cent to southern Europe, 26 per cent to the
West Indies and a mere 1 per cent to Africa. It is clear from Table 9.2
that Great Britain overwhelmingly dominated the import trade to all
regions, although the import trade from the West Indies was not
insignificant, especially to New England and the middle colonies. The
values of commodity imports from Africa and southern Europe were a
very small part of total imports.

An alternative perspective is to view the importance of each region's
trade compared to total trade with each overseas area. Table 9.3 shows
in percentage terms each region's share of total commodity exports to
each overseas area. Table 9.4 shows each region's share of total imports
from each overseas area. The southern regions dominated the export
trade to Great Britain and Ireland, with 57 per cent of all exports to
Great Britain coming from the upper south and 26 per cent coming from
the lower south. In the export trade to southern Europe, the middle
colonies were the most important (34 per cent of the total), but the
northern colonies held a significant share of this trade (25 per cent).

[1] These figures do not necessarily reflect the origin of the imports (or final destination of the
exports); for instance, most goods not of British or West Indian origin were channeled
through Britain and re-exported to the colonies.
[2] U.S. Bureau of the Census, *Historical Statistics of the United States, Colonial Times to 1957*
(Washington, D.C.: U.S. Government Printing Office, 1960), p. 766.

TABLE 9.3. *Regional shares of total commodity exports to each overseas area,*
1768–72 (in percentages)

	Great Britain and Ireland	Southern Europe	West Indies	Africa	All overseas areas
Northern colonies	2	25	2	0	6
New England	5	12	39	93	16
Middle colonies	8	34	32	5	19
Upper south	57	19	13	0	39
Lower south	26	10	14	2	20
Florida, Bahama and Bermuda Is.	1	0	0	0	1

Source: see Table 9.1.

TABLE 9.4. *Regional shares of total commodity imports from each overseas*
area, 1768–72 (in percentages)

	Great Britain and Ireland	Southern Europe	West Indies	Africa	All overseas areas
Northern colonies	10	10	1	—	8
New England	20	23	43	—	24
Middle colonies	26	42	32	—	28
Upper south	29	14	14	—	26
Lower south	13	9	9	—	12
Florida, Bahama and Bermuda Is.	2	2	1	—	2

Source: see Table 9.1.

New England and the middle colonies together dominated the export
trade to the West Indies, and New England overshadowed all others in
the trade to Africa. Out of the total commodity export trade to all
areas, 60 per cent came from the southern regions and 40 per cent came
from the colonies to the north of Maryland.

The percentage of total colonial imports to each region from each
overseas area was relatively evenly balanced, especially on the import
trade from Great Britain (and from all areas combined). However,
in the trade from southern Europe and the West Indies, the middle
colonies and New England took the largest shares of imports from these
areas. It seems likely that there was some redistribution of these imports
in the coastal trade.

It should be stressed that the above percentages show the relative
importance of overseas markets and regions only in terms of commodities traded. When the sales of ships, the sales of shipping and other
merchandizing services and the slave trade are considered, the picture
does change. Specifically, in the export trade, the West Indies market
appears to have been even more important to the middle colonies and
New England. The West Indies market also becomes more important to

all the colonies taken together. Moreover, the dominance of the southern regions in the export trade also alters when ship sales and invisible earnings are included, making the northern and southern regions more evenly balanced from the viewpoint of foreign exchange earnings. This is shown above in Chapter 6 to have had a similar equalizing effect on the per capita earnings of foreign exchange of the various regions. With regard to debits in the balance of payments, when expenditures on slaves are considered, the African trade becomes more significant, surpassing southern Europe in importance. The lower south accounted for the major share of such expenditures.

The general importance of the African trade has probably been exaggerated. Clearly, as a market for colonial exports Africa was of very little significance. It was primarily English shippers rather than colonial shippers who dominated the slave trade. Africa was an important source of labor but most descriptions of African–colonial commerce have greatly exaggerated the importance of Africa as a market for colonial products.

The estimates of imports from Great Britain show the effectiveness of the various non-importation agreements of 1769 and 1779 in the colonies. These agreements were the political means adopted by the colonists to resist the Townshend Acts and to compel the British government to repeal them. The Townshend Acts, passed by Parliament in 1767, authorized colonial courts to issue writs of assistance, created the American Customs Board, and levied duties on paper, glass, lead, painters' colors and tea. Non-importation agreements, which had been successful in getting the Stamp Act repealed, were reached in varying forms in each colony (except New Hampshire) and were in effect through 1769 and most of 1770. It is interesting to note how successful each of the regions was in boycotting British imports. The yearly values of imports from Britain into the colonies between 1768 and 1772 (in thousand pounds sterling) were:

	1768	1769	1770	1771	1772
New England	441	228	457	1,446	1,912
Middle colonies	1,005	325	717	1,551	979
Upper south	728	774	1,117	1,339	1,100
Lower south	399	429	261	572	635

The sharp decline in the value of imports from Britain into New England, the middle colonies, and the lower south in 1769 and 1770 clearly shows that the non-importation agreements were effective in these regions. To the extent that other European goods were substituted for British goods in these years, these figures do not show the full impact of the agreements on British products. Nevertheless, the steady increase in the value of imports from Britain into the upper south strongly suggests that the non-importation agreements were ineffective in Virginia and Maryland. It is interesting to note that the relaxation of the agreements in late 1770 brought forth a tremendous increase in British imports, more than doubling the flow to New England, the middle colonies and the lower south between 1770 and 1771. The steady increase of imports to the upper south through 1771 indicates there was no pent-up demand there as was apparently the case in the other colonies.

Our estimates of exports substantiate the importance of such goods as tobacco, rice, and indigo. These goods are typically given great stress in most descriptions of colonial trade. The average annual values of the five highest-valued commodities exported over the five years 1768–72 were: tobacco, £766,000; bread and flour, £412,000; rice, £312,000; dried fish, £287,000; and indigo, £117,000. These comprised more than 60 per cent of the total value of commodity exports. The importance of bread and flour, which came primarily from the middle colonies, but which were also becoming important exports of the upper south, has not been properly emphasized. Recent research on the trade of the upper south suggests that the grain trade (mainly corn, wheat, and flour) from there was becoming an increasingly important spur to the growth of that area in the late colonial period.[1] When shipping services are included the traditional picture does change. Average annual shipping earnings (1768–72) were £610,000, most of which were earned by New England and middle colonial shippers. Shipping services were the colonies' most important export except for tobacco during this period. In general, however, foodstuffs taken together were the most important class of colonial exports. Significant exports of foodstuffs (especially bread, flour, and wheat) went to Great Britain in 1768 and 1769, due to the poor British crops of the late 1760s. Southern Europe also imported large amounts of colonial foodstuffs. The variations in colonial exports to these areas were related to the success of their crops. The West Indies was also an important recipient of a variety of colonial foodstuffs and provisions, such as bread and flour, fish, Indian corn, spermaceti candles, beef and pork, livestock, and wood products. Wheat exports to the West Indies were of negligible importance. It was apparently to their advantage to import flour and bread rather than manufacture them from imported wheat. This permitted them to devote more of their resources to the production of sugar and other tropical and semi-tropical goods. Finally, cotton, despite its later importance, was never a significant colonial export. Almost ten times as much cotton was imported over the period 1768–72 as was re-exported to Great Britain.

Our estimates of imports indicate that the descriptions by historians

[1] See David Klingaman, 'The significance of grain in the development of the tobacco colonies,' *Journal of Economic History*, xxix, 2 (June 1969), pp. 268–78.

of the colonial import trade have been reasonably accurate. When the imports from each overseas area and the exports to each overseas area are compared, however, the typical descriptions of the balances of trade are substantially changed. Of course, the colonies did incur very large deficits in their commodity trade with Great Britain. The largest share of these deficits was incurred by the northern colonies, New England, and the middle colonies, but the southern colonies also incurred small deficits to Great Britain. What has been frequently overlooked is that the West Indies commodity trade was also unfavorable,[1] although the deficits were very small. Also, when the importation of slaves is taken into account, sizable deficits resulted from trade with Africa. The value of exports to Africa was very small relative to the value of imported slaves. These deficits were incurred principally by the southern regions. The trade with southern Europe was the only one in which a large surplus was earned from commodity trade alone; and all the regions except Florida, the Bahamas and Bermuda shared in it.

These statements indicate that the general description of the balances of colonial trade has not been accurate. Except for the southern European trade, surpluses earned in the commodity trades with other areas did not help pay for the deficits with Great Britain. This fact clearly substantiates the importance of viewing the entire current account and other possible sources of foreign exchange earnings, if we are to understand how the colonies were able to pay for their imports. An analysis of commodity trade alone does not permit this. Total invisible earnings were relatively large and offset 62 per cent of the estimated overall deficit of commodity trade. These earnings substantially reduced the deficits of New England and the middle colonies and raised to a surplus position the balances of the southern regions. Also, the small deficit incurred by the colonies taken as a whole in their commodity trade with the West Indies is radically changed by including invisible earnings, and the surpluses earned there approach those earned in southern Europe. The expenditure of foreign exchange on indentured servants and slaves, which were not included in the debits from commodity trade, were more than offset by the earnings from the sales of ships and the foreign exchange arising from British civil and defense expenditures in the colonies.

Because the trade among the colonies probably altered the final regional balances, and because the geographical incidence of the British civil and defense expenditures cannot be determined with reasonable accuracy, it is difficult to specify accurately the final regional balances. Nevertheless, these balances do suggest that the tobacco-growing regions together with the lower south did not face a

---

[1] It should be remembered that the estimates of export values are based on F.O.B. prices and the estimates of import values on C.I.F. prices.

growing indebtedness to Great Britain, as is so frequently asserted (see p. 131, note 2).[1] We suggest that the growing indebtedness of the colonies with Great Britain was due to other areas. If long-term investments had been made by the British investors, it seems that the investment opportunities in the southern colonies would have been the more favored ones from their viewpoint, and it seems less likely that long-term British capital would have gone to the middle colonies and to New England. We therefore hazard the conclusion that whatever deficits were incurred by New England and the middle colonies, such deficits were relatively small, and that long-term foreign investments in the thirteen colonies were nil. Longer-term investments were undoubtedly made by the British in their effort to develop and settle East Florida during the 1760s and 1770s, and such investments, or unilateral transfers, by the British government may have gone to the northern colonies as well.

The relatively small size of foreign capital inflows into the thirteen colonies suggests that the growing stock of capital in these colonies was due to domestic saving rather than foreign investment. This does not belittle the importance of overseas trade to these colonies, but only the importance of foreign borrowing. It appears that the typical stages of foreign borrowing were not universally valid for the thirteen colonies, and that these colonies experienced a long period of relative self-sufficiency with regard to capital accumulation.

As with capital flows, no direct evidence of monetary flows to and from the colonies exists. There are no records of bullion or specie exports from the colonies, but contemporary accounts of trade are filled with complaints about the lack of 'hard' money in the colonies, and about the tendency of all such money that came into the colonies rapidly to be shipped out to pay British debts. Of course, the long-run net exports of specie or bullion would not have been large, because the colonies had no domestic source of precious metals other than trade.[2] Deficits with Great Britain, however, did not in themselves keep the colonies from building or increasing their supply of 'hard' money. The colonists evidently preferred to import British goods rather than invest in an improved domestic monetary system. Their preference was to substitute other forms of media of exchange for specie, rather than to manage with less British and European manufactured goods.

---

[1] Of course, this does not rule out the growing indebtedness of particular individuals. What the surplus balances for the upper south imply is no growth of net aggregate indebtedness during the period.

[2] The extensive use of bills of exchange is another factor that would have limited the absolute size of these flows.

DATA FROM THE NAVAL OFFICE LISTS AND ESTIMATES OF TRADE WITH SOUTHERN EUROPE AND THE WEST INDIES FOR EARLIER YEARS IN THE EIGHTEENTH CENTURY

The 'Naval Office Lists'[1] were records prepared by each colonial naval officer for his particular port district. These records were 'itemized accounts of all vessels trading to and from the area and which when forwarded to London, were used by the authorities as the principal source of information on the nature and extent of trading activities.'[2] The naval officers were appointed by the colonial governors, who along with the customs officials were responsible for the enforcement of the Acts of Trade in each colony. As an appointee of the governor, the naval officer in theory was independent of the customs organization. Indeed, in later years in the seventeenth century he had acted independently, and at times was in conflict with the customs officials. By 1710, however, 'the naval officer had become a subsidiary of the customs officials and was indeed little more than a keeper of the official port records.'[3]

These records were prepared and submitted to London on a quarterly basis. Only a portion of the original lists have survived (probably most of those lost were destroyed in a fire in the Plantation Wing of the London Customs House in 1814).[4] Lists for some ports have not survived at all. The fact that all the Philadelphia lists have been lost creates an important gap in the data, and the lists for no port are complete. Compilations from these Naval Office Lists have been prepared by a Works Progress Administration project entitled 'Trade and Commerce of the English Colonies in America'[5] and conducted under the direction of Lawrence A. Harper at the University of California, Berkeley. For selected years for which all four quarters of the Naval Office Lists have survived, Professor Harper has punched the data from the W.P.A. compilations onto I.B.M. cards. Tables 1 and 2 have been constructed from these cards with the permission of Professor Harper. These tables include entries for those years and for those ports for which the data from all four quarters have survived. The commodities included in the tables were those which were relatively the more valuable exports from the colonies to southern Europe and the West Indies during 1768–72 (based upon the estimates of values in Chapter 6).

[1] The surviving Naval Office Lists are in the Public Record Office in London and are usually cataloged as C.O.5. See *Historical Statistics*, p. 743.
[2] Thomas C. Barrow, *Trade and Empire: The British Customs Service in Colonial America, 1660–1775* (Cambridge, Mass.: Harvard University Press, 1967), p. 78.
[3] *Ibid.*
[4] *Ibid.*, p. vii.
[5] *Historical Statistics*, p. 743.

TABLE I. *Exports (in quantities) of selected commodities from various British North American colonial ports to southern Europe and the Wine Islands, for various years, 1715–69*

Fish from New England ports (quintaux and barrels)[a]

	New Hampshire	Salem and Marblehead	Boston
1715		58,079 qn	5,040 qn
1743	3,415 qn[b]		
	3 bbl		
1744	29 qn		
	53 bbl		
1754	10,046 qn[c]	69,618 qn	26,869 qn
	59 bbl	42,355 bbl	296 bbl
1755	3,318 qn		39,803 qn
	29 bbl		
1762	60 qn		
1767	530 qn		
	2 bbl		
1768	120 qn		
	20 bbl		

[a] Includes small quantities of fish other than cod.
[b] To Holland.
[c] Includes 40 quintaux and 4 barrels exported to Africa.

Bread from middle colonial ports (tons and barrels)

	New York	Perth Amboy	Bridlington
1726		3 tn	
		3 bbl	
1733		4 tn	
		24 bbl	
1741			20 bbl
1744		4 bbl	
1745		21 bbl	
1763	9 bbl		

Flour from middle colonial ports (tons and barrels)

	New York	Perth Amboy	Bridlington
1725		1 tn	
		147 bbl	
1726		4 tn	
		173 bbl	
1733	80 tn	11 tn	
		295 bbl	
1734	69 tn		
1735	127 tn		
1741			500 bbl
1744		754 bbl	
1745		84 bbl	
1754	39 tn		

TABLE I   *(continued)*

Indian corn[d] from Virginia ports (bushels)

	Accomac	South Potomac	Rappa- hannock	Port York	Port Hampton	Upper James River
1726				0	0	0
1727	1,000			0	1,812	2,164
1731	600				1,100	0
1732				1,300		0
1733				458	3,285	
1734					7,054	
1743					0	0
1744					4,375	0
1745				1,492	1,620	300
1746						2,754
1752		1,480	1,000	7,511	37,539	
1754		1,049				65,245
1755		1,800	9,915	2,170	2,100	
1761			0		0	0
1762			0		5,000	0
1763					8,500	0
1766		2,862			3,000	
1768	11,397		13,065	12,333		19,755
1769			17,753			46,409

[d] Includes all entries of 'Indian corn and peas.'

Wheat from Virginia ports (bushels)

	Accomac	South Potomac	Rappa- hannock	Port York	Port Hampton	Upper James River
1726				0	9,185	800
1727	700			1,800	1,524	7,744
1731	1,200				20,818	0
1732				4,074		6,832
1733				1,854	12,368	
1734					6,503	
1743					0	0
1744					0	7,482
1745				3,226	197	2,111
1746						0
1752		824	1,700	7,375	28,404	
1754						1,534
1755			0	796	1,780	
1761			0		0	0
1762			0		0	0
1763			0		2,000	4,950
1766					22,901	
1768			4,300			33,551
1769			2,814			195,905

Rice from South Carolina (barrels)[e]

	South Carolina
1724	0
1731	6,403
1732	8,284
1734	10,538
1735	14,232
1758	12,490
1759	12,163
1762	11,008
1766	25,136

[e] Entries recorded as shipments and bags were not included.

TABLE 2. *Exports (in quantities) of selected commodities from various British North American colonial ports to the West Indies, for various years, 1715–69*

Fish from New England ports (quintaux and barrels)

	New Hampshire	Salem and Marblehead	Boston
1715		140 qn	1,709 bbl
		1,012 bbl	
1727	28 qn		
	474 bbl		
1743	70 qn		
	788 bbl		
1744	149 qn		
	573 bbl		
1754	704 qn	279 qn	450 qn
	470 bbl	9,878 bbl	21,281 bbl
1755	1,030 qn	335 qn	144 qn
	802 bbl	11,626 bbl	20,717 bbl
1761	1,231 qn	1,367 qn	
	638 bbl	13,894 bbl	
1762	2,009 qn		
	366 bbl		
1763	762 qn		
	78 bbl		
1767	4,550 qn		
	1,581 bbl		
1768	3,847 qn		
	1,304 bbl		

Bread from middle colonial ports (tons and barrels)

	New York	Perth Amboy	Bridlington
1725		37 tn	
		238 bbl	
1726		61 tn	
		50 bbl	
1732			2 tn
			184 bbl
1733		17 tn	
		135 bbl	615 bbl
1744		134 bbl	
1745		190 bbl	
1763	133 bbl		

Flour from middle colonial ports (tons and barrels)

	New York	Perth Amboy	Bridlington
1727	1 tn		
1732			1,161 bbl
1733	2,924 tn	465 bbl	760 bbl
1734	2,061 tn		
1735	1,860 tn		
1742			250 bbl
1744		857 bbl	
1745		712 bbl	
1754	6 tn		
1763	137 tn		
	1,548 bbl		

TABLE 2 *(continued)*

Indian corn[a] from Virginia ports (bushels)

	Accomac	South Potomac	Rappa-hannock	Port York	Port Hampton	Upper James River
1726		5,700		8,300	67,306	10,219
1727	10,060	2,900		13,373	74,315	6,667
1731	6,262	3,200			59,720	9,707
1732	1,300			11,724		9,554
1733		1,790		10,294	92,570	
1734					85,969	
1743					77,344	4,026
1744					65,079	14,293
1745		2,000		11,630	60,523	0
1746	3,500					8,647
1752	21,160	13,843	16,530	38,370	110,609	
1754		13,400				37,458
1755		4,645	20,688	38,466	111,369	
1761	8,500	2,140	4,285	22,684	189,473	25,110
1762	12,500		7,772	14,379	92,821	8,700
1763					106,205	6,477
1766		7,977			99,070	
1768	18,140		40,233	43,422		42,594
1769			34,317			31,176

[a] Includes all entries of 'Indian corn and peas.'

Rice[b] from South Carolina (barrels)

	South Carolina
1724	1,249
1731	1,872
1732	1,504
1734	1,234
1735	715
1758	6,384
1759	6,206
1762	21,624
1766	15,124

[b] Entries recorded as shipments and bags were not included.

Commodities in the Naval Office Lists were recorded in many different units. For construction of the different quantity series in Tables 1 and 2, these various units were converted for convenience into a single unit, or, in the cases of bread, fish, and flour, into two units. The conversion equivalencies for the various units recorded in the Naval Office Lists that were used for most of the commodities listed in the tables (with certain exceptions noted below) were:[1]

1 keg = $\frac{1}{7}$ barrel = $4\frac{1}{2}$ gallons
1 firkin = $\frac{1}{4}$ barrel = 8 gallons
1 barrel = $31\frac{1}{2}$ gallons = 3.38 bushels
1 tierce = $1\frac{1}{3}$ barrels = 42 gallons = 4.51 bushels

[1] These equivalencies were taken from various sources. See especially the discussion of colonial units in Appendix IV, and in the text to Chapter Z, *Historical Statistics*, pp. 743–55, especially pp. 750–1. Also see Marion Rawson, 'Old weights and measures,' *Antiques*, XXI, 1 (January 1932), pp. 17–18. The colonial container could vary widely in size, but it is hoped these sizes reflect the average quantity held by these various containers.

1 hogshead=2 barrels=63 gallons=6.77 bushels

1 puncheon=2⅔ barrel=84 gallons

1 pipe = 4 barrels = 126 gallons

1 ton (tun)=252 gallons=2,240 pounds

1 quarter=28 pounds

1 hundredweight=112 pounds

1 quintal=100 pounds

1 last=80 bushels

Several exceptions to the use of these equivalencies were made. The rice barrel evolved into a considerably larger container over the eighteenth century. Around 1720 it averaged about 350 pounds, then gained about an average of ten pounds per year until 1730. It apparently stayed at this average weight of 450 pounds until after 1740 when it began to increase by an average of about five pounds per year until it reached its pre-Revolutionary peak weight of about 525 pounds.[1] A bushel of rice was assumed to have weighed 65 pounds.[2] Finally, it was assumed that a cask, which was a general term, was a barrel of 31½ gallons (except for the rice barrel, which varied in the way described above).[3]

It is difficult to say very much about the validity of these data from the Naval Office Lists. A few comparisons can be made with the American Inspector-General's Ledgers (Customs 16/1) for 1768 and 1769 for several of the Virginia ports. These comparisons yield results ranging from perfect agreement to large differences between the two sets of data. With regard to Indian corn and wheat exports, which are the easiest to compare because they are listed in the same unit (bushels) in both sets of records, they vary from complete agreement in two instances in 1768 to a 46 per cent difference for corn for the Upper James River district in 1769 (46,409 bushels according to the Naval Office Lists compared with 31,809 bushels from Customs 16/1). It is likely that the data on exports from the Naval Office Lists is more accurate than that for imports. Comparisons made from the two sets of records of imports of molasses, rum, and salt (not shown in Tables 1 and 2) result in greater differences. For example, the Naval Office Lists recorded imports of 25,883 gallons of molasses into New Hampshire for 1768, but in Customs 16/1 over ten times as much (260,266 gallons) was recorded. Molasses from the foreign West Indian islands was dutiable, so there was a well-known incentive to engage in smuggling. This does not explain why one set of official records varied so much from the other, but it does point to the possibility that perhaps more faith can be placed in the export data from the Naval Office Lists than in the data on imports. This must be especially true for molasses. One author has stated that it does not appear that rum was smuggled into the colonies from the West Indies in significant amounts, but that import figures for molasses are probably not valid for the periods of

[1] *Historical Statistics*, pp. 750–1.

[2] Lewis C. Gray, *History of Agriculture in the Southern United States to 1860* (Gloucester, Mass.: Peter Smith, 1958), I, p. 284.

[3] *Historical Statistics*, p. 750.

the Molasses Act (1733–64) and the Sugar Act (enacted in 1764) before it was modified in 1766.[1] By 1763 probably 1,500,000 gallons of molasses were being imported annually into Massachusetts, of which probably 60 per cent was consumed within the province and 40 per cent was exported both as rum and as molasses[2] (this is significantly more than the quantities of molasses indicated by the Naval Office List data). Most of this molasses came from the foreign areas of the Caribbean.

There are several other reasons why the data in Tables 1 and 2 probably understate the true quantities of exports. For one thing, some entries were recorded simply as 'shipments' and could not be translated into the units used in Tables 1 and 2. Then, too, in some instances the overseas port of origin or destination was listed as 'unknown', and thus could not be classified by overseas area and so was not included. There were some other minor definitional problems. Some entries, for example, were given as 'Indian corn and peas', making it impossible to determine just the quantity of corn involved. In this instance, quantities of 'corn and peas' were simply included in the total for the year for Indian corn. The same is true for fish; this category includes small quantities of kinds of fish other than cod. Also, Table 2 includes exports to the Bahamas and the Bermuda Islands (unlike the estimates of exports to the West Indies for 1768–72 in Chapter 6). It is probable, however, that these problems do not affect significantly the data in Tables 1 and 2.

If two assumptions are made at this point, it is possible to make some educated guesses about the total magnitudes of the trade of the colonies with southern Europe and the West Indies for earlier decades. First, let us assume that each port for which records have survived exported approximately the same proportion of a commodity from a region as it did in the 1768–72 period. Secondly, let us assume that each commodity comprised about the same proportion of total exports from each region as it did in 1768–72. For example, from 1768 to 1772 nearly 21 per cent of the quantity of Indian corn exported to southern Europe from the upper south came from the Lower James River district of Virginia. Indian corn, in turn, was about 12 per cent of the value of total commodity exports to southern Europe from the upper south in the period 1768–72. If we had data for earlier years only from the Lower James River district for corn exports, we might infer (on the basis of the above two assumptions) that total exports from the upper south were about forty times the value of this corn exported from the Lower James. If additional data were available on other commodities and other ports in a region, then such data could easily be incorporated into the above procedure. The more data used, the more accurate the estimates would be.

If this procedure is followed, estimated annual average values of those commodity exports to southern Europe and the Wine Islands listed in Table 1 (in pounds sterling rounded to the nearest thousand), by decade, are:

[1] Gilman M. Ostrander, 'The Molasses Trade of the Thirteen Colonies' (unpublished M.A. thesis, Department of History, University of California, Berkeley, 1948), p. 18.

[2] *Ibid.*, pp. 22 and 67–77. These estimates are based on consumption estimates for Massachusetts and export data. According to the Massachusetts Naval Office Lists, the colony exported twice as much molasses and rum as it imported from 1753 to 1756 (*ibid.*, p. 67).

	New England	Middle colonies	Upper south	Lower south
1721–30	—	—	5,000	—
1731–40	—	8,000	8,000	20,000
1741–50	—	—	—	—
1751–60	45,000	—	26,000	27,000

The estimate for New England is based upon fish, that for the middle colonies upon bread and flour; Indian corn and wheat were used for the upper south and rice for the lower south. Boston prices were used to value the fish exports; Philadelphia prices to value bread, flour, corn, and wheat; and Charleston prices to value rice. Values were averaged for each port by decade. Extension to the estimated totals for each region was then made on the basis of the above two assumptions. The lack of an estimate for any particular decade was due to the lack of quantity data, the lack of price (or exchange rate) data (prices on fish, for example, are not available before 1752), or because this procedure resulted in what appeared to be unlikely results. The latter was true for the middle colonies in the 1740s, for example, when quantity data were available only for Perth Amboy and Bridlington. Because these ports furnished a very small part of bread and flour exports in the period 1768–72, basing the estimates for the middle colonies solely on these two ports would have resulted in very high – and probably inaccurate – estimates for the 1740s. Using the above procedure, the estimates for the West Indies are (in pounds sterling rounded to the nearest thousand):

	New England	Middle colonies	Upper south	Lower south
1721–30	—	—	24,000	—
1731–40	—	81,000	21,000	5,000
1741–50	—	—	14,000	—
1751–60	45,000	—	51,000	29,000

These estimates were based upon the same commodities as were exports to southern Europe for the respective regions, with the exception of wheat, which is not given in Table 2 and was not used in the calculations for the upper south because it was not an important export to the West Indies.

The above estimates would suggest that exports to southern Europe were probably in the range of £50,000 to £60,000 in the 1720s and 1730s, on the average, rising to £125,000 to £150,000 in the 1750s, and were possibly greater. Exports to the West Indies were larger, as they were in the later colonial period, being in the probable range of £125,000 to £150,000 in the 1720s and 1730s, and rising to £175,000 to £200,000 in the 1750s. If surpluses earned in these trades constituted the same proportion of total exports in earlier decades as in 1768–72, then they would have been in the vicinity of £140,000 to £160,000 for the 1720s and 1730s and £250,000 to £300,000 for the 1750s. The data from the Naval Office Lists pertaining to imports from southern Europe do indicate that surpluses earned there were probably large relative to total exports (as they were in 1768–72). Data from the Naval Office Lists on West Indian imports indicate that surpluses earned in the West Indian trade in earlier years may have been a relatively larger proportion of total exports than in the later period. For reasons stated earlier, however, these data may understate actual imports; therefore no reliance has been placed on them at this point (and for this reason import data from the Naval Office Lists have not been included here).

The question of how much faith to place in these estimates must rest upon the validity of the above two assumptions (that is, whether the pattern of exports in 1768–72 differed significantly from the pattern that prevailed in earlier years) as well as the accuracy of the existing evidence. Certainly, the relative export position of some ports (and regions) changed with respect to others. Philadelphia, for example, was a latecomer to prominence in trade; and it exported relatively less in earlier years than it did by the end of the colonial period. If this is true, then the estimates for the middle colonies would overstate the actual values of exports. Undoubtedly, the composition of exports and the relative importance of various commodities also changed over time. Bread and flour exports from the middle colonies and upper south, for instance, probably increased as a proportion of total exports. Further adjustments could be made in an attempt to correct for these possibilities. For example, it might reasonably be assumed that exports of a region were related to its population. Since Pennsylvania's population increased relative to New York's over the century, adjustments to the estimated values of exports from the middle colonies could be made on this basis of relative change in population.[1] This adjustment could have been made in the case of the middle colonies, but because of the particularly acute lack of data for this region, it was felt that the likely margin of error would have been so large as to outweigh any gain in accuracy from such an adjustment.

The resulting estimates admittedly are crude, but they probably give reasonable approximations of the magnitudes of colonial trade with these areas in earlier years. The suggested magnitudes of the surpluses earned in these trades are perhaps even more tenuous. The evidence indicates that nevertheless some surpluses were earned, and they need not have been large to have offset the deficits incurred in the English trade before 1745.

---

[1] Extrapolation back from 1768–72 could be made using the earlier incomplete Naval Office List data and using population as a related series. For this procedure see Milton Friedman, 'The interpolation of time series by related series,' *Journal of the American Statistical Association*, LVII, 300 (December 1962), pp. 729–57.

APPENDIX II

OFFICIAL VALUES AND REAL VALUES OF ENGLISH EXPORTS TO THE COLONIES

The origin of the official values calls for a brief explanation. In 1696 the office of the Inspector-General of Imports and Exports was established in England in order

> to make and keep a particular, distinct, and true account of the importacions and exportacions of all commodities into and out of this kingdome, and to and from what places the same are exported or imported, and out of the said account once in every yeare and as often as he shalbe thereto required by us or any three or more of us, or by the lord high treasurer or any three or more of the commissioners of the treasury for the time being, make and present a faire and exact scheme of the ballance of trade (as it then stands) between England and any other part of the world, ...[1]

The values recorded in the English Inspector-General's Ledgers were a product of the quantities of commodities imported and exported that were collected by the Inspector-General's office (from bills of entry in London, and from the searcher's books in the outports), and of 'official rates' which were set in 1696 to value the quantities of these commodities passing through customs. It is not clear how these rates were established, but the second Inspector-General wrote that his 'worthy predecessory...set a valuation upon all the respective goods...by the judgment of the ablest foreign merchants.'[2] Imports were rated on the basis of the estimated cost of the goods in the country of origin, exports of English manufacture on the basis of the estimated cost to English exporters, and re-exports on the same basis as exports of English manufacture (i.e. at rates which included insurance and freight charges for bringing the goods into England, an allowance for merchants' profits, and, in the case of re-exports 'out of time,' duty).[3] At this

---

[1] Constitution of the first Inspector-General of Imports and Exports, September 11, 1696, quoted from G. N. Clark, *Guide to English Commercial Statistics, 1696–1782* (London: The Royal Historical Society, 1938), pp. 6–7.

[2] Quoted from *ibid.*, p. 10.

[3] See Phyllis Deane and W. A. Cole, *British Economic Growth, 1688–1959* (London: Cambridge University Press, 1964), p. 318. Re-exports 'out of time' were those for which duties could not be 'drawn back' (refunded) because the time limitation had expired. Re-exports 'in time' were those commodities re-exported within the allotted time, and for which duties could therefore be drawn back. Note that imports into England would thus be valued at F.O.B. rather than C.I.F. The early Inspectors-General were very much aware of this, and listed this as one reason why their statistics would not give an accurate balance of trade. See, for example, 'An Essay Towards Finding the Ballance of our Whole Trade Annually

time, then, these rates were supposed to be approximate average prices for the particular commodity which they were used to value. With this in mind the first Inspector-General, William Culliford (whose term was 1696–1703), revised from year to year the rates of some commodities which appeared to get out of line with market values. The next two Inspectors-General, Charles Davenant and Henry Martin (whose terms were 1703–13 and 1713–21 respectively), revised downward the rates for most of the categories of woolens, which occupied an important part of the value of total exports of British manufacture. After 1721, this list of official rates was not changed. These rates did not disappear from use until the year 1870 (although in 1798 declared values began to be given alongside the official values for exports of British manufacture, and in 1854 imports and re-exports began to be based upon values calculated on the basis of current prices ascertained each month by experts).[1]

Even if the official values did approximate fairly accurately the actual values of English trade at the beginning of the eighteenth century, the changing structure of relative prices and of general price levels over the century must have produced at least some divergence between them and the actual values of trade by the late colonial period. The question that we must answer is: What was the direction and magnitude of this change? Opinions have been pessimistic regarding the possibility of approximating real values from the official values.[2] It is a problem, however, which cannot be avoided. We thus turn to the discussion of the evidence that bears on the relation of these official values to real values.

A price index has been constructed by Elizabeth B. Schumpeter for the eighteenth century, using prices of British manufactured goods and re-exported commodities (she used the price data gathered by the Beveridge group).[3] This index, averaged for five-year periods, is given in Table 1. The index admittedly is a crude one. Because it is based on contract prices, which were likely to have been less sensitive to market conditions than prices paid in the market-place, it probably has doubtful significance for short-term price fluctuations. But as the author states, the index does 'give a reasonably good

---

from Christmas of 1698 to Christmas 1719,' printed in Clark, pp. 69–149. Clark credited this essay to John Oxenford, who became Assistant Inspector-General of Imports and Exports in 1722 (see Clark, pp. 25–6), but recent evidence found since Clark wrote would suggest that Henry Martin, English Inspector-General of Imports and Exports, probably wrote the essay not long before his death in 1721. See T. S. Ashton's 'Introduction' in Elizabeth B. Schumpeter, *English Overseas Trade Statistics, 1697–1808* (Oxford: The Clarendon Press, 1960), p. 3. This will not be of concern in the present study, however, because we are only going to consider exports of British manufacture and re-exports from the English records.

[1] Werner Schlote, *British Overseas Trade from 1700 to the 1930s*, trans. W. O. Henderson and W. H. Chaloner (Oxford: Basil Blackwell, 1952), pp. 5–6.

[2] See, for example, Clark, pp. 38–9; and Albert H. Imlah, *Economic Elements in the Pax Britannica* (Cambridge, Mass.: Harvard University Press, 1958), p. 21.

[3] In England Lord William Beveridge headed the research on price and wage history that was sponsored by the International Scientific Committee on Price History. Part of this material was published in Beveridge, *Prices and Wages in England from the Twelfth to the Nineteenth Century* (London: Longmans, Green & Co., 1939), I, but Schumpeter used their material before this volume was published.

TABLE I. *Index of English prices of consumer goods (other than cereals) for five-year periods, 1696–1725 and 1761–1805*[a]

Five-year period[b]	Index[c]
1696–1700	115
1701–1705	97
1706–1710	95
1711–1715	104
1716–1720	96
1721–1725	94
1761–1765	93
1766–1770	93
1771–1775	100
1776–1780	103
1781–1785	109
1786–1790	109
1791–1795	116
1796–1800	144
1801–1805	154

Source: B. R. Mitchell and Phyllis Deane, *Abstract of British Historical Statistics* (London: Cambridge University Press, 1962), pp. 468–9.

[a] Prices for the following commodities were used in constructing the index: beef for salting, butter, cheese, pork, ale, beer, cider, hops, malt, pepper, raisins, sugar, tea, tallow candles, coal, broadcloth, hair, felt hats, kersey, leather backs, Brussels linen, Irish linen, and blue yarn stockings. The index was constructed using the unweighted arithmetic mean of the price series for the above goods. The sources were mainly contract prices paid by institutions.

[b] The years are from Michaelmas of the preceding year to Michaelmas of the stated year.

[c] The source gives the index numbers annually. For the less exacting purpose of looking at long-run price trends a simple average of the annual numbers has been constructed for five-year periods.

idea of the trend of prices over long periods...'[1] There were fluctuations in the general level of prices, as shown by the index over the century up to 1790. The 'ups' correspond quite closely to the various wars in which England became engaged, and the 'downs' to years of peace. But underlying these cycles is a horizontal trend of prices up to the beginning of the Napoleonic Wars in 1793. From the time the official rates used to value imports and exports became established and fixed (1696–1721) to the beginning of the Revolution, it would appear from this index that the general level of prices over the long run went neither decisively up nor down. This horizontal trend might thus indicate that in the late colonial period the official values of English exports were not greatly out of line with market values.

Assuming that the index is based on prices that were close to those prevailing in the English market-place, and that the official values originally approximated market values in the early eighteenth century, then the conclusion that official values closely approximated real values of English exports depends upon whether an unweighted index like this can accurately indicate the price trends of those English goods that were being exported to America. Certainly the foodstuffs included in the index are not relevant for our purposes; but most of the other items, especially the woolens and

[1] Elizabeth B. Schumpeter, 'English prices and public finance, 1660–1822,' *Review of Economic Statistics*, xx, 1 (February 1938), p. 33.

linens, are relevant. Let us consider one final piece of evidence regarding Schumpeter's index.

In 1800 Thomas Irving, the English Inspector-General of Imports and Exports, published an examination he had made of the divergence between the official values and market values for the years 1796–8.[1] 'Irving's estimates were very detailed, and a comparison of the prices he used for imports and re-exports with those quoted for the period in Tooke's *History of Prices* suggests that they were also remarkably accurate.'[2] Irving's comparison of the official values of exports of British manufacture with market values was less detailed, and perhaps less reliable, than those of imports and re-exports. Nevertheless, it is possible to compare his estimates with Schumpeter's index, which averages 135 for the years 1796–8.[3] The ratio of Irving's estimates of market values to the official values of exports of British manufactures in 1796–8 was 1.64, and 0.87 for re-exports.[4] An average of these ratios, weighted by Irving's estimated real values of exports and re-exports, is 1.43.[5] Had we estimated the real value of exports in the years 1796–8 using Schumpeter's index we would have been within 6 per cent of Irving's estimates. This is not a large difference when one considers that Schumpeter's index often fluctuates more than this from year to year. There is no guarantee that we would be as close if her index were used to value English exports for the years prior to 1775, but it does inspire more confidence in the index.

If one examines the eighteenth century up to the beginning of the Napoleonic Wars one fails to find any autonomous forces that might drastically affect price levels. Prior to the period under study it was not a century of great technological change, which, other things being equal, would have tended to lower prices. The developments in cotton textiles, iron, and steam power were just beginning to take place more rapidly, and their impact cannot have been widespread before this time. Improvements in organization in the woolen and linen industries may have increased productivity to some extent, but these were certainly not of the magnitude of the changes that were to come later. The wars of the eighteenth century did raise price levels, but they were not of the scale to cause the inflation that the Napoleonic Wars brought at the end of the century. Within the bounds of English mercantilism, competition between Englishmen for colonial markets undoubtedly had the effect of keeping monopolistic influences on prices of

[1] See Deane and Cole, pp. 43–4, and their Appendix 1.
[2] *Ibid.*, p. 43.
[3] B. R. Mitchell and Phyllis Deane, *Abstract of British Historical Statistics* (London: Cambridge University Press, 1962), p. 469.
[4] Ashton, p. 8, states: 'According to estimates made by the Inspector-General in the year 1800, the official prices of imports in general were only 55 per cent, and those of British-produced exports only 61 per cent, of actual prices. On the other hand, the official prices of re-exports at this time were 15 per cent *above* current market prices.' Turning Ashton's ratios around, we have 1.00/0.61 = 1.64, and 1.00/1.15 = 0.87.
[5] The official value of exports from England for the three years 1796–8 was £52,072,000, and £36,686,000 for re-exports (Schumpeter, *English Overseas Trade Statistics*, pp. 15–16). Revaluing these by Irving's ratios, his estimates of real values would be £85,398,000 for exports and £31,917,000 for re-exports, or 72.8 per cent and 27.2 per cent, respectively, of total exports of £117,315,000. Using these percentages of estimated real value to weight the ratios – 1.64 for exports and 0.87 for re-exports – the average of the two ratios is 1.43.

manufactured goods negligible. The correspondence of colonial importers is filled with reference to their ability and willingness to give their business to other firms unless they obtained satisfaction from the ones with which they were dealing at the time.

Further evidence of a horizontal secular trend of prices for English exports and re-exports can be found. Bezanson states:

> From the mass of comments by contemporary merchants, supported by the prices of osnaburgs on record, one may conclude that the movements in prices of British goods during the Colonial period roughly correspond to the fluctuations already noted in London loaf sugar, Liverpool salt, pepper, and tea... The most significant aspect of the behaviour of the prices of British goods, so far as the prices of osnaburgs are typical, is that from 1720 to 1775 there was a horizontal trend underlying the successive swings.[1]

This and the other evidence discussed above lacks the directness that one

TABLE 2. *Official values of linens, selected woolens, metal products, and goods at declared value exported from England to the thirteen colonies, 1768–72[a]* (pounds sterling)

Commodity	Year				
	1768	1769	1770	1771	1772
Linens:					
Above bounty price	126,817	77,347	70,197	201,148	194,881
British, 6d. to 18d. per yard	48,069	47,581	49,006	64,233	48,455
Irish, 6d. to 18d. per yard	88,544	66,022	106,411	145,856	108,887
Sailcloth	13,838	14,195	26,261	18,697	15,765
Total value of linen exported	277,268	205,145	251,875	429,934	367,988
Per cent of total exports[b]	16.1	18.8	16.0	13.9	14.3
Woolens:					
Baize minikin	39,562	38,882	78,363	146,505	165,730
Cloths, long	30,866	15,249	25,550	45,869	36,168
Cloths, short	138,299	88,124	139,827	275,756	153,618
Stockings, men's worsted	53,192	31,139	36,516	95,984	94,328
Stuffs	171,584	67,450	116,935	279,307	230,762
Total	433,503	240,844	397,191	843,421	680,606
Per cent of total exports[b]	25.2	22.1	25.2	27.3	26.5
Wrought iron	132,553	95,847	143,126	242,955	217,737
Per cent of total exports[b]	7.7	8.8	9.1	7.9	8.5
'Goods of Several Sorts'	277,487	181,644	228,470	477,937	393,412
Per cent of total exports[b]	16.2	16.7	14.5	15.5	15.3

Source: London, Public Record Office, Customs 3/68–72.

[a] Exports of British and Irish manufacture.

[b] The percentage is of the total 'official value' of exports of British and Irish manufacture to the thirteen colonies.

[1] Bezanson, *et al.*, *Prices in Colonial Pennsylvania*, pp. 291–2. Osnaburg was a coarse, heavy linen made originally in Osnaburg, Germany, and was used most often for sacking and bagging (P. L. White, *The Beekmans of New York in Politics and Commerce, 1647–1877*, p. 652). Bezanson does not publish the prices of osnaburgs, but says that they follow the same horizontal secular trend as the prices of the London loaf sugar, Liverpool salt, pepper and tea.

might desire. It does, however, negate the possibility of any drastic changes in the prices of British goods imported into the colonies from the beginning of the century to the end of the colonial period, and it clearly points to the likelihood that the official values of British exports to the colonies were not far removed from the market values that actually prevailed in this trade.

It is possible, however, to go beyond the above evidence and examine more closely the British and Irish customs records for at least a few of the more important commodities for which some prices can be observed. Let us first examine the following categories used in the English Inspector-General's Ledgers – linens, woolens, metals, and 'goods of several sorts.'

There were four types of linens listed in the English customs ledgers that were made in Great Britain and Ireland and exported to the colonies. For purposes of illustration, the official values for these four types, and the percentages that these values were of total exports to the colonies, are given in Table 2 for each of the five years 1768–72. The bounty of 1½d. per yard given to both British and Irish linen exported from Great Britain applied to linen worth 18d. per yard or less. The linen in these categories, i.e. British and Irish linen of 6d. to 18d. per yard, was valued at 12d. per yard. Linen that sold for prices above the bounty price was valued at 35s. per piece.[1] Linen sailcloth was valued at 12d. per ell.

From invoices received by colonial merchants from English exporters, it has been possible to compute average prices for Irish linen that would have been eligible for the bounty. These are presented in Table 3. Since only one observation was found for a year covered by this study, observations for two earlier years and one later one are also given. If these observations are representative[2] it would appear that Irish linen was undervalued in the official values by about 10 per cent. It must be realized, however, that what might look like small absolute differences in the average price per yard would mean substantial percentage differences between the actual values and the official values. For example, a difference in the observed average price of 1d. per yard would suggest a difference of around 8 per cent between the actual values and the official values. It is for this reason that the observed average prices must be considered as only rough approximations.

The observed price of about 13d. per yard is substantiated, however, by testimony concerning the state of the linen industry in Great Britain and Ireland in 1773.[3] Mr Richard Harris, a wholesale linen draper in London who dealt both in exporting and in domestic sales of linens, stated in 1773 that 'the Medium Price of Irish Linen printed for Garments is about 1s. and

---

[1] The rate used in the outports was 18d. per ell. Only a negligible amount of linen in this category was exported from the outports, however. An ell was 45 inches in English usage and 27 inches in continental usage. If this price was per English ell, the equivalent price in yards would be 14.4d. This is below the bounty price, however, and thus does not make much sense. If the price is per continental ell, then the equivalent price is 24d. per yard. Presumably the customs officers meant ells of 27 inches.

[2] The sample is admittedly too small to make this claim. Nevertheless, it is the only evidence that has heretofore been found relating directly to this question.

[3] Great Britain, Parliamentary Papers (*Reports from Committees from the House of Commons*, Vol. 3), May 25, 1773. 'Report from the Committee Appointed to Enquire into the State of the Linen Trade in Great Britain and Ireland,' pp. 99–133.

1d. per Yard.'[1] This statement does support the average prices shown in Table 3. The conclusion that can be drawn from the above evidence is that linen prices were probably slightly higher (up to 10 per cent) than the rates used to value linen in the English Inspector-General's Ledgers.

TABLE 3. *Observed average sterling prices of Irish linen imported into the British North American colonies, 1757–1783*[a]

Year	Average price (pence per yard)	No. of yards in observation
1757	12.21[b]	1,720
1759	13.59[b]	872
1770	13.85[c]	2,270
1783	13.84	1,806
Weighted average	13.39	6,668

Sources: Invoice from John Peach, Bristol, to James W. Beekman, New York, September 8, 1757 (New-York Historical Society, The Beekman Papers, Box 13, Folder No. 5, 1757); invoice from John Peach, Bristol, to James W. Beekman, New York, April 30, 1759, printed in *The Beekman Mercantile Papers, 1746–1799*, III, ed. Philip L. White (New York: New-York Historical Society, 1956), p. 1410–11, invoice from Thomas Greer, Dungannon, Ireland, to John Reynell, Philadelphia, September 3, 1770 (Harvard University, Baker Library, Manuscript Division, Mss: Reynell and Coates, Vol. 1, 1744–85); and invoice from Harrison Ansley and Co., London, to J. J. Amory, Boston, April 4, 1783 (Baker Library, Mss: Amory, Vol. 13).

[a] The average prices were computed by weighting each price observed by the number of yards imported at that price. Only linen eligible for the bounty (18d. per yard or less) has been included.

[b] Net of bounty of 1½d. per yard, which was passed on to the American importer.

[c] Shipped from Ireland, thus the British bounty was not applicable. Converted from Irish prices at rate of 13 Irish shillings to 12 English shillings (see Conrad Gill, *The Rise of the Irish Linen Industry* (Oxford: The Clarendon Press, 1925), p. 158).

Woolens as a group were the most valuable single English export to the colonies. Again for purposes of illustration, the official values of the five most valuable types of woolen textiles from the English records are given in Table 2, along with the percentage they formed of total exports to the colonies. All woolens together comprised 35 to 40 per cent of total exports during the five-year period 1768–72.[2] Because this was the most valuable group of goods that was exported to the colonies, the relation of the official values to actual values hinges to an important extent on this group. Unfortunately, it is difficult to relate the woolens as they were listed on invoices sent to colonial merchants to the particular categories listed in the customs ledgers; thus the problem is one of comparing the prices found in the invoices to the rates used in the ledgers. A few comparisons, nevertheless, can be made. In an invoice dated 1758, 990 yards of woolen flannel were valued at an average of 12.2d. per yard.[3] In another invoice from the same firm in

---

[1] *Ibid.*, p. 105.

[2] This percentage is based upon nearly complete recordings made of the official values of all woolens listed in the English records for the years 1768–72.

[3] Invoice from Peach and Pierce, Bristol, to James W. Beekman, New York, April 28, 1758, printed in *The Beekman Mercantile Papers, 1746–1799*, III, ed. Philip L. White (New York: New-York Historical Society, 1956), p. 1406.

1768 the price averaged 13.1d. per yard for 491 yards of flannel.[1] The rate used to value flannel in the English records was from 8d. to 24d. per yard for exports from London to Virginia and Maryland, and from 8d. to 18d. per yard for exports to all other colonies. The midpoint of these ranges was used, which meant the official values are based on rates of 16d. per yard for exports to Virginia and Maryland, and 13d. per yard for exports to the other colonies. The observed prices are slightly under the rates used in the English customs records. Another invoice from a Leeds, England, woolen merchant to a Philadelphia firm in 1771[2] lists 41 pieces of woolen broadcloth which averaged £6 16s. 4d. per piece. This was probably classified by English customs as 'cloths, short,' which were rated at £7 to £9 per piece from London and from £10 to £13 per piece from the outports. If this was the proper customs classification, these woolens were over-valued. On the other hand, 763 yards of kersies[3] shipped to New York in 1758[4] averaged 49.9s. per piece, while the official rate from the outports (from where most kersies were shipped) was from 20s. to 50s. per piece. The official value of this shipment of kersies was only 70 per cent of the actual value.

From these scattered observations no definite conclusions can be drawn regarding the actual values of woolens imported into the colonies. They do not, however, detract from the view expressed above that the official values of English exports to the colonies were not greatly out of line with the actual value of these exports.

The customs categories for metals and metalwares were 'iron, wrought,' 'brass, wrought,' 'copper, wrought,' 'iron nails,' 'pewter,' and 'steel.' The official values of wrought iron exports to the colonies, and the importance of this category in each year relative to the total official value of exports from England of British and Irish manufacture, are given in Table 2 as an illustration of the magnitude of these exports.

Little can be done to relate most of the various categories of metals listed by weight in the English records to the specific items of metalware found in the invoices. There is one important exception, however, and that is iron nails. Prices of nails can be found and compared with the rate used to value nails in the English customs records, which was 30s. to 40s. per hundredweight. If the same relation held between the official and actual value of nails imported into the colonies as did for the other metal categories, then this relation can be used to infer what the ratios of actual to official values of all metal and metalware imports were. The prices of iron nails which were found ranged from averages of 30.9s. to 34.6s. per hundredweight, or from about 88 per cent to 99 per cent of the 35s. official rate.[5] Based on this evi-

---

[1] New-York Historical Society, *The Beekman Papers*, 1768.

[2] Invoice for three bales of woolens from Samuel Elam, Leeds, England, to Reynell and Coates, Philadelphia, February 12, 1771, Baker Library, Mss. Reynell and Coates, Vol. 1, 1774–85.

[3] A type of coarse woolen cloth made chiefly in Kent and Devonshire.

[4] Invoice from Peach and Pierce, Bristol, printed in *The Beekman Mercantile Papers*, III, p. 1407.

[5] Invoices from Thomas Plumstead and Son to Samuel Powel, Philadelphia (1748), Pennsylvania Historical Society, Samuel Powel Invoice and Day Book, 1748–50; and invoice from Richard Debell to John Reynell, Philadelphia, February 9, 1736, Pennsylvania Historical Society, Samuel Coates–John Reynell Papers, Letters from England, 1730–1802.

dence, it is suggested that the actual values of metals and metalwares were slightly less than or nearly identical with (but no greater than) the official values.

There was one final category of exports that was important enough to mention at this time. This was evidently a 'catch-all' category into which were put any unrated goods that did not fit any specific description. The official values of this category are listed in Table 2. The values comprised about 15 per cent of the total official value of exports of British manufacture from England to the colonies during this period.

Commodities in this category entered the customs records 'at value,' i.e. at the value declared by the exporter. Since there were no export duties[1] we may hope that the declared values were close to the actual value of the goods.

The categories discussed above accounted for between 70 and 80 per cent of the total official value of exports from England of British and Irish manufacture. The evidence is not adequate to say with any high degree of accuracy what the actual values of these exports from England were. The evidence suggests, however, that the actual values were not radically different from the official values, and that, if anything, the official values were perhaps slightly below the actual values. The best evidence is that concerning linens and the declared values in the miscellaneous category ('goods of several sorts,' which hopefully were close to the actual values of the goods included in this category). Each category made up about 15 per cent of total exports, and should thus be given equal weight. It has been suggested that linens may have been undervalued by about 10 per cent, and that the declared values of the miscellaneous category approximated the actual values of these goods. It will thus be assumed that the official values of exports from England of British and Irish manufacture were 95 per cent of the actual value of these exports.

It must also be remembered that these values were F.O.B. England, and that to make them comparable with the C.I.F. values of imports from other areas an allowance must be made for insurance, freight, and other costs of getting these goods into the hands of colonial importers. All of these costs were usually listed on invoices sent to colonial merchants.[2] Freight was normally $2\frac{1}{2}$ per cent of the value of goods shipped. Commissions, when charged, ranged from 2 to $2\frac{1}{2}$ per cent. A commission was charged only if the goods were purchased through an agent who passed on the goods at the prices charged by the manufacturer or dealer, and took only the commission in return for his services of getting the order together and shipping it.

---

[1] The Townshend Acts levied duties on tea, paper, glass, lead, and painters' colors, which, with the exception of tea, were probably placed in this category. These duties, however, were import duties to be collected in the colonies, and thus should not have mattered to the English exporter who was declaring the value of these goods.

[2] Sometimes freight charges were paid by the merchant in the colonies upon receipt of the goods, and in such cases freight was not included in the charges on the invoice. No evidence was found to indicate the basis for the freight charges when paid by colonial merchants. Freight rates were said to be £2 to £3 per ton from England to the colonies, and colonial merchants, when paying the freight charges, may have paid upon the basis of tonnage. Nevertheless, the customary practice of charging $2\frac{1}{2}$ per cent of the value of goods shipped should accurately reflect the costs of sending British goods from England to the colonies.

Other exporters acted as dealers, i.e. they purchased the goods on their own account and obtained the return for their services by marking up the prices that were charged to the colonial merchant. In either case it is assumed that the return to the exporter for his services was $2\frac{1}{2}$ per cent, and that this return was not included in the official values. Insurance costs (including commission on the sale of insurance) ranged consistently from $2\frac{1}{4}$ to $2\frac{3}{4}$ per cent of the value of the shipment, and can be estimated accurately at $2\frac{1}{2}$ per cent of the value of the goods shipped.[1] Miscellaneous costs consisted of charges for such items or services as packing and transporting the goods to the nearest port (if the merchant was in an inland town, such as Birmingham, Manchester or Leeds); certificates of entry and searchers' fees; wharfage, porterage, boatage, and primage fees;[2] debentures[3] (usually one-half of these charges were passed on to the colonial merchant); bills of lading; and sometimes the postage of letters concerning the order and shipment. These charges were invariably small, and together did not usually average more than $\frac{1}{2}$ per cent of the value of the goods shipped. Thus an estimated allowance of 8 per cent ($2\frac{1}{2}$ per cent for freight, $2\frac{1}{2}$ per cent for merchants' profits, $2\frac{1}{2}$ per cent for insurance, and $\frac{1}{2}$ per cent for miscellaneous costs of shipment) of the value of goods shipped must be added to the adjusted official values to convert them to C.I.F. values in the colonies.

For re-exports it is possible to construct a price index based on three commodities – tea, linen entered as 'Germany narrow,'[4] and pepper – which comprised on the average for the five-year period about 34 per cent of the official value of all re-exports (the official values of these three commodities are given in Table 4). Prices for tea and pepper can be obtained from Bezanson.[5] Tea was entered at customs at declared values, which averaged about 4s. per pound during this five-year period. This was considerably more than tea prices averaged in Philadelphia (except for one year, 1770, when the non-importation agreements had the effect of raising the prices of most British imports).

German linens also were apparently valued higher than their actual values. They were rated at £4 to £7 per 112 ells, or 15.7d. per yard, in the English ledgers. Their average actual value was said to be 14.5d. per yard

---

[1] This is something of an overstatement because this was a peacetime period, and merchants did not always insure for the full value of the cargo. A common practice, for example, was to insure for half the value of the goods shipped, in which case the colonial merchant was bearing one-half the risk, and, in effect, providing one-half his own insurance. To the extent that colonial merchants were self-insured, this portion should not be a debit to the colonies in their balance of payments with Great Britain.

[2] Primage was an allowance or tip given to the ship captain in order to promote care in handling the cargo.

[3] A debenture was a customs office certificate given to a merchant re-exporting goods on which a drawback of import duties was allowed, or for exporting goods of British or Irish manufacture on which a bounty was granted. It certified that the holder was entitled to the amount stated on the debenture.

[4] This was a customs category in which most German linens $\frac{7}{8}$ of a yard wide or less were placed. The category included linens called Silesias, garlix, osnaburgs, dowlass, etc. See 'Report from the Committee Appointed to Enquire into the State of the Linen Trade in Great Britain and Ireland,' p. 115.

[5] *Prices in Colonial Pennsylvania*, pp. 418 and 421.

before the drawback of import duties on re-exportation which averaged
1.75d. per yard.[1] Since the drawbacks were usually passed on to the colonial
importer, the price net of drawbacks is the relevant one for our present
purposes. This price was 12.75d. per yard. It is not comparable with the
prices of tea and pepper from Philadelphia, however, because the use of the
latter results in C.I.F. values, whereas the use of the average German linen
price at the place of re-exportation in England results in F.O.B. values. We
must add to the linen price an allowance for the freight, insurance, and
miscellaneous costs of getting this linen to the colonies. This allowance has
earlier been estimated in this section to have been 8 per cent. The average
price of German linen is therefore raised by 8 per cent to 13.8d. per yard.

TABLE 4. *Official values of tea, German linens, and pepper re-exported from
England to the thirteen colonies, 1768–72* (pounds sterling)

Commodity	Year				
	1768	1769	1770	1771	1772
Tea	168,759	45,328	21,726	71,830	52,829
German linens	71,818	63,688	95,145	140,384	94,468
Pepper	9,997	3,370	8,447	21,310	6,961
Total	250,574	112,386	125,318	233,524	154,258

Source: London, Public Record Office, Customs 3/68–72.

From these average colonial prices for tea, pepper, and German linen, the
following price relatives (estimated actual average prices divided by the
official rates times 100), and a composite index constructed from the price
relatives weighted by the official values from Table 4, can be given in Table
5. The official values of re-exports to the colonies will be revalued according
to this price index. This will result in estimated C.I.F. values for goods
re-exported from England to the colonies.

TABLE 5. *Price relatives of tea, pepper, and German linen, and a composite price
index for these commodities, 1768–72*

Year	Price relatives			Price index
	Tea	Pepper	German linen	
1768	65.2	195.7	87.9	77
1769	57.7	207.7	87.9	79
1770	102.7	235.4	87.9	100
1771	74.5	125.5	87.9	87
1772	63.2	129.2	87.9	81

Source: see Table 4 and accompanying text.

One final qualification about the use of the English official values should
be mentioned. The balances of trade estimated in Chapter 7 are based upon
data from both the British and American customs records. Yet the data from

[1] 'Report from the Committee Appointed to Enquire into the State of the Linen Trade,'
p. 104. The average price of such linens was said to have been 1s. 2d. to 1s. 3d. before duties
were drawn back. This average price was substantiated from invoices that were received by
colonial merchants.

these sources are not strictly comparable because of the shipping lag, i.e. the time from when the goods passed through English customs, were loaded on board the ship, and were transported across the Atlantic, to the time when they finally passed through American customs. Goods leaving England in 1768, for example, might not have been recorded by American customs until 1769. There is no way to correct for these time period discrepancies. It should be borne in mind by the reader, however, when making comparisons concerning the balance of trade in any one year, that this potential source of error exists; and when import values fluctuated, as they did during and following the non-importation agreements, the balance of trade for any one year as estimated in Chapter 7 may differ from the balance of trade that actually did exist.

QUANTITATIVE DATA RELATED TO SHIPPING

The data and information are given in the following sequence under the titles:

1. Freight rates on oil: Boston to London
2. Freight rates on currency and bullion: New York to London
3. Freight rates on flour: New York to Jamaica
4. Freight rates on tobacco: Maryland to London
5. Freight rates on wine: southern Europe to London
6. Freight rate sources and codes
7. Explanation of base year weights to Table 4.5
8. Average size of vessels trading in the Port of Boston, 1688–1765
9. Average size of vessels trading in the Chesapeake, 1693–1768
10. Average size of vessels trading at Barbados, 1681–1773
11. Average size of vessels trading at Jamaica, 1686–1768
12. Ratios of tons, guns, and men for Boston, 1716–65
13. Ratios of tons, guns, and men for New York, 1715–64
14. Ratios of tons, guns, and men for Virginia, 1732–68
15. Ratios of tons, guns, and men for Barbados, 1696–1773
16. Ratios of tons, guns, and men for Jamaica, 1729–68
17. Average voyage times and average knots by route, 1686–1765
18. Average port times in New England
19. Average port times by rig in Philadelphia
20. Average port times in the southern colonies
21. Average port times in the West Indies
22. Explanation of t-tests
23. Ton–men ratios of armed and unarmed vessels at Jamaica (1729–31)
24. Ton–men ratios of armed and unarmed vessels at Barbados (1696–8)
25. Ton–men ratios of armed and unarmed vessels at Charleston (1735–9)

1. *Freight rates on oil: Boston to London*

Date	Rate per ton[a]	Source by code[b]
Nov. 1700	3/10/0	10
Aug. 1700	3/10/0	10
Aug. 1701	4	10
Aug. 1701	4	10
Aug. 1702	4/10/0	10
Jan. 1724	2/10/0	5

1. Freight rates on oil: Boston to London – continued

Date	Rate per ton*a*	Source by code*b*
May 1725	2/10/0	5
Feb. 1732	2/10/0	11 (Vol. 8)
July 1732	2/10/0	11 (Vol. 8)
Aug. 1739	2/10/0	5
July 1754	2	12
Jan. 1764	2/10/0	11 (Vol. 8)
Aug. 1767	2/5/0	11 (Vol. 28)
Oct. 1767	2/10/0	11 (Vol. 8)
Dec. 1767	2/10/0	11 (Vol. 8)
Jan. 1768	2/5/0	11 (Vol. 28)
Jan. 1768	2/5/0	11 (Vol. 28)
Feb. 1771	2/5/0	11 (Vol. 28)
July 1771	2	11 (Vol. 28)
May 1774	2/5/0	11 (Vol. 28)

a These rates are expressed in pounds sterling with eight barrels equaling one ton.
b See part 6 of this appendix.

2. Freight rates on currency and bullion: New York to London

Date	Rate in per cent	Source by code*a*
Sept. 1699	2.0	1
Sept. 1699	2.0	1
Oct. 1699	4.2*b*	2
Oct. 1699	2.0	1
April 1700	2.0	1
April 1700	2.0	1
May 1701	2.0	1
May 1701	2.0	1
June 1701	2.0	1
June 1701	2.0	1
June 1701	2.0	1
Dec. 1701	2.5	3
Nov. 1704	2.5	3
Nov. 1705	2.5	3
Nov. 1705	2.5	3
Jan. 1712	2.5	4
Jan. 1712	2.5	4
Jan. 1712	2.5	4
June 1720	2.0	4
June 1720	2.0	4
July 1721	2.0*c*	4
Nov. 1723	2.0	4
May 1724	2.0	4
Oct. 1725	2.0*b*	5
April 1736	1.0*b*	5
Nov. 1736	2.0*b*	5
Mar. 1787	1.0	6
Mar. 1789	1.0*c*	6
July 1789	1.0	7

a See part 6 of this appendix.
b This route is Boston to London.
c This rate was explicitly stated as being customary.

3. *Freight rates on flour: New York to Jamaica*

Date	Rate per ton[a]	Source by code[b]
Oct. 1699	5	1
Dec. 1699	5/10/0	1
Feb. 1700	5/10/0	1
April 1700	5/5/0	1
April 1700	5/5/0	1
April 1700	5/5/0	1
May 1700	5/5/0	1
Aug. 1700	5	1
Aug. 1700	5	1
Sept. 1701	6	1
Dec. 1701	6	1
June 1702	6	1
June 1702	6	1
June 1702	6	1
Nov. 1702	7	3
May 1704	6/10/0	3
May 1704	7	3
Sept. 1704	7/10/0	3
Dec. 1704	8	3
Dec. 1704	7/10/0	3
Dec. 1704	8/5/0	3
April 1705	8/5/0	3
May 1705	8/5/0	3
May 1705	8/5/0	3
July 1705	8/5/0	3
Nov. 1705	8/5/0	3
Dec. 1705	8	3
June 1719	3/17/6	4
July 1720	4	4
Dec. 1720	3/17/6	4
Aug. 1721	5	4
Nov. 1721	5	4
Nov. 1721	5	4
Mar. 1722	4	4
April 1722	3/17/6	4
April 1722	3/17/6	4
June 1722	3/17/6	4
Dec. 1722	3/17/6	4
June 1723	5	4
Dec. 1729	4/10/0	8
Dec. 1729	4/10/0	8
Dec. 1729	4/10/0	8
Nov. 1766	3/10/0	9
Dec. 1768	3/10/0	9

[a] Expressed in pounds sterling with 16 half barrels equaling one ton.

[b] See part 6 of this appendix.

4. *Freight rates on tobacco: Maryland to London*[a]

Year	Rate per ton[b]	Source by code[c]
1630–9	(12)	16
1657	7	17
1654–60	7–7/10/0	18
1675	(7)	18
1677	10	18
1678	(7–10)	18
1680	6	18
1680	(6/10/0)	18
1684	(5/5/0)	18
1685	6/5/0	18
1689	14	18
1690	(14)	18
1690	(16)	18
1691	14	18
1692	13	14 (#16)
1692	12/10/0	14 (#16)
1696	8/10/0	18
1697	(8)	18
1697	6/10/0	14 (#16)
1705	15	17
1706	15	17
1707	16	17
1708	14–16	17
1709	16	17
1711	12–13	17
1712	11–12	17
1713	8	17
1714	6	17
1715	5–8	17
1716	6–7	17
1717	6–7	17
1718	6	17
1719	6–7	17
1720	7–8	17
1721	7–8	17
1722	7	17
1723	7	17
1724	6	17
1725	6–7	17
1726	7	17
1727	7	17
1728	7	17
1729	7	17
1730	6–7	17
1731	7	17
1732	7	17
1733	7	17
1734	7	17
1735	7	17
1736	7	17
1737	7	17
1738	7	17
1739	7	17
1740	9–10	17

4. *Freight rates on tobacco: Maryland to London[a] – continued*

Year	Rates per ton[b]	Source by code[c]
1741	9	17
1742	9	17
1743	9	17
1744	9–12	17
1745	12–13	17
1746	13–14	17
1747	16	17
1748	8–16	17
1749	7	17
1750	7	17
1751	7	17
1752	7	17
1753	7	17
1754	7	17
1755	7	17
1756	9	17
1757	13–14	17
1758	12	17
1759	12	17
1760	12	17
1761	10–12	17
1762	11–13	17
1763	7	19
1764	7[d]	19
1765	7	19
1766	7	19
1767	7	19
1768	7	19
1769	7	19
1770	7	19
1771	7	19
1772	7	19
1773	7	19
1774	7	19
1775	7	19

[a] Rates in parentheses are from Virginia to London.

[b] These rates are expressed in pounds sterling with 4 hogsheads equaling one ton.

[c] See part 6 of this appendix.

[d] The 1764–73 Virginia rate was £8 per ton; see Jones Family Collection, Vols. 1–13, Library of Congress (Manuscripts Division), Washington, D.C.

5. *Freight rates on wine: southern Europe to London*

Year	Rate per ton[a]	From	Source by code[b]
1640–9	3/10/0–4/5/0	Malaga	13
1660–9	2/10/0–3	Lisbon	13
1696	8	Cadiz	14 (#17)
1696	8	Cadiz	14 (#16)
1696	8	Cadiz	14 (#16)
1700	2	St Sebastian	14 (#30)
1701–2	4	Lisbon	14 (#18)
1702	4	Lisbon	14 (#18)
1702	6	Lisbon	14 (#31)
1754	1/10/0	Oporto	15
1755	1/10/0	Oporto	15
1757	4	Oporto	15
1757	4	Oporto	15
1758	4	Oporto	15
1760	3/10/0	Oporto	15
1762	2/15/0	Oporto	15
1764	2	Oporto	15
1764	2	Oporto	15
1765	2	Oporto	15
1765	1/10/0	Oporto	15
1766	1/15/0	Oporto	15
1766	1/15/0	Oporto	15
1783	'normally 2, (some at 1/10/0)'	Oporto	13

[a] These rates are expressed in pounds sterling where two pipes of wine equals one ton.
[b] See part 6 of this appendix.

6. *Freight rate sources and codes*

Code	Source
1	Shipping book of Jacobus Van Cortlandt, New-York Historical Society (hereafter, N.-Y.H.S.), New York.
2	Chancery Masters' Exhibits (hereafter C.M.E.) C104–16, Public Record Office (hereafter P.R.O.), London.
3	Shipping book of Jacobus Van Cortlandt, owned by Mr John Fleming of New York, N.Y.
4	Nathan Simpson freight book, C.M.E., C104–13, P.R.O.
5	Dolbeare Papers, Massachusetts Historical Society (hereafter M.H.S.), Boston.
6	Mercantile Papers and Shipping, New York Public Library (hereafter N.Y.P.L.), New York.
7	Hudson Collection, Box 2, N.Y.P.L.
8	J. Lathan Manuscripts, N.-Y.H.S.
9	S. Gilford Manuscripts, N.-Y.H.S.
10	Accounts of various vessels, C.M.E. C104–16, P.R.O.
11	Thomas Hancock Papers, Baker Library, Boston (Vol. 8 and Vol. 28).
12	J. Stone Papers, Connecticut Historical Society, Hartford, Connecticut.

13   Ralph Davis, *The Rise of the English Shipping Industry* (London: Macmillan & Company Ltd, 1962), p. 239.

14   High Court of the Admiralty, H.C.A.–15, P.R.O. (numbers 16, 17, 18, 30, 31).

15   Accounts of Ship *Caroline*, C.M.E. C103–146, P.R.O.

16   Lewis C. Gray, *History of Agriculture in the Southern United States to 1860* (Washington, D.C.: The Carnegie Institution of Washington, 1933), p. 223.

17   John M. Hemphill, II, 'Freight rates in the Maryland tobacco trade, 1705–62,' *Maryland Historical Magazine*, LIX, 1 and 2 (March and June 1959), pp. 36–58, and 154–87.

18   V. J. Wycoff, 'Ships and shipping of seventeenth century Maryland,' *Maryland Historical Magazine*, XXIV, pp. 60, 282.

19   Hill Papers, Maryland Historical Society, Baltimore.

7. Explanation of Base Year Weights

The purpose of this section is to make explicit the assumptions made and sources used to determine the weights given in Table 4.5, Chapter 4. What is meant by a representative year is in some sense polemic, but early peace-time base years have been chosen to be 'representative' in each case. The estimated utilized tonnages (or percentage of earnings in the case of bullion) are discussed individually by commodity route.

Bullion. The average yearly tonnage sailing from New York to London, 1716–17 was 1153 (Naval Office Lists of New York, C.O. 5–1222, Public Record Office, London). This figure includes all tonnage going specifically to London and one-half that amount designated to Great Britain, the specific port being unstated. The percentage of this tonnage actually occupied by bullion was no doubt small. However, a capacity measure would in this case understate its share of earnings since the freight was levied as a per-centage of value. Nettels states that 'several independent reports from New York for the period 1697–1718 asserted emphatically that gold and silver made up the principal exports of the province to England' (Curtis P. Nettels, *The Money Supply of the American Colonies Before 1720*, Madison, Wis.: University of Wisconsin Studies in the Social Sciences and History, Number 20 (1934), p. 91). Consequently, assuming that bullion made up approximately 25 per cent of earnings to London, one-quarter of the average tonnage, or 288, represents the base year weight for bullion.

Flour. The average yearly tonnage sailing from New York to Jamaica between 1716 and 1717 was 758 (C.O. 5–1222, P.R.O., London). From a very early period flour was a chief export of New York. 'The trade of this province,' wrote Lord Cornbury, 'consists chiefly of flour, and biscuit, which is sent to the islands' (Nettels, p. 115). It is assumed that 40 per cent of this outward tonnage to Jamaica was used in carrying flour; thus, 303 is the tonnage weight for the flour series.

Oil. In 1716, 3,194 tons of shipping left Boston for England and of this amount 2,029 went to London (Naval Office Lists of Boston, C.O. 5–848, P.R.O., London). The major exports of New England 'in order of their

importance – were whale products, ship timber, other naval stores, and furs'
(Nettels, p. 74). In 1709, 800 tons of oil were shipped from Massachusetts to
England, and this was approximately the yearly average for 1721–3 (Nettels,
p. 74). Since the overwhelming percentage of New England trade was
channeled through Boston, the tonnage utilized by oil to London is assumed
to be roughly 550 tons (550≈800 × 2,029/3,194).

Wine. In 1686, sixty-eight ships averaging 126 tons per vessel entered
London from southern Spain carrying wine only (Davis, p. 231). Assuming
that these vessels were under-utilized by an amount roughly equal to that
amount of wine which was shipped in vessels carrying other goods as well as
wine, gives us the weight of 8,568 tons.

Tobacco. The average yearly aggregate tonnage of the tobacco fleet from
Maryland to London (1690–1700) was 6,290 tons (Arthur P. Middleton,
Tobacco Coast: A Maritime History of Chesapeake Bay in the Colonial Era (Newport
News: The Mariner's Museum, 1953) p. 250). Assuming 90 per cent utiliza-
tion gives a weight of 5,661 tons.

Sugar. In 1686, 225 vessels, averaging 150–200 (or approximately 175 tons)
arrived in London from the West Indies (Davis, p. 286). This 39,375 tons of
shipping carried sugar in the ratio of approximately 23:33 in proportion to
total goods (Davis, p. 184). Assuming that one-fifth of this tonnage was
unutilized, 23:33 of the utilized tonnage (31,500) equals that shipping
carrying sugar, or 21,954 tons. Giving Jamaica and Barbados equal weight
for this early period, and assuming that these two major islands made up
about 80 per cent of the sugar shipment, each of these series is weighted
8,782 tons.

8. *Average size of vessels trading in the port of Boston, 1688–1765*

Year	Average size of vessels	Observations
1688	46.5	249
1716	49.6	354
1753	51.7	321
1764–5	61.4	447

Source: Naval Office Lists of Massachusetts (hereafter, for this and other colonies, by call
number only) C.O. 5–848, 849, and 850, P.R.O., London.

9. *Average size of vessels trading in the Chesapeake, 1693–1768*

Year	Average size of vessels[a]	Observations
1693–1700	113.3	538
1726	89.5	220
1732–5	58.5	528
1749 and 1754–5	106.5	419
1764 and 1768	77.1	513

Source: C.O. 5–749, 750, 1441, 1442, 1443, 1444, 1445, 1446, and 1450, P.R.O., London.
[a] Further evidence on the average size of vessels engaged in the Chesapeake is given in
Arthur P. Middleton, *Tobacco Coast* (Newport News, Virginia: The Mariner's Museum,
1953), pp. 254–5. His findings indicate that the average size of vessels in the tobacco fleet
actually fell.

10. *Average size of vessels trading at Barbados, 1681–1773*

Year	Average size of vessels	Observations
1681–2	68.4	297
1697–8	90.0	369
1716	56.9	934
1731	53.4	269
1747	102.4	168
1764	49.7	338
1773	59.4	406

Source: C.O. 33–13, 14, 15, 16, and 17, P.R.O., London, plus photocopies of Barbados Naval Office Lists for 1773 owned by Professor Lawrence A. Harper of the University of California, Berkeley.

11. *Average size of vessels trading at Jamaica, 1686–1768*

Year	Average size of vessels	Observations
1686	51.2	179
1698–9	112.1	89
1711–12	90.4	165
1729	69.8	287
1753–4	85.9	411
1768	91.2	158

Source: C.O. 142–13, 14, 15, 16, and 17, P.R.O., London.

12. *Ratios of tons, guns, and men for Boston, 1716–65*

Ratio	1716			1753			1764–5		
	T/M	T/G	G/M	T/M	T/G	G/M	T/M	T/G	G/M
Colonial-owned	6.9	135	0.05	9.3	540	0.02	10.3	1,000+	0.00
British-owned	8.1	21	0.38	11.6	228	0.05	11.5	597	0.02
All	7.1	60	0.12	9.5	488	0.02	10.2	1,000+	0.00

Source: C.O. 5–848, 849, and 850, P.R.O., London.

13. *Ratios of tons, guns, and men for New York, 1715–64*

Ratio	1715–19			1735–9			1763–4		
	T/M	T/G	G/M	T/M	T/G	G/M	T/M	T/G	G/M
Colonial-owned	4.3	27	0.16	5.9	14	0.41	6.6	122	0.05
Non-colonial-owned	4.7	26	0.18	6.7	19	0.35	7.7	77	0.10
All	4.4	27	0.16	6.1	15	0.40	6.9	104	0.07

Source: C.O. 5–1222, 1225, 1226, and 1228, P.R.O., London.

14. *Ratios of tons, guns, and men for Virginia, 1732–68*

Ratio	1732–5			1754–5			1768		
	T/M	T/G	G/M	T/M	T/G	G/M	T/M	T/G	G/M
Colonial-owned	6.4	25	0.26	10.0	140	0.07	8.3	1,000+	0.00
British-owned	8.5	30	0.28	10.4	104	0.10	11.5	1,000+	0.00
All	7.1	29	0.26	10.1	123	0.08	10.2	1,000+	0.00

Source: C.O. 5–1443, 1444, 1447, and 1450, P.R.O., London.

15. *Ratios of tons, guns, and men for Barbados, 1696–1773*

Ratio	1696-7			1747			1764			1773		
	T/M	T/G	G/M	T/M	T/G	G/M	T/M	T/G	G/M	T/M	T/G	G/M
Colonial-owned	7.8	35	0.22	7.6	25	0.30	8.0	327	0.02	9.1	1,000+	0.00
West Indies-owned	7.0	15	0.43	6.5	10	0.63	5.6	510	0.01	7.3	1,000+	0.00
British-owned	7.2	14	0.51	6.6	14	0.48	7.0	110	0.06	10.8	134	0.08
All	7.3	17	0.44	7.0	16	0.43	7.2	207	0.04	9.1	313	0.03

Source: C.O. 33-13, 14, 16, and 17, P.R.O., London.

16. *Ratios of tons, guns, and men for Jamaica, 1729–68*

Ratio	1729-30			1753-4			1768		
	T/M	T/G	G/M	T/M	T/G	G/M	T/M	T/G	G/M
Colonial-owned	5.6	26	0.22	7.9	46	0.17	7.9	1,000+	0.00
West-Indies owned	3.0	7	0.46	4.3	15	0.28	5.6	1,000+	0.00
British-owned	7.3	19	0.40	8.0	34	0.24	8.7	131	0.07
All	6.0	18	0.34	7.5	32	0.23	8.5	162	0.05

Source: C.O. 142-15, 16, and 17, P.R.O., London.

17. *Average voyage times and average knots by route, 1686–1765*

Year	Route[a]	Average days	Average knots[b]	Observations
1686-8	N.E.–Barbados	45.9 —	1.72 —	62 —
	N.E.–Jamaica	44.5 (52.8)	1.55 (1.31)	24 (14)
1715-19	N.E.- Barbados	40.6 (30.7)	1.94 (2.56)	61 (6)
	N.E.–Jamaica	43.7 (48.8)	1.58 (1.42)	14 (8)
	N.Y.–Barbados	36.1 (32.1)	2.08 (2.38)	58 (40)
	N.Y.–Jamaica	30.9 (47.2)	1.99 (1.30)	22 (11)
1742-8	N.E.–Barbados	46.0 (28.0)	1.72 (2.81)	13 (2)
	N.E.–Jamaica	— —	— —	— —
	N.Y.–Barbados	— —	— —	— —
	N.Y.–Jamaica	40.0 (52.3)	1.53 (1.18)	22 (6)
1764-5	N.E.–Barbados	38.6 (51.2)	2.05 (1.59)	22 (4)
	N.E.–Jamaica	45.4 (46.9)	1.53 (1.47)	22 (19)
	N.Y.–Barbados	— (39.0)	— (1.77)	— (2)
	N.Y.–Jamaica	33.7 (41.6)	1.82 (1.48)	16 (12)

The sources used to derive these voyage times were the Naval Office Lists of Massachusetts (C.O. 5-848, 849, and 850), New York (C.O. 5-1222, 1223, 1224, 1225, 1226, 1227, and 1228), Barbados (C.O. 33-13, 14, 15, 16, and 17), and Jamaica (C.O. 142-13, 14, 15, 16, 17, and 18), all in the P.R.O., London. The method used was to match a vessel clearing a port against its entry in another. For instance, a ship clearing Boston for Jamaica was recorded from the Naval Office List of Boston by name, captain, tonnage, and date clearing. This information was then sought in the Naval Office Lists of Jamaica among the ships entering. If the matching vessel stated an entry into Jamaica from Boston, the voyage time was recorded. Where matching entries were found, but the vessel gave a point of last departure other than Boston, the voyage was discarded on the assumption it had stopped over at another port of call. The reader should be cautioned that vessels sometimes recorded a clear or enter out a few days before leaving port. Consequently, the actual length of some voyages (and the averages) may be understated absolutely. Similarly, speeds may be somewhat overstated absolutely. This error is not likely to be large, however, and the estimates do adequately reflect *changes* in

voyage times. Whatever the degree of understatement of voyage times, it would have per-
sisted throughout the period; thus the estimates properly reflect the *trend* in voyage times.

  a N.E. and N.Y. are abbreviations for New England and New York, respectively. The two
computations given in each column are averages going to and returning from the Caribbean.
The number in parentheses is the return figure.

  b The nautical distance used is the international nautical mile of 6,076 feet.

18.   *Average port times in New England*

| | 1686–8 | | 1725 | | 1764–9 | | Percentage change |
| | Average port times | Obser-vations | Average port times | Obser-vations | Average port times | Obser-vations | Early year base |
Port							
Boston	36.0	81	—	—	48.0	154	+33.3
Piscataqua	—	—	63.9	23	53.0	48	−17.1
Total	36.0	81	63.9	23	49.2	202	—

  Source: C.O. 5–848, 849, and 850, P.R.O., London.

19.   *Average port times by rig in Philadelphia*

| | 1732–3 | | 1749–50 | | Percentage change |
| | Average port times | Obser-vations | Average port times | Obser-vations | 1732–3 base |
Rig					
Ship	64.4	69	56.8	92	−11.8
Snow	51.0	22	50.6	52	− 0.8
Brig	54.8	85	41.6	125	−24.1
Schooner	24.4	140	20.9	193	−14.3
Sloop	23.7	29	25.1	27	+ 5.9
Total	41.6	345	36.3	489	−12.7

  Source: These port times were computed from data given in an unpublished paper given
by Professor William I. Davisson at the meetings of the Western Economic Association in
1965. The paper, entitled 'The use of a computer in analysing the colonial trade of Philadelphia,' gives data on shipping movements gathered from the *Pennsylvania Gazette*.

20.   *Average port times in the southern colonies*

| | 1694–1701 | | 1762–8 | | Percentage change |
| | Average port times | Obser-vations | Average port times | Obser-vations | 1694–1701 base |
Colony					
Maryland	105.6	88	41.4	57	60.8
Virginia	93.6	77	48.9	174	47.8
Total	99.9	165	47.1	231	52.9

  Source: C.O. 5–749, 750, 1441, and 1450, P.R.O., London.

21. *Average port times in the West Indies*

Colony	1686–99 Average port times	Observations	1711–16 Average port times	Observations	1730–1 Average port times	Observations	1764–8 Average port times	Observations	1773 Average port times	Observations
Jamaica	59.4	89	39.7	165	—	—	53.7	72	—	—
Barbados	49.1	220	34.9	661	34.3	253	21.8	100	22.8	308
Total	52.1	309	35.9	826	34.3	253	35.1	172	22.8	308

Source: C.O. 142–13, 14, 15, 16, 17, and 18, and C.O. 33–13, 14, 15, 16, and 17, plus photocopies of Barbados Naval Office Lists for 1773 owned by Professor Lawrence A. Harper of the University of California, Berkeley.

22. *Explanation of 't'-tests*

The following tables of ton-men ratios show the extent to which armed and unarmed vessels of the same size had different manning characteristics. For forty-one out of forty-five comparisons, armed vessels had lower ton–men ratios than unarmed vessels. Statistical *t*-tests have been applied to test the significance of these differences, and for the means of the totals, eight of the fourteen comparable differences (there were no unarmed vessels at Jamaica over 150 tons) prove to be statistically significant at the 5 per cent confidence level. These eight statistically significant differences are for the following tonnage classes: Jamaica, 20–49, 50–99, 100–149; Barbados, 20–49, 50–99; and Charleston, 20–49, 50–99, and 100–149. Along with the totals, tests have been made by the origins of the voyages (Great Britain, etc., West Indies, and mainland colonies). Jamaica has eight possible comparisons of which three are statistically significant (at a 5 per cent confidence level). For Barbados, with ten possible comparisons, five are statistically significant (however, one of these is from the West Indies for the tonnage classification 50–99, which is contrary to the general case), and Charleston has thirteen possible comparisons with eight being statistically significant (however, one of these...7.1 vs. 5.4 from Great Britain, etc. ...is also contrary to the general case).

23. *Ton–men ratios of armed and unarmed vessels at Jamaica (1729–31)*

Entered from	0–19 tons		20–49 tons		50–99 tons		100–149 tons		over 150 tons	
	Armed	Unarmed	Armed	Unarmed	Armed	Unarmed	Armed	Unarmed	Armed	Unarmed
Great Britain, southern Europe, and Africa	—	—	3.9 (6)	5.5 (5)	5.7 (30)	6.4 (11)	7.0 (35)	8.8 (8)	8.7 (22)	—
West Indies	1.4 (2)	3.1 (7)	3.3 (24)	4.7 (20)	5.1 (7)	6.3 (1)	8.3 (1)	—	5.3 (4)	—
Mainland colonies	—	3.2 (7)	5.0 (27)	5.2 (59)	7.3 (10)	7.3 (18)	8.2 (4)	—	12.1 (3)	—
Totals	1.4 (2)	3.2 (14)	4.2 (57)	5.1 (84)	5.9 (47)	6.9 (30)	7.2 (40)	8.8 (8)	8.6 (29)	—

Source: The Naval Office Lists of Jamaica, C.O. 142–15, P.R.O., London. Only the ships entering are recorded, and the number of observations is given in parenthesis.

24. *Ton–men ratios of armed and unarmed vessels at Barbados (1696–8)*

Entered from	0–19 tons		20–49 tons		50–99 tons		100–149 tons		over 150 tons	
	Armed	Unarmed	Armed	Unarmed	Armed	Unarmed	Armed	Unarmed	Armed	Unarmed
Great Britain, southern Europe, and Africa	—	—	5.7 (7)	5.1 (15)	7.0 (38)	8.6 (44)	9.4 (13)	10.6 (4)	9.8 (38)	12.8 (2)
West Indies	—	3.5 (2)	7.1 (5)	8.1 (16)	11.4 (6)	10.3 (7)	—	—	15.8 (1)	—
Mainland colonies	3.3 (1)	3.6 (3)	5.3 (14)	7.4 (57)	8.4 (34)	9.7 (43)	8.4 (3)	10.3 (4)	13.5 (13)	—
Totals	3.3 (1)	3.5 (5)	5.8 (26)	7.1 (88)	8.0 (78)	9.3 (94)	9.2 (16)	10.4 (8)	10.7 (52)	12.8 (2)

Source: The Naval Office Lists of Barbados, C.O. 33–13, P.R.O., London. Only the ships entering are recorded, and the number of observations is given in parenthesis.

25. *Ton–men ratios of armed and unarmed vessels at Charleston (1735–9)*

Entered from	0–19 tons Armed	Unarmed	20–49 tons Armed	Unarmed	50–99 tons Armed	Unarmed	100–149 tons Armed	Unarmed	over 150 tons Armed	Unarmed
Great Britain, southern Europe, and Africa	—	—	7.1 (4)	5.4 (4)	7.5 (56)	9.5 (41)	8.8 (55)	11.9 (3)	11.9 (15)	11.9 (3)
West Indies	3.1 (2)	2.5 (54)	4.5 (26)	5.6 (68)	8.2 (23)	8.8 (28)	10.3 (16)	10.8 (4)	13.0 (3)	—
Mainland colonies	1.7 (2)	3.4 (29)	4.8 (19)	6.0 (79)	7.9 (15)	8.6 (31)	10.2 (9)	11.8 (23)	11.7 (10)	12.0 (7)
Totals	2.4 (4)	2.8 (83)	4.8 (49)	5.8 (151)	7.7 (94)	9.0 (100)	9.3 (80)	11.7 (30)	12.0 (28)	12.0 (10)

Source: The Naval Office Lists of Charleston, South Carolina, C.O. 5–510, P.R.O., London. Only the ships entering are recorded and the number of observations is given in parenthesis.

COMMODITY EXPORTS AND IMPORTS, 1768–72[1]

THE QUANTITY DATA FROM THE CUSTOMS RECORDS

The quantity data upon which the estimates of the values of exports in Chapter 6 are based have been taken from the American Inspector-General's Ledgers (London, Public Record Office, Customs 16/1). Apparently these records were a product of the American Board of Customs established in 1767 under the Townshend Acts with headquarters in Boston. It is not known why the records end with the year 1772, but probably the work of compiling them (which evidently took place in England) was several years behind, and when the Revolution began they were not continued. Quantities of all commodities legally exported from and imported into the British North American colonies for the period January 5, 1768 to January 5, 1773 were listed for 42 colonial port districts[2] in these records. Exceptions to this were that ships sold abroad were not recorded, and imports from Great Britain and Ireland were recorded for only three years, January 5, 1769 to January 5, 1772. The number and tonnage of ships entering and clearing these colonial port districts, and the duties collected on dutiable imports, were also recorded. No values were given for any commodities except for miscellaneous entries called 'sundries'; and these values were not significant magnitudes. The five years covered by these records thus represent the only period for which we have data that purport to be a complete coverage of colonial overseas trade.

There were various idiosyncrasies in these records that raised problems of interpretation,[3] and in several cases entries that seemed highly unlikely were

[1] A more extensive set of appendixes concerning these estimates is given in two papers by James F. Shepherd, 'Commodity exports from the British North American colonies to overseas areas: magnitudes and patterns of trade,' and 'Commodity imports into the British North American colonies from southern Europe and the West Indies, 1768–1772,' Institute for Research in the Behavioral, Economic, and Management Sciences, No. 258 (1969) and No. 270 (1970), Purdue University, Lafayette, Ind.

[2] These districts are described in Thomas C. Barrow, *Trade and Empire: The British Customs Service in Colonial America, 1660–1775* (Cambridge, Mass.: Harvard University Press, 1967), p. 269–72. A forty-third district, the Island of St Johns (Prince Edward Island), which had been separated officially from the government of Nova Scotia in 1769, began to be listed separately in the customs records in 1771. The port district for Newfoundland pertained only to St Johns. Hudson Bay was not included in the American records.

[3] For example, in some instances a commodity would be listed in different units, and it was not clear whether such entries represented different physical quantities of the commodity, or the same quantity specified in different units. In several important cases, such as tobacco exported from Virginia and Maryland in 1769–72, and rice exported from Charleston and St Augustine in 1771, it would appear that it was the same quantity given in different units. In other cases it would appear that the different units refer to different quantities that were exported.

changed. (For a complete discussion of these problems of interpretation and errors, see the Appendices to the papers cited on p. 204, note 1.) These records did not distinguish Africa from southern Europe and the Wine Islands for 1768. Estimated quantities of exports of spermaceti candles and American and West Indian rum to Africa in 1768 were derived by obtaining the ratios of these commodities exported in the other four years (1769–72) to southern Europe and Africa; and these ratios were applied to the quantities of these three commodities given for 1768. It was assumed that all other commodities listed for 1768 were exported to southern Europe, and that none went to Africa (in the years 1769–72 exports of some other commodities were made to Africa, but the magnitudes were not significant).

VALIDITY OF THE CUSTOMS DATA

The validity of the estimates of all the export values, and of the import values from southern Europe and the West Indies, in Chapter 6 depends, of course, upon the validity of the quantity data contained in the American customs records. Although errors of omission, over-entry, and arithmetic undoubtedly were incorporated into the final compilations of trade found in these records, it is the fact that they pertain only to the legal trade of the colonies which has usually posed the most serious question regarding their validity. In the export trades there was little or no incentive to engage in smuggling. Export duties were either nonexistent, or, as in the case of tobacco, very low relative to the value of the goods exported; so it seems unlikely that smuggling would have been of any significance to the export estimates in Chapter 6. With regard to imports, however, it may well have been important, because there were incentives on the part of the merchant to avoid paying import duties on such commodities as coffee, molasses, sugar, and wine. The estimates will understate the actual value of imports by the value of the goods that were smuggled. Smuggling is a factor, however, that must be considered commodity by commodity. The amount of smuggling of any commodity must have depended upon such factors as whether there was a duty, the relative magnitude of any such duty, and the ease of smuggling. In the case of molasses and sugar imported from the foreign West Indian islands, if it was entered falsely into colonial ports as British molasses or sugar (as some was), our estimates are not affected. To the extent that foreign molasses or sugar were smuggled, the quantities in Table 5 will understate the true quantities imported. But the values (computed using colonial prices) probably overstate the actual expenditures of foreign exchange, given the lower prices that prevailed in the foreign islands. The colonial prices must have covered costs of importing molasses and sugar, and such costs would have included the risks of smuggling. These risks, however, were largely borne by colonial merchants; thus the estimated values of such molasses and sugar would tend to overstate the actual expenditures of foreign exchange, and thus compensate (to some unknown degree) for the value of these commodities that were smuggled. Furthermore, for the period after 1763 when considerably increased effort was devoted to the enforcement of customs regulations and the collection of duties by the colonial customs administration, it is difficult to imagine that the value of goods smuggled comprised a very large part of the value of all goods imported. Nevertheless, the reader must be warned, and the foregoing estimates qualified, because of this unknown factor.

It is possible to make some checks of the American records using data from the English and Scottish customs records.[1] The annual data of the American and British records are not strictly comparable because of differences in the time required for shipping across the Atlantic and the clearing of British customs. Nevertheless, comparisons of two major exports to Britain, tobacco and rice, reveal only very small discrepancies. For tobacco exported from the colonies to Britain in 1770–2[2] the American records listed quantities that were about $5\frac{1}{2}$ per cent higher than the British records. When we consider, however, that the landed weight of tobacco in Britain was about 5 per cent less than the shipping weight from the colonies,[3] the above comparison makes the two sources look very close. If we make the same comparison for rice exported from the colonies to Great Britain, the difference is less than 1 per cent for the period 1768–72. These two comparisons are encouraging when assessing the accuracy of the customs data.

UNITS OF MEASURE

Various problems regarding the quantities recorded in the customs records arose when estimating the export and import values. Specific comments in most of these instances have been made in the notes to Tables 2 through 8. In those instances where the quantities of a commodity given in the customs records were listed in different units from the prices, it was necessary to know the equivalent of one unit in terms of another. The following equivalencies were used to convert to common units.

Bar iron	1 bar = 65 pounds
Beef and pork	1 barrel = 221 pounds
Bread and flour	1 barrel = 196 pounds
Coffee	1 hundredweight = 112 pounds
Pitch	1 hogshead = 2 barrels
Rice	1 barrel = 525 pounds = 4 firkins
Salt	1 hogshead = 10 bushels
Muscovado sugar	1 hogshead = 16 hundredweight
Wine	1 tun = 252 gallons

Units of colonial weights and measures could not be considered very exact by modern standards. The number of pounds the barrel or hogshead held could vary considerably for the same commodity. Under such circumstances, it is the average number of pounds which a barrel or hogshead held which is the relevant fact. It is hoped that the above equivalencies accurately reflect these averages.

[1] London, Public Record Office, Customs 3 and 14, respectively. The Scottish records for 1769 are not in the P.R.O. and are apparently missing.

[2] The 1768 figure in the American records was given only in hogsheads, and the 1769 figure from the Scottish records was missing, so no comparison was made for these two years.

[3] *Historical Statistics*, p. 748. The difference in weight was due to loss of moisture during the trans-Atlantic shipment.

The availability of price data has governed which commodity exports, and which imports from southern Europe and the West Indies, could be valued. The same commodities were valued for all regions (a commodity for which prices were available, but which was not exported from, or imported into, a region in any of the five years, does not appear under that region in Tables 2 through 8).

The price histories published by Bezanson and Cole[1] provided most of the prices used in the computations. These prices are monthly and annual average prices compiled largely from prices current that were published in colonial newspapers. Bezanson and her co-authors collected and published Philadelphia prices, and these were reprinted in Cole along with prices for Boston, New York and Charleston. If they were given for a particular commodity, Boston prices were used to compute the value of exports from or imports into the northern and New England colonies; Philadelphia prices were used for the middle colonies and the upper south; and Charleston prices were used for the lower south and Florida, the Bahamas, and the Bermuda Islands. If the price of a particular commodity was not given for the appropriate port, the price from the nearest port was used. For example, only Philadelphia prices of naval stores were available. These were used to compute the value of naval stores exported from all colonies.

Bezanson gave both monthly and annual average prices for most of the commodities which she listed. The annual average prices were used in the value computations. Cole gave only monthly average prices; unweighted annual average prices were computed from these and used in the value computations. Admittedly, this is not a satisfactory procedure unless one can assume that exports or imports of each commodity were distributed evenly over the year; but weighted average prices could not be computed because the quantity data were available only on an annual basis. The prices listed by Bezanson and Cole were given in the monetary unit of their respective colony. British pounds sterling were chosen as a common unit, and the prices were converted to sterling using the exchange rates given by Bezanson and Cole.

The commodities valued using prices from Bezanson and Cole were: beef and pork, bread and flour, spermaceti candles, cotton, dried fish, flaxseed, Indian corn, rice, wheat, hemp, indigo, bar iron, pig iron, molasses, pitch, tar, turpentine, potash, American rum, West Indian rum, Madeira wine, pine boards (from the lower south and Florida, the Bahamas, and the Bermuda Islands), salt, staves and muscovado sugar. Various problems arose associated with relating these prices to the quantities of commodities given in the customs records. For a complete discussion of how they were handled for each commodity, see the Appendixes to the papers cited on p. 204, note 1.

Prices for the other commodities valued in Tables 2 through 8 that were not taken from the price histories were found in various sources. Prices of beeswax, deerskins and whale oil were taken from Henry Lloyd's Letter

[1] Cited on p. 92, note 1.

Book.[1] A price of 54 shillings (Rhode Island currency) per 1,000 hoops, quoted by Richard Pares,[2] was used to value this commodity. Average prices of £6 and £10 per head were used to value cattle and horses respectively.[3] The price histories gave only Charleston prices for pine boards. According to statements by Victor S. Clark,[4] Charleston prices were higher than those which prevailed in the colonies to the north. The Charleston prices were thus used to value only exports of pine boards from the lower south and from Florida, the Bahamas and the Bermuda Islands. The following average annual prices (in pounds sterling per 1,000 feet) were constructed from prices quoted by Clark[5] and used to value pine boards from the other colonies:

	Northern and New England colonies, New York and New Jersey	Pennsylvania, Delaware, Maryland and Virginia
1768	1.35	2.00
1769	1.35	2.00
1770	1.60	2.25
1771	1.60	2.25
1772	1.70	2.35

Given that about one-quarter of the total value of colonial exports was tobacco, it is especially important that accurate prices be used to value the tobacco exported by Maryland and Virginia. Because the correspondence of a tobacco factor in Virginia, Roger Atkinson of Petersburg, suggested that current prices of tobacco in Virginia were substantially different than the prices given by Bezanson for Philadelphia, Atkinson's prices, which are listed in Table 1, were averaged and used to value tobacco exported from Virginia (and all other colonies except Maryland).[6] Since Maryland tobacco prices usually averaged less than Virginia prices, the Virginia prices were modified by a differential suggested by Gray[7] to obtain a series of average annual prices. The following average annual prices (in shillings per 100 pounds) were used to value tobacco exports:

	Maryland	Virginia and other colonies
1768	15.00	18.00
1769	17.00	20.00
1770	17.00	20.00
1771	13.67	16.67
1772	13.67	16.67

[1] Baker Library, Harvard University, Boston, Mass.
[2] *Yankees and Creoles: The Trade between North America and the West Indies before the American Revolution* (Cambridge, Mass.: Harvard University Press, 1956), p. 90.
[3] Invoice of the sales of the sloop *Biddeford*, September 10, 1766, Bourn Papers, Baker Library, Boston, Mass.
[4] *History of Manufactures in the United States, 1607–1860* (Washington, D.C.: The Carnegie Institution, 1916), pp. 136–7.
[5] *Ibid.*, pp. 587–8.
[6] *Roger Atkinson Letter Book, 1769–1776*, University of Virginia Library, Charlottesville, Va.
[7] Lewis C. Gray, *History of Agriculture in the Southern United States to 1860* (Gloucester, Mass.: Peter Smith, 1958; originally published by the Carnegie Institution of Washington, 1933), I, p. 274.

TABLE I.   *Quotations of tobacco prices in Virginia, 1767–72*

Dates	Prices per 100 lb (quoted in Virginia currency, shillings and pence)	Exchange rates[a]	Sterling prices (shillings)
Nov. 1767	20s.	1.25	16.00
Dec. 1767	22s. 6d.	1.25	18.00
Summer 1768	23s.–23s. 6d.	1.25	18.40–18.80
Fall 1768	22s. 6d.–25s.	1.25	18.00–20.00
July 1769	22s. 6d.–27s. 6d.	1.225	18.37–22.45
Aug.–Nov. 1769	25s.	1.225	20.41
Feb.–May 1770	25s.	1.15	21.74
July 1770	25s.	1.175–1.20	20.83–21.28
Nov. 1770	22s. 6d.–25s.	1.175–1.20	18.75–21.28
Dec. 1770–Sept. 1771	20s.	1.20	16.67
March 1772	20s.–25s.	1.20	16.67–20.83

Source: *Roger Atkinson Letter Book, 1769–1776*, University of Virginia Library, Charlottesville, Virginia.

[a] The exchange rates for 1767 were taken from Victor S. Clark, *History of Manufactures in the United States, 1607–1860* (Washington, D.C.: The Carnegie Institution of Washington, 1916), p. 586. No rates were quoted by Atkinson or Clark for 1768, so par of 1.25 was assumed. All other rates are from Atkinson's Letter Book.

POSSIBLE SOURCES OF ERROR IN THE ESTIMATES OF EXPORT VALUES

The possibility of errors resulting from inaccurate quantity data and smuggling have been mentioned above. It is obvious, too, that the price data used must accurately reflect what prices averaged over the years in this study. The fact that the use of unweighted average annual prices may have resulted in errors in the estimates has also been mentioned above.

The export values are supposed to represent the earnings of foreign exchange, and thus it is necessary that the commodities exported were owned by colonial residents. For one commodity, whale oil, there is evidence which suggests that part of these oil exports was not owned by colonial residents, but probably was taken by British-owned whaling ships and trans-shipped from the colonies. For 1771 and 1772, the English customs records noted that 3,244 tons (42 per cent of the total) of whale oil imported into Great Britain in these two years were London-owned. This was, however, the only commodity for which the British records noted British ownership of imports from the colonies. If this was actually the case, then this would not have been a significant source of error.

A more serious possible source of error may exist concerning the regional breakdowns of the estimates of total exports in Table 6.1 and imports from southern Europe and the West Indies (Table 6.2). It was assumed that the values of those commodities which were calculated (in Tables 2 through 8) comprised a certain percentage of total exports or imports. This percentage was taken from two contemporary estimates where the value of exports (Table 9) and imports from southern Europe and the West Indies (Table

10) had been estimated for all the colonies together, and no breakdown by both commodity and region was given. For some regions, use of this percentage may overstate the value of the commodities which were calculated and included in Tables 2 through 8, and thus understate total exports from that region. This may be the case with regard to the northern colonies, where furs from Quebec were important exports for which values were not computed in Table 2 due to lack of prices (for an attempt to correct for this factor for Quebec, see Table 3.2, Chapter 3, and the accompanying text). This same problem may affect the reliability of some of the other regional estimates. For example, exports of lumber and wood products from New Hampshire may be a similar case, and total exports from New England thus may be understated. The resulting regional estimates, then, must be viewed with more caution than the estimates of total exports from all colonies.

THE STATISTICAL EVIDENCE

The following tables contain the statistical evidence described in Chapter 6 and this Appendix which enables us to estimate the magnitudes of exports from and imports into the British North American colonies for the period 1768–72. Tables 2 through 6 present exports from each colonial region to the five major overseas areas of trade. Tables 7 and 8 contain estimates of the value of imports into each region from southern Europe and the West Indies. Table 9 presents the contemporary estimates of export values from the colonies for 1768 and 1770. Table 10 gives the contemporary estimate of the value of imports from southern Europe and the West Indies for 1768. Table 11 lists commodity imports (in quantities) from Africa for 1768–72. Finally, Tables 12 and 13 give the official value of imports from England and Scotland respectively for 1768–72.

TABLE 2. *Quantities and estimated values (in pounds sterling) of selected commodities exported from the British North American colonies to Great Britain, 1768–72[a]*

Commodity (unit)	1768		1769		1770		1771		1772	
	Quantity	Value	Quantity	Value	Quantity	Value	Quantity	Value	Quantity	Value
From northern colonies										
Bread and flour (tn)					0.60	6				
Deerskins (lb)[b]	11,696	5,556	104,116	10,050	145,821	14,392	209,042	20,420	103,120	10,468
Fish, dried (qn)			13,321	6,607	12,082	6,174	11,362	5,783	16,952	8,502
Grain, wheat (bu)	45	10			39	8	40	9	5,940	1,443
Iron										
bar (tn)			0.57	8			19.57	294		
pig (tn)							186.39	900	200.72	1,016
Naval stores										
pitch (bbl)	55	24	393	126	20	7	13	5	5	2
tar (bbl)									5	3
turpentine (bbl)										
Oil, whale (tn)	690.36	8,284	309.14	3,710	918.47	11,022	2,342.71	28,113	815.44	9,785
Potash (tn)	8.13	178	35.20	772	41.19	1,153	35.74	1,101	65.12	1,478
Rum, West Indian (gal)							13,500	1,364		
Wood products										
pine boards (1,000 ft)	167	225	271	366	203	325	180	290	220	374
staves and headings (1,000)	265	723	377	1,008	78	237	243	764	188	599
Total, northern colonies		15,000		22,647		33,324		59,043		33,670
From New England										
Beef and pork (bbl)[a]	939	1,776							40	93
Beeswax (lb)	1,731	86	3,933	197	7,373	369	2,758	139	6,874	344
Bread and flour (tn)	8.25	84					0.60	6		
Cotton (lb)	17,072	851	500	22			300	13	19,930	917
Deerskins (lb)[b]			10	5	4	2	2,000	1,018	1,800	225
Fish, dried (qn)									7	4

TABLE 2. *Quantities and estimated values (in pounds sterling) of selected commodities exported from the British North American colonies to Great Britain, 1768–72[a] – continued*

Commodity (unit)	1768 Quantity	1768 Value	1769 Quantity	1769 Value	1770 Quantity	1770 Value	1771 Quantity	1771 Value	1772 Quantity	1772 Value
Flaxseed (bu)	5,256	870	6,370	812	4,407	738	7,190	1,409	9,014	2,461
Grain										
Indian corn (bu)	140	11		100						
rice (bbl)	1	2	9	24	9					
Indigo (lb)	1,790	270			102	252	77	184	6	20
Iron										
bar (tn)	40.03	721	11.06	163	7.00	126	1.12	17		
pig (tn)	144.83	714	183.48	918	235.85	1,191	178.50	863	118.80	601
Naval stores										
pitch (bbl)	1,646	709	473	178	240	90	51	18	12	5
tar (bbl)	8,506	2,815	5,041	1,618	3,413	1,256	11,303	4,239	11,317	5,025
turpentine (bbl)	2,615	1,246	2,883	1,334	1,813	814	1,055	456	215	112
Oil, whale (tn)	3,594.26	43,130	3,870.52	46,446	4,011.42	48,137	2,838.68	34,064	2,536.46	30,438
Potash (tn)	926.62	20,340	880.42	19,316	760.53	21,294	952.62	29,359	953.28	21,639
Rum										
American (gal)[c]	1,700	104	21,340	1,366	600	38	700	43	117	7
West Indian (gal)			324	34	6,158	600	1,600	162		
Wood products										
pine boards (1,000 ft)	1,622	2,190	2,486	3,356	3,303	5,286	1,596	2,552	1,432	2,435
staves and headings (1,000)	867	2,378	720	1,920	981	3,008	947	2,966	1,205	3,825
Total, New England		78,297		77,718		83,201		77,508		68,151
From middle colonies										
Beeswax (lb)	65,450	3,273	21,152	1,058	37,198	1,860	50,618	2,531	39,805	1,990
Beef and pork (bbl)[a]	471	891	123	264	54	113	115	228	24	56
Bread and flour (tn)	3,111.87	31,586	2,102.83	19,977	48.00	490	5.05	53	24.68	310
Cotton (lb)	11,100	572	6,480	282	6,097	262	9,600	360	14,093	557

TABLE 2. *Quantities and estimated values (in pounds sterling) of selected commodities exported from the British North American colonies to Great Britain, 1768–72[a] – continued*

Commodity (unit)	1768 Quantity	1768 Value	1769 Quantity	1769 Value	1770 Quantity	1770 Value	1771 Quantity	1771 Value	1772 Quantity	1772 Value
Deerskins (lb)[b]	7,692	1,273	7,250	752	31,775	2,927	22,330	2,271	19,802	1,726
Flaxseed (bu)	5,384	415	4,305	549	2,142	359	3,821	749	3,383	923
Grain										
Indian corn (bu)	480	1,200	128	336	346	858	35	4	45	5
rice (bbl)	38,321	7,262	6,547	1,133			3,723	8,883	1,282	4,358
wheat (bu)	1,487	224	380	69					1,644	395
Indigo (lb)										
Iron										
bar (tn)	617.84	8,804	1,075.23	15,860	1,378.10	20,741	1,192.50	17,339	541.50	9,092
pig (tn)	2,029.30	10,005	1,831.80	9,159	2,645.10	13,358	2,014.31	9,729	1,221.25	6,180
Naval stores										
pitch (bbl)	613	264	462	174	221	83	51	19	572	258
tar (bbl)	5,309	1,758	1,423	457	1,794	660	3,007	1,128	6,987	3,102
turpentine (bbl)	6,676	3,181	4,047	1,871	2,910	1,307	141	61	1,134	587
Oil, whale (tn)	361.46	4,338	352.52	4,230	272.24	3,267	122.38	1,469	25.27	303
Potash (tn)	402.62	8,837	320.03	7,022	365.30	10,228	679.43	20,940	622.80	14,137
Rum										
American (gal)[c]	47,098	3,156	3,664	249	24,394	2,378	2,027	134		
West Indian (gal)			1,170	122			845	86	504	54
Wood products										
pine boards (1,000 ft)	99	175	257	486	545	1,093	260	463	118	263
staves and headings (1,000)	643	1,762	387	1,033	708	2,171	1,065	3,337	754	2,392
Total, middle colonies		88,976		65,083		62,155		69,784		46,688
From upper south										
Beef and pork (lb)[d]	5,250	263	3,100	155	7,672	384	4,200	210		
Beeswax (lb)									4	9

TABLE 2. *Quantities and estimated values (in pounds sterling) of selected commodities exported from the British North American colonies to Great Britain, 1768–72[a] – continued*

Commodity (unit)	1768 Quantity	1768 Value	1769 Quantity	1769 Value	1770 Quantity	1770 Value	1771 Quantity	1771 Value	1772 Quantity	1772 Value
Bread and flour (tn)	275.01	2,792	152.73	1,451	214.20	2,185	208.30	2,202	214.60	2,697
Cotton (lb)	43,350	2,233	2,950	128	1,727	74	1,400	53	2,484	98
Deerskins (lb)[b]	5,636	933	69,188	5,972	175,260	14,282	168,263	13,724	197,592	16,304
Flaxseed (bu)			434	55	140	23	2,514	493	48	13
Grain										
Indian corn (bu)	91,276	7,028								
rice (bbl)	9	22					10	24		
wheat (bu)	66,422	12,587	38,231	6,614	11,700	2,246	47,029	9,618	6,524	1,566
Hemp (tn)	398.41	10,187	124.77	3,645						
Indigo (lb)	2,700	408	7,087.00	1,283	2,741	495			2,423	626
Iron										
bar (tn)	2,568.11	35,740	1,068.89	15,766	717.24	10,795	921.43	13,398	443.89	7,453
pig (tn)	943.68	4,653	2,678.00	13,390	2,866.25	14,475	2,873.00	13,876	2,375.95	12,022
Naval stores										
pitch (bbl)	7,916	3,412	564	213			949	349	12	5
tar (bbl)	14,978	4,958	17,004	5,458	12,792	4,707	17,993	6,747	21,006	9,327
turpentine (bbl)	472	225	10,317	4,772	1,665	721	4,053	1,750	1,411	730
Oil, whale (tn)	13.49	296	2.89	63	5.91	165	1.00	12	5.12	116
Potash (tn)							0.10	3		
Rum										
American (gal)[c]	1,430	96					685	45		
West Indian (gal)							1,200	121	3,530	376
Tobacco (cwt)	691,520	585,794	831,196	792,523	764,186	723,286	1,102,001	860,120	1,043,514	818,916
Wood products										
pine board (1,000 ft)	100	202	115	230	667	1,502	93	210	34	81
staves and headings (1,000)	2,229	6,112	2,734	7,291	2,602	7,980	3,414	10,699	3,464	10,995
Total, upper south		677,941		859,009		783,320		933,654		881,334

TABLE 2. Quantities and estimated values (in pounds sterling) of selected commodities exported from the British North American colonies to Great Britain, 1768-72[a] – continued

Commodity (unit)	1768 Quantity	1768 Value	1769 Quantity	1769 Value	1770 Quantity	1770 Value	1771 Quantity	1771 Value	1772 Quantity	1772 Value
From lower south										
Beeswax (lb)	11,224	561	20,471	1,023	10,551	528	18,722	937	8,623	432
Beef and pork (bbl)[d]	147	185	83	122	3	4	1	2	36	62
Bread and flour (tn)	8.41	85	0.75	7			2.30	24		
Cotton (lb)	3,300	170	554	25	2,444	105	2,615	98	1,128	45
Deerskins (lb)[b]			392,739	39,838	328,832	31,731	438,344	42,241	359,482	34,563
Flaxseed (bu)	133	22	702	90	92	15	854	167		
Grain										
Indian corn (bu)	8,361	732							4,355	662
rice (bbl)	91,671	214,886	79,692	173,838	73,625	128,907	95,521	191,567	96,085	283,750
Hemp (tn)	9.27	237	101.35	2,961	4.31	151	6.28	207	1.10	38
Indigo (lb)	517,301	78,113	416,436	75,375	573,017	103,430	454,207	106,285	758,677	196,118
Iron, bar (tn)	16.80	345								
Naval stores										
pitch (bbl)	11,489	4,951	12,293	4,635	7,666	2,871	6,330	2,329	5,362	2,419
tar (bbl)	59,155	19,581	59,466	19,089	60,012	22,084	71,575	26,841	60,280	26,764
turpentine (bbl)	14,373	6,849	19,745	9,132	8,697	3,905	8,947	3,865	6,240	3,229
Oil, whale (tn)	1.50	18	5.00	60						
Potash (tn)	1.50	33	1.00	22						
Rum										
American (gal)[c]	1,240	108	970	81	6,080	593	200	15	640	68
West Indian (gal)							370	37		
Tobacco (cwt)	3,671	3,304	8,256	8,256	900	900	23,085	19,241	22,226	18,525
Wood products										
pine boards (1,000 ft)	231	644	137	377	218	649	198	596	105	325
staves and headings (1,000)	581	1,802	877	2,784	547	1,737	628	2,136	463	1,551
Total, lower south		332,626		337,715		297,610		396,588		568,551

TABLE 2. *Quantities and estimated values (in pounds sterling) of selected commodities exported from the British North American colonies to Great Britain, 1768–72*^{a} – *continued*

Commodity (unit)	1768		1769		1770		1771		1772	
	Quantity	Value	Quantity	Value	Quantity	Value	Quantity	Value	Quantity	Value
From Florida, Bahama and Bermuda Is.										
Beeswax (lb)									600	30
Cotton (lb)	6,672	344	27,900	1,214	24,457	1,051	7,587	285	4,600	182
Deerskins (lb)^b			103,969	12,200	117,932	12,358	248,947	25,696	204,530	21,185
Grain, rice (bbl)			340	61	1	2	20	40	192	567
Indigo (lb)	486	73			8,835	1,595	43,399	10,155	46,583	12,042
Naval stores										
pitch (bbl)	326	141	94	35	138	52				
tar (bbl)			119	38	84	31				
Rum, West Indian (gal)			100	10					11,176	1,190
Tobacco (cwt)							240	200		
Wood products										
pine boards (1,000 ft)	1	2			5	17	2	7	6	19
staves and headings (1,000)										
Total, Florida, Bahama and Bermuda Is.		560		13,558		15,106		36,383		35,215
Total, British North American colonies		1,193,400		1,375,730		1,274,716		1,572,960		1,633,609

^{a} All quantities and values have been rounded to the nearest whole number (except for several commodities for which fractional units of quantities were converted to decimals; and pine boards and staves and headings, which are given in units of 1,000 ft and 1,000 number, respectively).

^{b} Deerskins were not given by the source for 1768.

^{c} The source did not distinguish between American and West Indian rum for 1768. Exports of rum in 1768 have been listed and valued as American rum, but West Indian rum may be included in the 1768 quantities.

^{d} The source gave beef and pork in tons for 1768 and 1769. It was converted to barrels assuming an average barrel weight of 221 lb (Cole, *Wholesale Commodity Prices*, p. x).

TABLE 3. *Quantities and estimated values (in pounds sterling) of selected commodities exported from the British North American colonies to Ireland, 1768–72*ᵃ

Commodity (unit)	1768 Quantity	1768 Value	1769 Quantity	1769 Value	1770 Quantity	1770 Value	1771 Quantity	1771 Value	1772 Quantity	1772 Value
From northern colonies										
Grain, wheat (bu)	2,293	1,089			3,500	709	49,983	11,396		
Fish, dried (qn)	4,541	752	480	238	450	230	6,119	3,115	2,850	1,429
Flaxseed (bu)	73.76	885	6.30	76	22.25	267	143.90	1,727	48.34	580
Oil, whale (tn)										
Wood products										
pine boards (1,000 ft)ᵇ	1	1	10	14	8	12				
staves and headings (1,000)	8	21	57	152	1	4	19	60	10	30
Total, northern colonies		2,748		480		1,222		16,298		2,039
From New England										
Bread and flour (tn)			10.90	104	1.11	11				
Flaxseed (bu)			16,233	2,069	5,743	962	2,500	490	5,745	1,569
Potash (tn)			1.98	43						
Rum, American (gal)ᶜ	3,574	218								
Wood products										
pine boards (1,000 ft)ᵇ	16	22	32	43					3	5
staves and headings (1,000)	55	150	86	230	30	92	29	91	65	206
Total, New England		390		2,489		1,065		581		1,780
From middle colonies										
Bread and flour (tn)	295.36	2,997	1,183.65	11,245	1,153.83	11,770	787.06	8,320	104.58	1,315
Flaxseed (bu)	240,295	39,769	165,516	21,104	256,948	43,039	147,517	28,914	157,874	43,100
Grain										
Indian corn (bu)	235	18	294	26	10,216	1,961	14,358	2,937		
wheat (bu)	1,100	208	44,131	7,634	64.25	967	24.00	349		
Iron, bar (tn)ᵈ	111.57	1,590	38.50	568			0.16	2		
Oil, whale (tn)	1.50	18								

TABLE 3. *Quantities and estimated values (in pounds sterling) of selected commodities exported from the British North American colonies to Ireland, 1768-72[a] – continued*

Commodity (unit)	1768		1769		1770		1771		1772	
	Quantity	Value	Quantity	Value	Quantity	Value	Quantity	Value	Quantity	Value
Potash (tn)	5.64	124	3.25	71						
Rum										
American (gal)[c]	22,368	1,499	2,020	137	7,931	563	4,560	301	1,815	123
West Indian (gal)			2,890	300	10,704	1,044	4,575	463	19,719	2,100
Wood products										
pine boards (1,000 ft)[b]	92	157	25	44	43	68	20	39	14	31
staves and headings (1,000)	1,684	4,616	1,426	3,801	1,963	6,021	1,680	5,265	1,270	4,031
Total, middle colonies		50,996		44,930		65,433		46,590		50,700
From upper south										
Bread and flour (tn)	173.89	1,765	1,095.85	10,411	2,361.68	24,089	1,438.30	15,203	119.85	1,507
Flaxseed (bu)	15,685	2,596	13,821	1,763	30,101	5,042	9,191	1,801	20,243	5,526
Grain										
Indian corn (bu)	4,860	374			150	18	8,500	897		
wheat (bu)	20,074	3,804	71,914	12,441	136,269	26,163	65,297	13,353	19,941	4,786
Iron, bar (tn)[d]	61.00	869	39.50	583	21.00	316	2.00	29	17.00	285
Rum, West Indian (gal)									540	58
Wood products										
pine boards (1,000 ft)[b]	107	213	60	121	4	8	5	12		
staves and headings (1,000)	312	855	430	1,148	805	2,467	939	2,941	884	2,808
Total, upper south		10,476		26,467		58,103		34,236		14,970
From lower south										
Bread and flour (tn)	2.63	27	42.10	400	66.50	678	62.00	655	5.50	69
Flaxseed (bu)	1,734	287	4,347	554			5,143	1,008	2,554	697
Grain, wheat (bu)					4,290	824				
Rum, West Indian (gal)							300	32		

TABLE 3. *Quantities and estimated values (in pounds sterling) of selected commodities exported from the British North American colonies to Ireland, 1768–72*[a] *– continued*

Commodity (unit)	1768		1769		1770		1771		1772	
	Quantity	Value	Quantity	Value	Quantity	Value	Quantity	Value	Quantity	Value
Wood products										
pine boards (1,000 ft)[b]	36	100	4	11	18	54	5	15		
staves and headings (1,000)	157	487	20	64	31	98	86	292	5	17
Total, lower south		901		1,029		1,654		2,002		783
Total, British North American colonies		65,511		75,395		127,477		99,707		70,272

[a] All quantities and values have been rounded to the nearest whole number (except for several commodities for which fractional units of quantities were converted to decimals; and pine boards and staves and headings, which are given in units of 1,000 feet and 1,000 number, respectively).

[b] Pine boards were not distinguished from other boards in the source for 1768. The quantities given as pine boards for 1768 may thus include oak and cedar boards.

[c] The source did not distinguish between American and West Indian rum for 1768. Exports of rum in 1768 have been listed and valued as American rum, but West Indian rum may be included in the 1768 quantities.

[d] The type of iron exported in 1768 was not specified. It has been assumed that it was bar iron.

TABLE 4. *Quantities and estimated values (in pounds sterling) of selected commodities exported from the British North American colonies to southern Europe and the Wine Islands, 1768–72[a]*

Commodity (unit)	1768[b] Quantity	1768[b] Value	1769 Quantity	1769 Value	1770 Quantity	1770 Value	1771 Quantity	1771 Value	1772 Quantity	1772 Value
From northern colonies										
Bread and flour (tn)							18.70	198	33.35	419
Fish, dried (qn)	127,106	60,376	168,465	83,558	185,867	94,978	404,995	206,142	265,306	133,051
Grain,										
Indian corn (bu)							1,180	124	260	30
wheat (bu)	23,362	5,256			29,584	5,991	103,269	23,545	121,856	29,611
Oil, whale (tn)	201.90	2,423	191.27	2,296	172.44	2,069	281.98	3,383	274.40	3,293
Rum, West Indian (gal)									915	97
Wood products										
pine boards (1,000 ft)[c]	8	10	51	69	98	158	29	46	2	3
staves and headings (1,000)	17	46	9	22	3	9	2	6	1	3
Total, northern colonies		68,111		85,945		103,205		233,444		166,507
From New England										
Beef and pork[d]	599	1,131	345	737	66	138	122	242	25	58
Beeswax (lb)	4,100	205	5,080	255	1,300	65	3,150	158	15,960	798
Bread and flour (tn)	186.12	1,889	525.65	4,994	71.31	728	196.88	2,081	79.35	997
Candles, spermaceti (lb)	5,316	359	19,093	1,289	10,867	723	5,850	384	8,760	623
Fish, dried (qn)	116,273	55,230	116,176	57,623	104,695	53,499	131,200	66,781	105,364	52,840
Grain										
Indian corn (bu)	7,773	598	4,379	388	13,561	1,587	7,466	788	3,018	345
rice (bbl)			322	844	32	79				
wheat (bu)	200	45	3,311	654	1,078	218	16,476	3,756		
Oil, whale (tn)	21.85	262	21.07	253	2.38	29	7.14	86	0.95	11
Rum										
American (gal)[e]	10,744	655	13,871	888	30,273	1,893	26,915	1,669	28,599	1,730
West Indian (gal)			1,820	190	3,904	381	1,080	109		
Wood products										
pine boards (1,000 ft)[c]	687	927	262	354	292	467	424	679	237	404
staves and headings (1,000)	409	1,119	322	859	145	444	274	858	203	647
Total, New England		62,420		69,328		60,251		77,591		58,453

TABLE 4. *Quantities and estimated values (in pounds sterling) of selected commodities exported from the British North American colonies to southern Europe and the Wine Islands, 1768–72[a] – continued*

Commodity (unit)	1768[b] Quantity	1768[b] Value	1769 Quantity	1769 Value	1770 Quantity	1770 Value	1771 Quantity	1771 Value	1772 Quantity	1772 Value
From middle colonies										
Beeswax (lb)	16,600	830	21,340	1,067	39,799	1,990	20,572	1,029	21,580	1,079
Beef and pork (bbl)[a]	205	387	301	646	159	331	122	243	39	91
Bread and flour (tn)	5,112.00	51,886	17,278.38	164,145	15,369.02	156,763	10,124.40	107,014	14,661.16	184,291
Candles, spermaceti (lb)	3,100	209	5,175	349	800	53	1,800	118	5,425	386
Fish, dried (qn)	288	137	60	30	824	421	683	348	12	6
Grain										
Indian corn (bu)	118,608	9,133	119,458	10,572	83,356	9,753	109,453	11,548	127,378	14,585
rice (bbl)	4	10			547	1,355	662	1,579	278	945
wheat (bu)	191,255	36,243	248,880	43,056	173,590	33,329	92,938	19,006	127,942	30,706
Rum										
American (gal)[e]	3,481	233			15,037	1,068	11,957	790	5,630	383
West Indian (gal)					5,077	495	1,060	107	100	11
Wood products										
pine boards (1,000 ft)[c]	67	106	114	157	52	102	47	75	106	183
staves and headings (1,000)	1,513	4,146	956	2,549	1,037	3,180	878	2,753	635	2,015
Total, middle colonies		103,320		222,571		208,840		144,610		234,681
From upper south										
Beeswax (lb)	4,786	240	13,012	650	5,100	255	2,857	143	13,400	670
Beef and pork (bbl)[a]	56	106	60	129			100	199		
Bread and flour (tn)	1,176.52	11,942	3,212.10	30,515	3,031.46	30,921	1,977.75	20,905	3,176.63	39,931
Candles, spermaceti (lb)	125	8							175	12
Fish, dried (qn)									30	15
Grain										
Indian corn (bu)	217,293	16,732	152,797	13,523	71,314	8,344	93,389	9,852	117,439	13,447
wheat (bu)	214,772	40,699	609,033	105,363	381,499	73,248	158,627	32,440	165,635	39,752
Rum										
American (gal)[e]	760	51								
West Indian (gal)										
Wood products										
pine boards (1,000 ft)[c]	117	234	63	125	20	45			50	119
staves and headings (1,000)	814	2,231	263	702	102	314	303	949	267	849
Total, upper south		72,243		151,007		113,127		64,488		94,948

TABLE 4. *Quantities and estimated values (in pounds sterling) of selected commodities exported from the British North American colonies to southern Europe and the Wine Islands, 1768–72ᵃ – continued*

Commodity (unit)	1768[b]		1769		1770		1771		1772	
	Quantity	Value	Quantity	Value	Quantity	Value	Quantity	Value	Quantity	Value
From lower south										
Beeswax (lb)	7,180	359	6,819	341	4,330	217	908	45	3,158	158
Beef and pork (bbl)[d]	10	13	342	502		304	2.50	26	125	9
Bread and flour (t)	14.44	146	36.00	342	29.76	166			46	23
Candles, spermaceti (lb)										
Fish, dried (qn)	136	65			2,500					
Grain										
Indian corn (bu)	7,897	691	16,850	1,669	6,989	734	3,865	483	7,942	1,207
rice (bbl)	30,027	70,387	152,147[f]	63,217	35,718	62,538	78,797	30,100	9,708	28,669
wheat (bu)	940	178	1,700	294	2,810	540				
Oil, whale (t)			4.00	48						
Rum										
American (gal)[c]	1,110	97	783	81	270	26	90	7	2,285	202
West Indian (gal)										
Wood products										
pine boards (1,000 ft)[c]	2		26	71					2	6
staves and headings (1,000)	505	1,563	500	1,587	404	1,284	364	1,241	365	1,223
Total, lower south		73,505		68,152		65,809		31,902		31,497
Total, British North American colonies		379,599		597,003		551,232		553,035		586,086

ᵃ Southern Europe and the Wine Islands consisted of European areas south of Cape Finisterre (primarily Spain, Portugal, and Italy), the Azores, and the Madeira, Canary, and Cape Verde Islands. All quantities and values have been rounded to the nearest whole number (except for several commodities for which fractional units of quantities were converted to decimals; and pine boards and staves and headings, which are given in units of 1,000 feet and 1,000 number, respectively).

ᵇ The source did not list Africa separately from southern Europe and the Wine Islands for 1768. Estimated exports of spermaceti candles and rum to Africa for 1768 were derived by obtaining the ratios of these two commodities exported during the four years 1769–72 to southern Europe and to Africa, and applying these ratios to the quantities of rum and candles given for 1768. It was assumed that all other commodity exports listed in this category for 1768 went to southern Europe.

ᶜ Pine boards were not distinguished from other boards in the source for 1768. The quantities given as pine boards for 1768 may thus include oak and cedar boards.

ᵈ The source gave beef and pork in tons for 1768 and 1769 for some colonies. These quantities were converted to barrels assuming an average barrel weight of 221 lb (Cole, *Wholesale Commodity Prices*, p. x).

ᵉ The source did not distinguish between American and West Indian rum for 1768. Exports of rum in 1768 have been listed and valued as American rum, but West Indian rum may be included in the 1768 quantities.

ᶠ Hundredweight.

TABLE 5. *Quantities and estimated values (in pounds sterling) of selected commodities exported from the British North American colonies to the West Indies, 1768–72[a]*

Commodity (unit)	1768		1769		1770		1771		1772	
	Quantity	Value	Quantity	Value	Quantity	Value	Quantity	Value	Quantity	Value
From northern colonies										
Beef and pork (bbl)[b]	22	42	15	33	81	168			50	117
Bread and flour (tn)[c]	1.75	18	3.20	30	103.80	1,059	76.38	808	57.70	725
Candles, spermaceti (lb)			1,073	73	250	17	125	8		
Fish, dried (qn)	13,883	6,594	13,065	6,480	13,248	6,770	18,426	9,379	35,447	17,776
Grain										
Indian corn (bu)	588	45	40	4	200	41	1,000	228		
rice (bbl)									25	85
wheat (tn)	24	48	37	74	32	65	39	79	18	35
Hoops (1,000)										
Livestock										
cattle (no.)	27	162								
horses (no.)	16	160	99	990	17	170	54	540		
Oil, whale (tn)	4.30	51	7.03	84	6.86	83	18.91	227	18.87	227
Wine (tn)							0.12	7		
Wood products										
pine boards (1,000 ft)[a]	96	130	195	263	289	464	158	253	148	253
staves and headings (1,000)					4	11	2	8	12	37
Total, northern colonies		7,250		8,031		8,848		11,537		19,255
From New England										
Beef and pork (bbl)[b]	8,473	16,012	8,891	19,028	8,038	16,800	5,434	10,811	6,555	15,274
Bread and flour (tn)[c]	768.49	7,799	1,625.31	15,440	1,966.81	20,061	1,462.12	15,455	972.42	12,223
Candles, spermaceti (lb)	225,210	15,202	239,745	16,182	324,650	21,589	346,170	22,674	220,066	15,625
Fish, dried (qn)	155,455	73,841	168,860	83,754	179,258	91,600	193,194	98,336	251,720	126,238
Grain										
Indian corn (bu)	12,690	977	9,846	872	11,174	1,308	14,437	1,523	5,995	686
rice (bbl)	35	87	148	388	551	1,366	247	589	12	41
wheat (bu)									16	4
Hoops (1,000)	2,724	5,515	3,091	6,257	3,204	6,486	3,564	7,216	3,909	7,916
Iron, bar (tn)	1.72	31	5.50	81	13.06	235	6.00	90	3.71	71

TABLE 5. *Quantities and estimated values (in pounds sterling) of selected commodities exported from the British North American colonies to the West Indies, 1768-72[a] – continued*

Commodity (unit)	1768 Quantity	1768 Value	1769 Quantity	1769 Value	1770 Quantity	1770 Value	1771 Quantity	1771 Value	1772 Quantity	1772 Value
Livestock										
cattle (no.)	3,561	21,366	2,683	16,098	3,038	18,228	3,287	19,722	3,719	22,314
horses (no.)	4,420	44,200	5,515	55,150	5,932	59,320	5,720	57,200	5,356	53,560
Oil, whale (tn)	192.01	2,303	242.71	2,912	189.85	2,278	105.99	1,272	170.30	2,043
Wine (tn)	2.82	162	5.24	319	0.48	31	1.73	104	1.65	111
Wood products										
pine boards (1,000 ft)[a]	24,291	32,794	23,854	32,204	25,716	41,145	27,992	44,789	28,167	47,883
staves and headings (1,000)	4,009	10,992	3,399	9,065	3,448	10,572	3,861	12,098	4,382	13,912
Total, New England		231,281		257,750		291,019		291,879		317,901
From middle colonies										
Beef and pork (bbl)[b]	6,460	12,206	7,728	16,538	8,373	17,498	6,453	12,842	5,077	11,829
Bread and flour (tn)[c]	10,393.87	105,498	15,593.21	148,135	17,360.54	177,078	16,720.88	176,740	19,711.24	247,770
Candles, spermaceti (lb)	30,200	2,039	17,260	1,165	22,950	1,527	22,150	1,451	22,275	1,581
Fish, dried (qn)	2,774	1,318	2,940	1,459	2,450	1,252	2,733	1,391	6,194	3,106
Grain,										
Indian corn (bu)	59,756	4,601	36,170	3,201	61,363	7,180	110,611	11,669	63,382	7,257
rice (bbl)	28	70	215	564	893	2,214	637	1,520	330	1,122
wheat (bu)					755	145	28	6	144	35
Hoops (1,000)	344	698	312	630	384	773	519	1,050	432	874
Iron, bar (tn)	196.97[e]	2,807	201.85	2,977	211.49	3,183	156.55	2,276	200.25	3,363
Livestock										
cattle (no.)	111	666	162	972	67	402	1	6	65	390
horses (no.)	139	1,390	199	1,990	250	2,500	272	2,720	151	1,510
Oil, whale (tn)	35.15	421	63.05	757	68.60	823	30.32	364	43.42	521
Wine (tn)	64.13	3,680	17.43	1,058	39.60	2,550	26.07	1,575	43.52	2,917
Wood products										
pine boards (1,000 ft)[a]	1,217	2,077	1,428	2,330	2,198	4,170	2,400	4,429	6,089	12,959
staves and headings (1,000)	3,886	10,653	3,013	8,033	3,848	11,802	4,410	13,817	6,278	19,930
Total, middle colonies		148,124		189,809		233,097		231,856		315,164
From upper south										
Beef and pork (bbl)[b]	4,686	8,855	7,377	15,787	7,112	14,863	4,442	8,840	5,305	12,360
Bread and flour (tn)[c]	1,575.88	15,996	2,810.85	26,703	3,610.15	36,824	3,181.86	33,632	2,710.25	34,068

TABLE 5. Quantities and estimated values (in pounds sterling) of selected commodities exported from the British North American colonies to the West Indies, 1768–72[a] – continued

Commodity (unit)	1768		1769		1770		1771		1772	
	Quantity	Value	Quantity	Value	Quantity	Value	Quantity	Value	Quantity	Value
Candles, spermaceti (lb)	5	2	525	35	250	17			250	18
Fish, dried (qn)			50	25	1,090	557	24	12	108	54
Grain										
Indian corn (bu)	454,707	35,013	447,939	39,643	275,809	32,270	419,431	44,250	396,650	45,417
rice (bbl)	28	70	53	106	148	299	25	60	60	24
Hoops (1,000)	195	396					146	295	279	566
Iron, bar (tn)	19.11	272	33.90	500	41.39	623	31.41	456	27.08	454
Livestock, horses (no.)	2	20	3	30	5	50	8	80	5	50
Oil, whale (tn)	2.29	27								
Wine (tn)	1.75	100	1.25	15	1.12	13	0.25	15	1.25	15
Wood products										
pine boards (1,000 ft)[a]	721	1,442	700	1,399	649	1,459	2,031	4,570	2,545	5,981
staves and headings (1,000)	1,874	5,137	1,222	3,257	2,096	6,426	2,773	8,691	3,449	10,952
Total, upper south		67,330		87,500		93,401		100,901		109,959
From lower south										
Beef and pork (bbl)[b]	5,735	7,225	6,740	9,907	5,172	7,292	3,706	5,632	3,834	6,633
Bread and flour (tn)[c]	132.63	1,346	296.95	2,821	319.95	3,264	292.64	3,093	118.09	1,485
Candles, spermaceti (lb)	3,600	243	1,350	91	2,150	143	3,060	200	1,125	80
Fish, dried (qn)	176	84	8	4	25	13	32	16	62	31
Grain										
Indian corn (bu)	95,141	8,326	85,044	8,419	88,505	9,293	60,053	7,507	73,907	11,233
rice (bbl)	16,042	37,605	21,620	47,161	39,488	69,139	30,576	61,318	21,869	64,582
Hoops (1,000)	62	126	113	229	51	103	27	54	19	38
Iron, bar (tn)	1.00	21	0.05	1	7.03	124				
Livestock										
cattle (no.)	37	222	42	252	79	474	97	582	217	1,302
horses (no.)	322	3,220	581	5,810	488	4,880	365	3,650	505	5,050
Oil, whale (tn)	1.27	15	0.63	8	0.99	11	5.09	61	7.50	330
Wine (tn)	64.46	2,096	5.24	180	2.78	123	1.16	51		
Wood products										
pine boards (1,000 ft)[a]	5,355	14,942	5,257	14,510	5,417	16,143	5,723	17,225	6,536	20,262
staves and headings (1,000)	701	2,173	1,663	5,280	1,684	5,345	1,876	6,380	2,019	6,764
Total, lower south		77,644		94,673		116,347		105,769		117,790

TABLE 5. *Quantities and estimated values (in pounds sterling) of selected commodities exported from the British North American colonies to the West Indies, 1768–72^a – continued*

Commodity (unit)	1768 Quantity	1768 Value	1769 Quantity	1769 Value	1770 Quantity	1770 Value	1771 Quantity	1771 Value	1772 Quantity	1772 Value
From Florida, Bahama and Bermuda Is.										
Beef and pork (bbl)^b	203	255	126	185	323	455	56	85	110	190
Bread and flour (tn)^c	149.98	1,523	124.43	1,182	98.98	1,010	125.91	1,331	29.20	367
Candles, spermaceti (lb)	8	4	200	14	1,375	91				
Fish, dried (qn)			32	16	10	5				
Grain										
Indian corn (bu)	7,400	648	10,503	1,040	3,575	375	3,840	480	5,628	855
rice (bbl)			210	458			65	130	123	363
Hoops (1,000)			1	10	2	3				5
Iron, bar (tn)									0.10	2
Livestock, horses (no.)						10	45	450	39	390
Oil, whale (tn)			2.04	24	0.87	24				
Wine (tn)			4.46	153	0.95	42	0.95	42	0.48	21
Wood products										
pine boards (1,000 ft)^d	51	142	46	126	124	370	87	262	169	523
staves and headings (1,000)	23	70	11	35	37	118	13	44	32	105
Total, Florida, Bahama and Bermuda Is.		2,642		3,243		2,479		2,824		2,821
Total, British North American colonies		534,271		641,006		745,191		744,766		882,890

^a The West Indies include all British and foreign islands and mainland parts of the Caribbean area. All quantities and values have been rounded to the nearest whole number (except for several commodities for which fractional units of quantities were converted to decimals; and pine boards, which are given in units of 1,000 feet, and hoops and staves and headings, which are given in units of 1,000 number).

^b The source gave beef and pork in tons for 1769 and 1770. These quantities were converted to barrels assuming an average barrel weight of 221 lb (Cole, *Wholesale Commodity Prices*, p. x).

^c The source gave bread and flour in barrels for 1768. These quantities were converted to tons assuming an average barrel weight of 196 lb (Cole, *Wholesale Commodity Prices*, p. x).

^d Pine boards were not distinguished from other boards in the source for 1768. The quantities given as pine boards for 1768 may thus include oak and cedar boards.

^e Includes 2,125 bars, which were converted to tons assuming an average bar weight of 65 lb (Clark, *History of Manufactures*, p. 172).

TABLE 6. *Quantities and estimated values (in pounds sterling) of selected commodities exported from the British North American colonies to Africa, 1768–72*[a]

Commodity (unit)	1768[b]		1769		1770		1771		1772	
	Quantity	Value'	Quantity	Value	Quantity	Value	Quantity	Value	Quantity	Value
From New England										
Spermaceti candles (lb)	4,564	308	9,564	646	7,914	526	3,980	261	6,460	459
Rum										
American (gal)[c]	181,884	11,095	308,482	19,742	274,506	17,157	211,999	13,138	373,247	22,581
West Indian (gal)			460	47			120	12		
Total, New England		11,403		20,435		17,683		13,411		23,040
From middle colonies										
Rum										
American (gal)[c]	6,454	432	12,901	877	14,460	1,027	19,908	1,313	24,011	1,633
West Indian (gal)			1,000	104						
Total, middle colonies		432		981		1,027		1,313		1,633
From lower south										
Rum										
American (gal)[c]			1,300	109			2,500	189	4,076	361
West Indian (gal)			1,000	104					9,832	1,047
Total, lower south		0		213		0		189		1,408
Total, British North American colonies		11,835		21,629		18,710		14,913		26,081

[a] All values have been rounded to the nearest whole number.
[b] The source did not list Africa separately from southern Europe and the Wine Islands for 1768. Estimated exports of spermaceti candles and rum to Africa for 1768 were derived by obtaining the ratios of these two commodities exported during the four years 1769–72 to southern Europe and to Africa, and applying these ratios to the quantities of rum and candles given for 1768.
[c] The source did not distinguish between American and West Indian rum for 1768. Exports of rum in 1768 have been listed and valued as American rum, but West Indian rum may be included in the 1768 quantities.

TABLE 7. Quantities and estimated values (in pounds sterling) of selected commodities imported into the British North American colonies from southern Europe and the Wine Islands, 1768-72[a]

Commodity (unit)	1768		1769		1770		1771		1772	
	Quantity	Value	Quantity	Value	Quantity	Value	Quantity	Value	Quantity	Value
To northern colonies										
Salt (bu)	86,785	4,096	62,725	3,208	103,941	5,940	209,859	10,137	191,340	11,829
Wine (tn)	35.39	2,031	13.44	815	1.72	111	28.52	1,722		
Total, northern colonies		6,127		4,023		6,051		11,859		11,829
To New England										
Salt (bu)	174,100	8,218	317,556	16,242	201,240	11,501	170,240	8,222	191,340	10,982
Wine (tn)	110.42	6,336	163.85	9,940	37.98	2,446	112.69	6,806	137.73	9,233
Total, New England		14,554		26,182		13,947		15,028		20,215
To middle colonies										
Salt (bu)	220,862	10,424	192,936	9,869	210,044	12,005	161,963	7,823	147,598	8,472
Wine (tn)	420.93	24,153	330.95	20,077	474.08	30,528	237.39	14,337	348.39	23,352
Total, middle colonies		34,577		29,946		42,533		22,160		31,824
To upper south										
Salt (bu)	50,200	2,369	27,038	1,383	6,000	343	8,500	411		
Wine (tn)	222.74	12,781	212.89	12,915	69.75	4,491	156.54	9,454	152.06	10,193
Total, upper south		15,150		14,298		4,834		9,865		10,193
To lower south										
Salt (bu)	1,200	57	7,855	402					3,000	172
Wine (tn)	189.36	6,156	120.26	4,123	162.13	7,147	156.91	6,917	210.62	9,285
Total, lower south		6,213		4,525		7,147		6,917		9,457
To Florida, Bahama and Bermuda Is.										
Wine (tn)	21.42	696	51.15	1,754	17.83	786	14.45	637	20.27	894
Total, Florida, Bahama and Bermuda Is.		696		1,754		786		637		894
Total, North American colonies		77,317		80,728		75,298		66,466		84,412

Sources: quantities were taken from the American Inspector-General's Ledgers (London, P.R.O., Customs 16/1). Values were computed using prices from Bezanson and Cole (note 1, p. 92).

[a] Southern Europe and the Wine Islands consisted of European areas south of Cape Finisterre (primarily Spain, Portugal, and Italy), the Azores, and the Madeira, Canary, and Cape Verde Islands. All quantities and values have been rounded to the nearest whole number, except that fractional units of wine have been converted to decimals.

Indies, 1768–72[a]

Commodity (unit)	1768 Quantity	1768 Value	1769 Quantity	1769 Value	1770 Quantity	1770 Value	1771 Quantity	1771 Value	1772 Quantity	1772 Value
To northern colonies										
Coffee (cwt)	56.00	227	37.11	156	4.50	21	1.50	6	6.30	26
Cotton (lb)	600	29	800	36						
Molasses (gal)	27,483	1,343	25,951	1,338	51,132	2,636	42,707	2,172	57,140	2,800
Rum (gal)	50,340	5,054	4,740	492	41,290	4,036	42,820	4,331	42,750	4,561
Salt (bu)	3,200	151	9,620	493	4,400	251	1,800	87	9,300	534
Sugar, Muscovado (cwt)	1,244.38	1,830	427.18	687	798.54	1,447	1,352.61	2,105	969.10	1,474
Wine (tn)	0.47	27	0.50		0.48	31				
Total, northern colonies		8,661		3,202		8,422		8,701		9,395
To New England										
Coffee (cwt)	582.44	2,362	945.96	3,973	620.68	2,906	1,025.90	3,854	644.92	2,622
Cotton (lb)	330,236	16,116	345,011	15,318	247,254	10,805	349,338	14,828	243,314	11,157
Molasses (gal)	2,305,885	112,758	2,771,523	142,872	2,546,897	131,293	2,915,049	148,230	3,503,128	171,654
Rum (gal)	591,608	59,397	805,843	83,727	942,422	92,122	546,346	55,263	784,071	83,661
Salt (bu)	284,180	13,413	358,956	18,360	308,279	17,619	598,615	28,913	460,650	26,441
Sugar, Muscovado (cwt)	13,500.88	19,860	31,372.89	50,448	27,044.72	49,032	18,278.34	28,440	35,734.98	54,352
Wine (tn)	3.73	215	0.50	30	1.10	71	0.69	42	2.50	168
Total, New England		224,121		314,728		303,848		279,570		350,055
To middle colonies										
Coffee (cwt)	1,273.54	5,164	2,074.87	8,715	2,716.38	12,718	252.62	950	2,800.69	11,386
Cotton (lb)	110,770	5,694	134,892	5,833	92,413	3,960	116,000	4,344	57,154	2,252
Molasses (gal)	595,220	32,380	839,621	47,185	869,006	52,488	443,367	23,698	1,003,767	54,505
Rum (gal)	745,530	74,852	1,051,928	109,296	1,131,890	110,642	784,015	79,303	1,293,557	138,023
Salt (bu)	38,266	1,806	26,504	1,355	68,601	3,921	83,602	4,037	79,925	4,588
Sugar, Muscovado (cwt)	19,245.24	26,848	47,584.56	79,276	49,195.21	82,746	31,391.77	48,217	44,647.08	68,086
Wine (tn)	1.19	68					5.00	302	0.96	64
Total, middle colonies		146,812		251,660		266,475		160,851		278,904
To upper south										
Coffee (cwt)	441.50	1,790	363.09	1,525	400.35	1,875	601.74	2,261	578.65	2,353
Cotton (lb)	6,187	318	12,543	543	11,195	480	18,446	691	9,350	369
Molasses (gal)	115,741	6,296	125,317	7,043	121,989	7,368	235,289	12,576	178,896	9,714

TABLE 8. *Quantities and estimated values (in pounds sterling) of selected commodities imported into the British North American colonies from the West Indies, 1768–72[a] – continued*

Commodity (unit)	1768 Quantity	1768 Value	1769 Quantity	1769 Value	1770 Quantity	1770 Value	1771 Quantity	1771 Value	1772 Quantity	1772 Value
Rum (gal)	512,368	51,442	608,269	63,199	679,442	66,415	628,044	63,527	805,420	85,939
Salt (bu)	31,351	1,480	45,943	2,350	29,604	1,692	36,175	1,747	65,629	3,767
Sugar, Muscovado (cwt)	6,777.46	9,454	9,043.40	15,067	11,733.03	19,735	12,116.36	18,611	8,936.32	13,628
Wine (tn)	4.48	257	3.50	212	1.24	80	0.75	45	8.93	599
Total, upper south		71,037		89,939		97,645		99,458		116,369
To lower south										
Coffee (cwt)	425.95	1,727	624.94	2,625	301.53	1,412	430.21	1,616	459.57	1,868
Cotton (lb)	6,080	313	2,097	90	5,529	237	4,800	180	1,000	39
Molasses (gal)	89,401	4,863	109,406	6,149	135,716	8,198	150,238	8,030	136,447	7,427
Rum (gal)	211,170	21,201	312,883	32,509	470,306	45,972	221,655	22,421	468,339	49,971
Salt (bu)	58,454	2,760	65,922	3,371	79,400	4,537	53,476	2,583	57,087	3,277
Sugar, Muscovado (cwt)	5,547.32	7,910	6,489.93	10,280	13,421.10	21,675	6,838.64[b]	9,424	7,159.30	9,866
Wine (tn)	61.11	1,987	6.15	211			36.67	1,616		
Total, lower south		40,761		55,235		82,031		45,870		72,448
To Florida, Bahama and Bermuda Is.										
Coffee (cwt)	59.10	240	51.11	215	21.78	102			1,084.15	4,408
Cotton (lb)	4,200	216	1,300	56	200	9	5,500	206	248	10
Molasses (gal)	2,659	145	7,997	449			1,211	65	4,032	219
Rum (gal)	27,060	2,716	51,089	5,308	23,020	2,250	24,768	2,506	24,237	2,586
Salt (bu)	21,265	1,004	20,840	1,066			24,950	1,205	21,137	1,213
Sugar, Muscovado (cwt)	1,858.82	2,651	1,237.16	1,960	776.71	1,255	738.80	1,018	1,201.45	1,656
Wine (tn)			0.25	9	0.37	16				
Total, Florida, Bahama and Bermuda Is.		6,972		9,063		3,632		5,000		10,092
Total, British North American colonies		498,364		723,827		762,053		599,450		837,263

Sources: see Table 7.

[a] The West Indies included all British and foreign islands and mainland parts of the Caribbean area. All quantities and values have been rounded to the nearest whole number, except that fractional units of coffee, sugar, and wine have been converted to decimals.

[b] Includes 22 hogsheads of sugar, which have been estimated to have been 16 hundredweight per hogshead (see David Macpherson, *Annals of Commerce* (London, 1805), III, p. 56).

TABLE 9. *Contemporary estimates of values of commodities exported to overseas areas from the British North American colonies, 1768 and 1770[a]* (pounds sterling)

Commodity	1768	1770[b]
To Great Britain		
Beeswax	4,183	3,140
Beef and pork	3,469	0
Bread and flour	37,439	2,876
Cotton	4,075	[c]
Deerskins	44,096	57,738
Fish, dried	7,025	12,576
Flaxseed	2,081	763
Grain, Indian corn	7,716	0
rice	207,815	166,667
wheat	15,718	2,051
Hemp	12,230	130
Indigo	126,913	131,539
Iron, bar	44,620	31,454
pig	15,589	28,738
Naval stores, pitch	12,829	2,892
tar	22,935	23,435
turpentine	10,856	6,051
Oil, whale	69,714	78,033
Potash	30,430	35,192
Rum[d]	5,790	37
Tobacco	662,980	904,982
Wood products, pine boards[e]	1,052	8,242
staves and headings	13,754	14,758
Total, above commodities	1,363,309	1,511,294
Per cent of total	(88.85)[f]	(86.24)
Total, all commodities in estimate	1,534,453	1,752,515
To Ireland		
Bread and flour	5,191	39,406
Fish, dried	1,376	263
Flaxseed	29,509	34,321
Grain, Indian corn	382	13
wheat	3,176	26,241
Iron, bar	2,541	1,271
Oil, whale	1,129	332
Potash	2,524	0
Rum[d]	2,918	496
Wood products, pine boards[e]	329	451
staves and headings	6,644	8,485
Total, above commodities	55,719	111,279
Per cent of total	(92.44)	(93.69)
Total, all commodities in estimate	60,279	118,777
To southern Europe		
Beeswax	1,633	2,527
Beef and pork	1,953	541
Bread and flour	73,604	203,537
Candles, spermaceti	819	886
Fish, dried	146,222	245,358

TABLE 9. (*continued*)

Commodity	1768	1770[b]
Grain, Indian corn	26,368	13,143
rice	67,570	81,664
wheat	64,580	103,004
Oil, whale	3,356	2,627
Rum[d]	12,777	2,832
Wood products, pine boards[e]	1,315	668
staves and headings	9,766	5,040
Total, above commodities	409,963	661,827
Per cent of total	(98.09)	(95.65)
Total, all commodities in estimate	417,954	691,912
To the West Indies		
Beef and pork	57,590	64,523
Bread and flour	148,504	257,927
Candles, spermaceti	16,188	21,975
Fish, dried	86,151	117,198
Grain, Indian corn	48,471	30,220
rice	36,285	92,089
wheat	0	171
Hoops	7,566	8,590
Iron, bar	2,650	4,084
Livestock, cattle	16,812	14,328
horses	45,891	60,228
Oil, whale	3,181	4,021
Wine (from Wine Islands)	7,966	c
Wood products, pine boards[e]	42,402	49,251
staves and headings	25,304	33,336
Total, above commodities	544,961	757,941
Per cent of total	(89.39)	(89.28)
Total, all commodities in estimate	609,629	848,934
To Africa		
Candles, spermaceti		495
Rum[d]		18,309
Total, above commodities		18,804
Per cent of total		(86.74)
Total, all commodities in estimate		21,678

Source: 1768, London, British Museum, Add. Mss 15485; 1770, David Macpherson, *Annals of Commerce* (London, 1805), III, pp. 572–3, reprinted in *Historical Statistics*, p. 761, with corrections.

[a] All values were rounded to the nearest pound sterling. Totals may not add because of rounding.

[b] The source for 1770 gave a breakdown by quantities of each commodity exported to the various overseas areas, but the value of each commodity was given only as a total for all areas. The total value of each commodity has been allocated to the various overseas areas on the basis of the quantity exported to each area.

[c] Not given in source. Macpherson includes only commodities produced in the colonies, and no re-exports like cotton and wine.

[d] In the 1768 source, rum includes both American and West Indian rum. The 1770 source includes only American rum.

[e] The 1768 source includes pine boards and planks. The 1770 source includes pine, oak, and cedar boards.

[f] This percentage is 85.97 when deerskins are not included. For 1768 this was the percentage used because deerskins were not included in Customs 16/1 for 1768.

TABLE 10.   *A contemporary estimate of values of commodities imported from the West Indies and southern Europe and the Wine Islands into the British North American colonies, 1768*

Commodity	Quantity[a]	Value[a] (pounds sterling)
From the West Indies		
Braziletto	115 tn	518
Cocoa	280,566 lb	7,014
Coffee	2,839 cwt	5,597
Cotton	448,558 lb	22,433
Ginger	1,416 cwt	633
Hides	5,022 No.	1,758
Indigo	1,105 lb	249
Lignum vitae	103 tn	464
Limes	1,866 bbl	2,799
Logwood	4,056 tn[b]	18,251
Mahogany	726,016 ft[c]	9,524
Molasses	3,146,389 gal	157,319
Pimento	50,128 lb	1,253
Rum	2,138,126 gal	240,539
Salt	436,416 bu	21,821
Sarsaparilla	27,360 lb[d]	7,606
Sugar, muscovado	48,254 cwt	78,471
white	78 cwt	175
Wine of the Azores	72 tn	4,321
Sundries, valued[e]		30,000
Total, West Indies		610,745
From southern Europe and the Wine Islands		
Salt	533,137 bu	26,657
Wine of the Azores	1,000 tn	60,014
Total, southern Europe and the Wine Islands		86,671

Source: London, British Museum, Add. Mss 15485.

[a] All quantities have been rounded to the nearest whole number; all values to the nearest pound sterling.

[b] Plus 11 pieces.

[c] Plus 1,871 pieces and 15 logs.

[d] Plus 805 bundles.

[e] All sundries are assumed to have been imported from the West Indies. The Navigation Acts allowed only salt and wine to be imported directly into the colonies from southern Europe.

TABLE 11. *Commodity imports into the British North American colonies from Africa, 1768–72* (in quantities)

Commodity (unit)	Year				
	1768	1769	1770	1771	1772
Barwood (pieces)					
middle colonies			4,164		
Beeswax (lb)					
middle colonies			16,553		1,250
upper south			672		
lower south				4,600	500
Camwood (tn)					
northern colonies		10			
lower south		9		15	
Dyewood (tn)					
middle colonies			70		
Ebony (tn)					
middle colonies			3.55		25
Gum copal (hhd)					
lower south		3			
Hides (no.)					
middle colonies			166		40
Ivory (teeth and lb)					
middle colonies (teeth)		93	113		
(lb)			3,453		1,400
upper south (teeth)			81		
(lb)			1,986		
lower south (teeth)					133
(lb)				3,136	4,300
Florida, Bahama and Bermuda Is. (lb)		500			

Source: London, P.R.O., Customs 16/1.

TABLE 12. *Official values of exports from England to the British North American colonies, 1768–72 (pounds sterling)*ᵃ

Destination	(Class of exports)ᵇ	1768	1769	1770	1771	1772
To the northern coloniesᶜ	(B)	150,810	197,698	298,683	260,178	295,184
	(F)	26,119	60,088	69,071	51,761	51,226
		176,929	257,786	367,754	311,939	346,410
To New England	(B)	289,676	133,553	277,250	734,738	690,593
	(F)	130,122	74,441	117,201	685,381	134,237
		419,798	207,994	394,451	1,420,119	824,830
To the middle colonies	(B)	703,015	212,664	514,545	1,142,832	733,186
	(F)	212,024	62,165	96,328	239,534	118,694
		915,039	274,829	610,873	1,382,366	851,880
To the upper south	(B)	408,813	411,779	594,069	782,491	659,453
	(F)	67,142	76,494	123,714	137,835	134,458
		475,955	488,273	717,783	920,326	793,911
To the lower south	(B)	316,434	330,765	189,061	425,257	483,887
	(F)	29,998	34,176	13,407	54,406	58,130
		346,432	364,941	202,468	479,663	542,017
To Florida, Bahama and Bermuda Is.	(B)	44,856	43,919	50,627	68,996	48,042
	(F)	4,995	4,895	4,977	6,296	5,777
		49,851	48,814	55,604	75,292	53,819
Total to the British North American colonies	(B)	1,913,604	1,330,378	1,924,235	3,414,492	2,910,345
	(F)	470,400	312,259	424,698	1,175,213	502,522
		2,384,004	1,642,637	2,348,933	4,589,705	3,412,867

Source: London, P.R.O., Customs 3/68–72.

ᵃ All figures were rounded to the nearest pound sterling.

ᵇ (B) designates exports of British or Irish manufacture from England; (F) designates re-exports from England.

ᶜ Exports to Hudson Bay that were recorded in Customs 3 have not been included.

TABLE 13. *Official values of exports from Scotland to the British North American colonies, 1768–72 (pounds sterling)*[a]

Destination	(Class of exports)[b]	1768	1769[c]	1770	1771	1772
To the northern colonies	(B)	3,353		2,199	557	4,234
	(F)	561		652	150	1,176
		3,914	3,871	2,851	707	5,410
To New England	(B)	8,010		15,170	12,772	16,429
	(F)	3,000		7,073	2,946	3,163
		11,010	15,702	22,243	15,718	19,592
To the middle colonies	(B)	14,414		7,747	16,798	20,493
	(F)	3,052		1,235	3,456	3,033
		17,466	6,083	8,982	20,254	23,526
To the upper south	(B)	128,665		177,824	200,960	148,580
	(F)	64,904		101,551	102,441	73,081
		193,569	226,581	279,375	303,401	221,661
To the lower south	(B)	9,363		20,673	29,277	26,267
	(F)	1,694		4,693	5,823	7,043
		11,057	20,484	25,366	35,100	33,310
To Florida, Bahama and Bermuda Is.	(B)	0		93	170	0
	(F)	0		0	161	0
		0	185	93	331	0
Total to the British North American colonies	(B)	163,805		223,706	260,534	216,003
	(F)	73,211		115,204	114,977	87,496
		237,016	272,906	338,910	375,511	303,499

Sources: London, P.R.O., Customs 14/1B; and David Macpherson, *Annals of Commerce* (London, 1805), III, p. 495.

[a] All figures were rounded to the nearest pound sterling.

[b] (B) designates exports of British manufacture from Scotland; (F) designates re-exports from Scotland.

[c] The Scottish ledger for 1769 is not in the P.R.O., and is apparently lost. The 1769 totals were taken from Macpherson, who did not give a breakdown between exports of British or Irish manufacture, and re-exports.

UTILIZATION OF SHIPPING CAPACITY

For the purpose of estimating shipping earnings by our method one must know what proportion of the tonnage entering and clearing colonial ports was being employed or utilized. Estimates of these proportions have been based on the conversion factors listed below, and they are expressed as percentages in Table 7.5.

The tons used by the English to register merchant ships prior to 1773 correspond most closely to what Frederic C. Lane has called 'measurement freight tonnage', 'freight tons', or 'tons burden', all of which were terms that represented the cubic volume of space available in a ship for carrying cargo.[1] The freight rates given in Table 7.4 were charges either for 'tons burden' of 60 cubic feet,[2] or for 2,240 pounds (a long ton) of freight if the freight occupied less than 60 cubic feet of shipping. The registered tons for merchant

---

[1] Frederic C. Lane, 'Tonnages, medieval and modern', *Economic History Review*, Second Series, XVII, 2 (December 1964), pp. 214–18. After 1773 all British merchant shipping tonnage was required to be registered on the basis of a formula which had been used by the Royal Navy and by shipwrights since the seventeenth century. Such tons have been commonly called 'measured tons' and the number of such tons probably exceeded 'tons burden' by some 50 per cent for the same ship. That is, a ship registered as 100 'tons burden' would have been rated as 150 'measured tons' under the Navy formula. Lane would say that the ship would have been rated as 133 'measured tons' (Lane, p. 228). In any case, this relationship was apparently highly variable from ship to ship (see Gary M. Walton, 'Colonial tonnage measurements: a comment', *Journal of Economic History*, XXVII, 3 (September 1967), pp. 392–7). 'Measured tons' do not concern the shipping tons given in Table 7.2, and thus should not be confused with them.

[2] Lane states that 40 cu. ft were not even roughly equivalent to the space 'occupied' by 2,240 lb of cargo, which Lane calls a 'deadweight ton.' Nevertheless, the space obtained by paying for a ton of freight became standardized fairly early at 40 cu. ft (Lane, p. 220; also see the quotation from Lane in Chapter 4). Ralph Davis considers 'tons burden' and 'deadweight tons' as synonymous (*The Rise of the English Shipping Industry in the Seventeenth and Eighteenth Centuries* (London: Macmillan & Company, Ltd., 1962), pp. 7n., 49, 74, 395–6), but Lane (p. 228) and N. Salisbury (in his review of Davis in *The Mariner's Mirror*, XLIX, 3 (August 1963), p. 236) are doubtful about this. Lane states that such a statement must have been made on the assumption that 2,240 lb occupied, on the average, 56 to 60 cu. ft – not 40 cu. ft. The problem of whether the 'ton burden' was 40 cu. ft or 56–60 cu. ft is not relevant to our method for the most part. What is crucial, however, is whether or not the equivalencies between the various commodities and 'tons burden' listed below are reasonably accurate, and whether the freight rates given in Table 7.4 were the rates charged for these estimated 'tons' of commodities from which the utilization percentages are calculated. The space occupied by two hogsheads of tobacco was closer to 60 cu. ft than to 40 cu. ft and two hogsheads are the basis for the trans-Atlantic freight rate of £3.5; hence 60 cu. ft is our choice. Note that this volume includes the space between the hogsheads as well as the volume of the hogsheads themselves.

shipping entering and clearing the colonies are shown in Table 7.2. To estimate utilization we have taken the major commodities shipped on each
route, and attempted to calculate the shipping tonnage that each commodity
occupied. The ratio of the converted total tonnages of commodities on each
route to the tonnage of ships entering and clearing colonial ports (the 'tons
burden' given in Table 7.2) then gives some idea of the proportion of shipping
capacity that was utilized on each route (these ratios are given as percentages
in Table 7.5). In some instances our calculations yielded percentages greater
than 100 per cent. When these occurred, they were expressed in Table 7.5
as 100 per cent.[1]

The following relations between the various commodities and 'tons
burden' were used in making these calculations.

(1) All commodities recorded by weight were converted to long tons (2,240
pounds). The assumption was made that one long ton occupied, on the
average, one 'ton burden' of shipping (60 cubic feet); or, if one ton of the
commodity occupied less than 60 cubic feet, the freight charge was based
on weight rather than volume. This same assumption was also made for
other commodities that were not recorded by weight, but which could be
converted to weight using the various relationships stated below. Two
exceptions were made to this assumption. One-third ton of cotton (747
pounds), which is a relatively light commodity, was assumed to have
occupied one 'ton burden.'[2] Bar and pig iron are relatively heavy, and
one ton occupied considerably less than 60 cubic feet. It nevertheless
was charged the going freight rate per ton (of weight) from most colonies,

---

[1] As would be expected, the estimated utilization rates that exceeded 100 per cent occurred
primarily in the export trades. The routes in which they exceeded 100 per cent by significant
amounts were the ones from the upper and lower south to Great Britain and Ireland (the
average calculated utilization rates for the five-year period were 124 per cent for the upper
south and 129 per cent for the lower south), and the routes from all the thirteen colonies to
the West Indies and to southern Europe (the average calculated utilization percentages
for the five-year period for shipping going to the West Indies were 166 for New England,
138 for the middle colonies, 129 for the upper south, and 131 for the lower south; and those
for the southern European routes were 125 for New England, 168 for the middle colonies,
117 for the upper south, and 122 for the lower south). These percentages indicate that the
above conversion factors must understate the quantities of these commodities that could be
carried in a 'ton burden.' For example, somewhat more than two hogsheads of tobacco
clearly were being carried in a 'ton burden' to Great Britain. By the end of the colonial
period, the American customs records gave the number of hogsheads of tobacco for 1768–2
as 433,085. The same records also gave the number of shipping tons ('tons burden') that
cleared Virginia and Maryland for Great Britain as 202,819 for the same period. Assuming
that ships were fully laden and carried nothing but tobacco, this results in an average of
2.14 hogsheads per ton. The ships did, of course, carry other goods (for example, iron), but
these goods very often occupied unused space among the tobacco hogsheads and, in any
case, were not of sufficiently large magnitudes to alter this average significantly. The fact
that this average was slightly more than two hogsheads per ton will not seriously affect our
estimates of shipping earnings from the British route, since only a small portion of shipping
in this route was owned in the colonies. In the routes from the colonies to the West Indies
and southern Europe, the result may be to understate actual shipping earnings from these
routes. If they do, then the tentative conclusions in Chapter 8 are strengthened. In any case,
these estimates, crude as they may be, support the assertion made in Table 7.5 that ships
carrying exports from the colonies tended to be fully loaded.

[2] The source for this assumption is Davis, p. 179.

but in ships clearing from Virginia and Maryland it was often packed in among the tobacco hogsheads and thus occupied what otherwise would have been wasted space. From these .colonial ports lower rates were charged for its carriage. It was thus assumed (for Virginia and Maryland) that two tons of iron occupied one 'ton burden.'[1]

(2) Whale oil and wine were recorded in liquid 'tuns', and it was assumed that one liquid 'tun' occupied one 'ton burden.'[2] Since 252 gallons equalled one liquid 'tun', commodities given in gallons (such as rum and molasses) were also converted to 'tons burden' using this same assumption.

(3) Barrels of rice weighed 525 pounds, on the average, in the late colonial period.[3] Therefore, it was assumed that four barrels of rice occupied approximately one 'ton burden'. The conversion factor for naval stores (pitch, tar, and turpentine) was based on eight barrels per ton, and this same conversion factor was assumed for pickled fish.[4] Barrels of flour were converted to tons (of weight) assuming an average of 196 pounds per barrel, and barrels of beef and pork were converted assuming an average of 221 pounds per barrel.[5]

(4) By the late colonial period approximately two hogsheads of tobacco occupied one 'ton burden' of shipping.[6]

(5) Quintaux of dried fish weighed 100 pounds.[7] Thus, 22.4 quintaux were assumed to have occupied one 'ton burden'.

(6) For commodities given in bushels, it was assumed that 44 bushels occupied one 'ton burden.'[8] These commodities were flaxseed, Indian corn, wheat and salt.

(7) For lumber, it was assumed that 600 board feet occupied one 'ton burden.'[9] A Pennsylvania Act of 1759 prescribed specific dimensions for staves and provided for their inspection. Pipe staves were to be '4 feet 8 inches long, 4 inches broad, and 1 inch thick on the sap side and $\frac{3}{4}$ inch on the heart side; hogshead staves 3 feet 6 inches long, $3\frac{1}{2}$ inches broad, $\frac{3}{4}$ inch thick on the sap side, $\frac{1}{2}$ inch thick on the heartside; and barrel staves from 28 to 32 inches long, and thickness the same as the hogshead staves.'[10] For staves it was assumed the hogshead stave was the average size stave being shipped. If so, and if tightly packed, about 1,100 staves occupied a

[1] See *ibid.*, p. 180.

[2] The original meaning of the 'ton burden' was that this volume held about one 'tun' (252 gallons) of wine. See the quotation from Lane in Chapter 4.

[3] U.S. Bureau of the Census, *Historical Statistics of the United States, Colonial Times to 1957* (Washington, D.C.: U.S. Government Printing Office, 1960), pp. 750–1.

[4] Sales Account and Invoice Book of Wallace, Davidson, and Johnson, 1775, Catalogue Number 153, Maryland Hall of Records, Annapolis, Maryland.

[5] Arthur H. Cole, *Wholesale Commodity Prices in the United States, 1700–1861: Statistical Supplement* (Cambridge, Mass.: Harvard University Press, 1938), p. x.

[6] See the discussion of the change in the size of tobacco hogsheads in Chapter 4, and p. 238, note 1.

[7] Cole, p. x.

[8] Davis, p. 185.

[9] Robert G. Albion, *Forests and Seapower: The Timber Problem of the Royal Navy, 1652–1862* (Cambridge, Mass.: Harvard University Press, 1926), p. 9.

[10] Anne Bezanson, *et al.*, *Prices in Colonial Pennsylvania* (Philadelphia: University of Pennsylvania Press, 1935), p. 119.

'ton burden' of 60 cubic feet. No references could be found describing the size of shingles that were shipped to the West Indies. It seems doubtful that an average shingle would have been smaller than 1 foot by 6 inches by $\frac{1}{2}$ inch. About 3,000 shingles of this size would have occupied one 'ton burden'.

(8) Cattle and horses were assumed to have occupied two 'tons burden' each.

(9) Slaves were assumed to have occupied half a 'ton burden' each.

The above equivalencies pertain to all the major commodities in all trade routes except imports from Great Britain and Ireland. These imports consisted mostly of woolen and linen textiles, a multitude of items of hardware, and various goods which were being re-exported from Great Britain, such as German linens and tea. Immigrants traveling to America also occupied tonnage entering from Great Britain and Ireland. To account for these British and Irish imports and immigrants, it has been assumed that commodity imports from Great Britain and Ireland occupied 20 per cent of the tonnage entering the upper and lower south and 40 per cent of the tonnage entering all other colonies.[1] To this must be added estimates of tonnage occupied by immigrants. The best guess of immigration into the colonies at this point is in the range of 11,000 to 19,000 per year, on the average, during the late colonial period.[2] Assuming that an immigrant occupied one 'ton burden' of shipping, the following regional utilization of ships entering from Great Britain and Ireland due to immigration was:[3]

Northern colonies	0%	Upper south	20%
New England	5%	Lower south	10%
Middle colonies	45%	Florida etc.	0%

Given the above assumptions it is possible to obtain some idea about the proportion of tonnage that was utilized on ships entering from Great Britain and Ireland.

[1] About one-half the tonnage entered New England and the middle colonies as entered the southern colonies from Great Britain. Yet the value of British and Irish imports was about the same in the two regions. Thus it would be expected that tonnage entering the colonial ports to the north (of Maryland) from Britain was more fully utilized.

[2] See the discussion on immigration in Chapters 3 and 8.

[3] These percentages are based upon an *average annual* immigration estimate of 18,000 persons. This estimated number of immigrants was distributed to each region by assuming 750 persons went to New England, 7,500 to the middle colonies, 7,500 to the upper south, and 1,500 to the lower south each year. This assumption was based upon the evidence discussed and cited in Chapter 8, which strongly suggests that the greatest number of immigrants went to the middle colonies and upper south. Since constructing these estimates of tonnage utilized by immigrants on ships entering from Great Britain and Ireland, the authors have revised slightly downward their estimates of immigration during the period 1768–72 (from an average of 18,000 annually to an average of 15,000; see Chapter 8). This would result in a reduction of total shipping earnings (as calculated in Chapter 7) of about £3,000 – an amount so small that it was not deemed worthwhile to perform the necessary recalculations in Chapters 7 and 8. If the reader wishes to make this adjustment, the percentages of regional utilization of tonnage entering from Great Britain and Ireland due to immigration of 15,000 persons annually would have been:

Northern colonies	0%	Upper south	16%
New England	4%	Lower south	8%
Middle colonies	38%	Florida etc.	0%

FOREIGN EXCHANGE EARNINGS FROM THE SALE OF SHIPS TO OVERSEAS BUYERS

Shipbuilding began in the colonies in 1631 when Governor Winthrop of Massachusetts built the *Blessing of the Bay*, a small sloop of 30 tons, for trade with other towns along the coast. As early as 1638 a colonial-built vessel visited London. According to Edward Randolph there had been 730 ships built in Massachusetts prior to 1676.[1] Most ships built in the colonies, especially in the seventeenth and early eighteenth centuries, were less than 50 tons burden and were constructed primarily for use in the fisheries and West Indian and coastal trades.[2] However, some larger ones were built to be used in the ocean trade, and by the late colonial period a sizable number of tons were built for sale in Great Britain. Often such ships were sent there with cargo, and both ship and cargo would be sold after arrival.

Since the customs records did not record ship sales to buyers in overseas areas, reliance must be placed upon such fragmentary evidence as does exist in order to obtain some estimate of the value of ships sold abroad. Evidence indicates that ship sales were consistent throughout the entire colonial period, but that they were not an item of large value relative to total exports. Bernard and Lotte Bailyn have placed ship sales by New England to the British Isles at 187 vessels totaling 20,601 tons during the years 1697–1714.[3] Governor Dudley, writing to the Council of Trade and Plantations from Boston in 1712, said 'Ships and vessels are built for sale in Great Britain and the West Indies to the numbers of 70 per annum.'[4] In an unsigned essay, written most likely by Henry Martin,[5] English Inspector-General of Imports and Exports, probably not long before his death in 1721, we find the following statement:

> The Act of Navigation is so very severe against the use of other foreign built ships that we may safely pronounce that none are sold in England, and as for those of our plantations they are generally very low prized,

---

[1] Emory R. Johnson, *et al.*, *History of Domestic and Foreign Commerce of the United States* (Washington, D.C.: The Carnegie Institution of Washington, 1915), I, pp. 72–3.

[2] *Ibid.*

[3] *Massachusetts Shipping, 1696–1714: A Statistical Study* (Cambridge, Mass.: Belknap Press, 1959), p. 53.

[4] Great Britain, Public Record Office, *Calendar of State Papers, Colonial Series, American and West Indies, 1711–1712*, XXVI (London: H.M. Stationery Office, 1925), p. 259.

[5] 'An Essay towards finding the Ballance of our whole Trade Annually from Christmas of 1698 to Christmas 1719,' printed in G. N. Clark, *Guide to English Commercial Statistics, 1696–1782* (London: Royal Historical Society, 1938), pp. 69–149 (see p. 176, note 3).

not above £300 or £400 one with another, so the purchase of 100 such ships in a year (and I never heard of so great a number) would hardly amount to £40,000 and would be very seldom to 3 not very often 2 per cent of the value of imports purchased by England per Table 10 [£1,891,000 in 1719].[1]

Such an item would have been relatively more important to the colonies than to England in 1719 when colonial exports to England were valued at £463,054.[2] At most, this would have been 9 per cent of total exports, but it was probably much less if Martin was correct.

By the eve of the American Revolution Richard Champion, a Bristol merchant writing in 1784, stated that out of a total of 7,694 British-owned ships, 2,342 had been built in the colonies.[3] This was just over 30 per cent. Based on this statement Jacob M. Price suggests 'a sale of about 100 colonial ships yearly, worth close to £100,000 exclusive of sails, cables, etc.'[4] Curtis P. Nettels suggests that before the Revolution about fifty ships were sold annually to Great Britain and that 'in 1763–66...the value of vessels annually built for sale (to Great Britain) in New England, Pennsylvania, and New York was only £80,000.'[5]

David Macpherson gives the shipbuilding statistics which are shown in Table 1 for three years in the late colonial period, namely 1769 through 1771. Macpherson did not say (and probably did not know) what part of this tonnage built in the colonies was sold abroad. Macpherson's tonnage can be valued by using prices at which colonial-built ships were sold during this period, or at the costs that were incurred to build them. One contemporary writer stated that costs of building ships in the colonies were £7 10s. to £8

---

[1] 'An Essay towards finding the Ballance,' in Clark, p. 104.

[2] U.S. Bureau of the Census, *Historical Statistics of the United States, Colonial Times to 1957* (Washington, D.C.: U.S. Government Printing Office, 1960), p. 757. This is the official value of exports to England from the colonies in this year.

[3] *Considerations on the Present Situation of Great Britain and the United States of North America, with a View to their Future Commercial Connections* (London: J. Stockdale, 1784), p. 14. According to Ralph Davis, *The Rise of the English Shipping Industry in the Seventeenth and Eighteenth Centuries* (London: Macmillan & Co., Ltd, 1962), p. 68, these numbers given by Champion pertain to 1773.

[4] 'Discussion,' *Journal of Economic History*, xxv, 4 (December 1965), p. 657. Price bases his estimate on average ship life of 20 to 25 years. Davis suggests a normal ship life of this length (p. 376). For a stock of 7,694 ships, over 300 ships would have needed to be replaced yearly, if they lasted approximately this long on the average. If about 30 per cent were purchased from the colonies, then this would have been about 100 ships sold by the colonies yearly to Great Britain. The quality of colonial-built ships was said to be lower than those built in Britain, and as a result of the growing proportion of colonial-built vessels in the British fleet the average life of an average British-owned ship may have been falling. Nevertheless, if 70 per cent of the fleet in 1774 was still of British build, then the average life may still have been around 20 to 25 years, if Davis is correct.

[5] *The Emergence of a National Economy, 1775–1815* (New York: Holt, Rinehart & Winston, 1962), p. 239; and *The Roots of American Civilization*, p. 435. The estimates of Price and Nettels are virtually the same when one considers that Nettels did not include any ships built in the southern colonies in his estimate. (See Table 1 for Macpherson's estimate of tonnage built in the southern colonies.)

TABLE I.   *Tonnage of ships built in the thirteen colonies, 1769–71ᵃ*

Place built	1769	1770	1771
New England	13,435	14,412	16,326
Middle colonies	2,507	3,314	3,075
Upper south	2,613	2,650	3,323
Lower south	1,446	234	1,350
Total	20,001	20,610	24,074

Source: Macpherson, *Annals of Commerce*, III, p. 570.
ᵃ These are the same figures given by Lord John Sheffield, *Observations on the Commerce of the American States* (London: Debrett, 1784), p. 96.

per ton in the late colonial period.[1] However, most sources give considerably lower costs for colonial shipbuilding. John G. B. Hutchins[2] has stated that shipbuilding costs were £3 and £4 per ton in the colonies, but the latter estimate probably does not include costs of rigging and outfitting a ship, and should be viewed as a minimum cost figure.[3] Davis lists prices of American ships in 1784 as being £6 8s. to £7 19s. per measured ton in New York and Philadelphia and £3 18s. to £5 9s. in New England.[4] We are not told whether they include costs of the initial fitting out of the ship, but since they are called the 'price of a ship of 200 tons' presumably they do. These figures suggest average prices of about £4 14s. per measured ton in New England and £7 4s. per measured ton in the middle colonies. The same higher quality oak ships were being built in the southern colonies as were built in the middle colonies, so the higher price would have also applied to both of

[1] Lord John Sheffield, *Observations on the Commerce of the American States* (London: Debrett' 1784), p. 162. Sheffield, a Tory propagandist, was writing with a definite bias, however. He did not want to see the new United States accorded any trading privileges within the British Empire, and thus had an incentive to state higher colonial prices for shipbuilding than perhaps may have actually prevailed. Champion, p. 17, writing expressly in rebuttal to Sheffield, stated that 'in New England shipbuilders will now (1784) contract for building ships at 3 pounds sterling per ton, including the joiner's work.'

[2] *The American Maritime Industries and Public Policy, 1789–1914: An Economic History* (Cambridge Mass.: Harvard University Press, 1941), p. 153. For a discussion of the secular trend of shipbuilding costs, see Chapter 4, p. 70, note 1.

[3] Certainly the value of rigging, sails, hardware, etc., used in equipping a ship should be credited as a colonial export. If such items were originally imported from Great Britain, as many were, their value would have been included in the value of imports from there. Some of the items, however, were of colonial manufacture. Ropewalks were fairly common around colonial shipbuilding centers, even though the hemp was usually imported. In either case, these items were exports not valued in Chapter 6, and should be taken into account here.

[4] Davis, p. 375. These were prices obtained when a number of informed persons were asked their views about the relative prices of a ship of 200 'measured tons'. These prices refer to 'measured tons', i.e. tons measured by rules which the shipwrights had developed and the basis on which they quoted their prices. Macpherson's figures are registered tons, or 'tons burden', which was a capacity measure of the ship. A vessel with registered tonnage of 100 tons was probably near 150 measured tons (see p. 237, note 1). Consequently, our measured ton prices must be adjusted upward appropriately when applied to Macpherson's 'ton burden' below.

these regions.[1] Based upon Davis' prices, which probably included the costs of rigging and outfitting a ship, the annual average value of Macpherson's tonnage of ships built in the colonies during 1769–71 was somewhere around £175,000 per year. This suggests, if the estimates of Price and Nettels are close to the mark, that about 57 per cent of the tonnage built in the colonies during this period was sold abroad. Since other evidence suggests that it is more likely that more than this was sold in the colonies,[2] these estimates may well be too high.

By using some information which exists about the stock of Massachusetts-owned shipping, it is possible to obtain a rough idea of what proportion of Macpherson's tonnage was sold abroad if one can assume that the amount purchased by Massachusetts residents was for replacement purposes. The Massachusetts-owned fleet was about 59,000 tons in the early 1770s.[3] By assuming, first, that Massachusetts was just maintaining this total stock of tonnage; secondly, that this replacement was made with ships built in Massachusetts; and, thirdly, that the average life of a Massachusetts-built ship was ten years;[4] then about 5,900 tons would have been required annually for replacement purposes and the remainder sold abroad. According to Macpherson the annual average tonnage built in Massachusetts during the three years 1769–71 was 7,664 tons. The residual, then, would have been roughly one-quarter of the tonnage built during this period. An average ship life of ten years, however, may have been low even for New England-built ships, which were said to be of lower quality (that is, less durable) than ships built in the middle and southern colonies and in England. If the average life of a Massachusetts-built ship was actually twenty years, then the residual assumed to have been the tonnage sold abroad would rise to about 60 per cent of the tonnage built. If the amount sold abroad by the other colonies was in this same range of approximately 25 to 60 per cent of the tonnage that Macpherson states was built in the colonies, then the range of possible foreign exchange earnings from the sale of ships for each colonial region would have been (in pounds sterling rounded to the nearest thousand):

	From	To
New England	£26,000	£62,000
Middle colonies	8,000	19,000
Upper south	8,000	18,000
Lower south	3,000	7,000
Total	£45,000	£106,000

[1] Davis, p. 375.

[2] Among other evidence, we see that a considerable part of the tonnage entering and clearing the colonies was colonial-owned (see Table 7.3). Macpherson gives the number and types of vessels built from 1769 through 1771 as being 359 square-rigged ships and 849 sloops and schooners. The latter were used mainly in the coastal and West Indian trades and in the fisheries (although Macpherson does not state whether he includes ships built for the fisheries) and were mostly owned in the colonies.

[3] Richard C. Berner, 'The Means of Paying for Colonial New England's Imports' (unpublished M.A. thesis, Department of History, University of California, Berkeley, 1950), p. 25. Berner estimates the tonnage of ships built in New England and sold to Great Britain in this way.

[4] This was the average life used by Berner, *ibid.*

It seems likely from the preceding discussion that the actual average annual earnings from this source were above £45,000, but probably below the estimates of Price and Nettels. In any case, it seems certain that earnings from the sale of ships to Great Britain[1] during the late colonial period were small relative to total commodity exports.[2]

---

[1] Some ships were sold to residents of the West Indies. It is not known whether the tonnage involved was significant.

[2] There were probably also some ships built in the northern colonies that were sold to Great Britain. It is doubtful that the number was significant, however. Champion, *op. cit.*, states that at the beginning of the Revolution, out of a total number of 7,694 British ships, 163 were built in 'British colonies still remaining (in 1784)' (Nova Scotia was probably the most important remaining colony for shipbuilding).

SELECT BIBLIOGRAPHY

BOOKS

Albion, Robert G. *Forests and Seapower: The Timber Problem of the Royal Navy, 1652–1862.* Cambridge, Massachusetts: Harvard University Press, 1962.

Andreano, Ralph L. (ed.). *New Views on American Economic Development.* Cambridge, Massachusetts: Schenkman Publishing Company, Inc., 1965.

Bailyn, Bernard and Lotte. *Massachusetts Shipping, 1696–1714: A Statistical Study.* Cambridge, Massachusetts: Belknap Press, 1959.

Barrow, Thomas C. *Trade and Empire: The British Customs Service in Colonial America, 1660–1775.* Cambridge, Massachusetts: Harvard University Press, 1967.

Baxter, W. T. *The House of Hancock.* Cambridge, Massachusetts: Harvard University Press, 1945.

Bezanson, Anne, *et al. Prices in Colonial Pennsylvania.* Philadelphia: University of Pennsylvania Press, 1935.

Bezanson, Anne, B. Daley, M. Denison and M. Hussey. *Prices and Inflation during the American Revolution, Pennsylvania, 1770–1790.* Philadelphia: University of Pennsylvania Press, 1951.

Bidwell, P. W. and J. I. Falconer. *History of Agriculture in the Northern United States, 1620–1860.* Washington, D.C.: Carnegie Institution of Washington, 1925.

Bruchey, Stuart (ed.). *The Colonial Merchant: Sources and Readings.* New York: Harcourt, Brace & World, Inc., 1966.

The Roots of American Economic Growth, 1607–1861: An Essay in Social Causation. London: Hutchinson & Co., Ltd., 1965.

Clark, G. N. *Guide to English Commercial Statistics, 1696–1782.* London: The Royal Historical Society, 1938.

Clark, Victor S. *History of Manufactures in the United States, 1607–1860.* Washington, D.C.: Carnegie Institution, 1916.

Cole, Arthur H. *Wholesale Commodity Prices in the United States, 1700–1861.* Cambridge, Massachusetts: Harvard University Press, 1938.

Davis, Ralph. *The Rise of the English Shipping Industry in the Seventeenth and Eighteenth Centuries.* London: Macmillan & Co., Ltd., 1962.

Deane, Phyllis and W. A. Cole. *British Economic Growth, 1688–1959.* London: Cambridge University Press, 1964.

Donnan, Elizabeth (ed.). *Documents Illustrative of the History of the Slave Trade to America.* Washington, D.C.: Carnegie Institution of Washington 1930–5, 4 Vols.

Gray, Lewis C. *History of Agriculture in the Southern United States to 1860.* Washington, D.C.: Carnegie Institution of Washington, 1933, 2 Vols.

Harper, Lawrence A. *The English Navigation Acts: A Seventeenth-Century Experiment in Social Engineering.* New York: Columbia University Press, 1939.

Hughson, S. C. *The Carolina Pirates and Colonial Commerce (1670–1740).* Baltimore: Johns Hopkins University Studies in Historical and Political Science, 1894. Vol. XII.

Hutchins, John G. B. *The American Maritime Industries and Public Policy, 1789–1914.* Cambridge, Massachusetts: Harvard University Press, 1941.

Imlah, Albert H. *Economic Elements in the Pax Britannica.* Cambridge, Massachusetts: Harvard University Press, 1958.

Jameson, John F. *Privateering and Piracy in the Colonial Period: Illustrative Documents.* New York: The Macmillan Company, 1923.

Johnson, Emory R., *et al. History of Domestic and Foreign Commerce of the United States.* Washington, D.C.: Carnegie Institution of Washington, 1915.

Macpherson, David. *Annals of Commerce, Manufactures, Fisheries, and Navigation.* London, 1805.

Mitchell, B. R. and Phyllis Deane. *Abstract of British Historical Statistics.* London: Cambridge University Press, 1962.

Nettels, Curtis P. *The Money Supply of the American Colonies Before 1720.* Madison, Wisconsin: University of Wisconsin Studies in the Social Sciences and History, No. 20, 1934; reprinted by Augustus M. Kelley, 1964.

The Roots of American Civilization. Second edition; New York: Appleton-Century-Crofts, 1963.

Pares, Richard. *Yankees and Creoles.* Cambridge, Massachusetts: Harvard University Press, 1956.

Pitman, Frank W. *The Development of the West Indies, 1700–63.* New Haven, Connecticut: Yale University Press, 1917.

Posthumus, N. W. *Inquiry into the History of Prices in Holland.* Leiden: E. J. Brill, 1946.

Salter, W. E. G. *Productivity and Technical Change.* London: Cambridge University Press, 1960.

Schlote, Werner, *British Overseas Trade from 1700 to the 1930's,* trans. W. O. Henderson and W. H. Chaloner. Oxford: Basil Blackwell, 1952.

Schumpeter, Elizabeth B. *English Overseas Trade Statistics, 1697–1808.* Oxford: The Clarendon Press, 1960.

Sheffield, John. *Observations on the Commerce of the American States.* London: Debrett, 1784.

Smith, Abbot E. *Colonists in Bondage: White Servitude and Convict Labor in America, 1607–1776.* Chapel Hill, North Carolina: University of North Carolina Press, 1947.

Sosin, Jack M. *Whitehall and the Wilderness: The Middle West in British Colonial Policy, 1760–1775.* Lincoln, Nebraska: University of Nebraska Press, 1961.

Weeden, William B. *Economic and Social History of New England*. Boston: Houghton, Mifflin, & Company, 1891. Vol. II.

White, Philip L. *The Beekmans of New York in Politics and Commerce, 1647–1877*. New York: New-York Historical Society, 1956.

Wycoff, V. J. *Tobacco Regulations in Maryland*. Baltimore, Maryland: The Johns Hopkins Press, 1936.

ARTICLES AND ESSAYS

Andrews, Charles M. 'Colonial commerce,' *American Historical Review*, xx (October 1914), pp. 43–63.

Barbour, Violet. 'Dutch and English merchant shipping in the seventeenth century,' *Economic History Review*, II (1930), pp. 261–90.

Bell, Herbert C. 'West India trade before the Revolution,' *American Historical Review*, xxII, 2 (January 1917), pp. 272–87.

Callender, Guy S. 'The early transportation and banking enterprises of the states in relation to the growth of the corporation,' *Quarterly Journal of Economics*, xvII, 1 (November 1902), pp. 111–62.

Caves, Richard E. ' "Vent for surplus" models of trade and growth,' in Robert E. Baldwin, *et al.*, *Trade, Growth and the Balance of Payments*. Chicago: Rand McNally & Company, 1965, pp. 95–115.

Edelman, Edward. 'Thomas Hancock, Colonial Merchant,' *Journal of Economic and Business History*, I (1928–9), pp. 77–104.

Fei, John C. H. and Gustav Ranis. 'Economic development in historical perspective,' *American Economic Review*, lix, 2 (May 1969), pp. 386–400.

Gallman, Robert E. 'The pace and pattern of American economic growth,' *American Economic Growth: An Economist's History of the United States*, ed. William N. Parker. New York: Harper & Row, 1972.

Hemphill, John M., II. 'Freight rates in the Maryland tobacco trade, 1705–62,' *Maryland Historical Magazine*, lix, 1 and 2 (March and June 1959), pp. 36–58 and 154–87.

John, A. H. 'The London Company and the marine assurance market of the eighteenth century,' *Economica*, xxv, 18 (May 1958), pp. 126–41.

Jones, Alice Hanson. 'Wealth estimates for the American middle colonies, 1774,' *Economic Development and Cultural Change*, xvIII, 4 (July 1970), Supplement, pp. 1–172.

Klingaman, David. 'The significance of grain in the development of the tobacco colonies,' *Journal of Economic History*, xxIx, 2 (June 1969), pp. 268–78.

Land, Aubrey C. 'Economic behavior in a planting society: the eighteenth century Chesapeake,' *Journal of Southern History*, xxxIII, 4 (November 1967), pp. 469–85).

Lane, Frederic C. 'Tonnages, medieval and modern,' *Economic History Review*, Second Series, xvII, 2 (December 1964), pp. 213–33.

Lydon, James G. 'Fish and flour for gold: southern Europe and the colonial American balance of payments,' *Business History Review*, xxxIx, 2 (Summer 1965), pp. 171–83.

McClelland, Peter D. 'The cost to America of British imperial policy,' *American Economic Review*, LIX, 2 (May 1969), pp. 370–81.

Nettels, Curtis P. 'England's trade with New England and New York, 1685–1720,' *Publications of the Colonial Society of Massachusetts*, XXVIII. (February 1933).

North, Douglass C. 'Sources of productivity change in ocean shipping, 1600–1850,' *Journal of Political Economy*, LXXVI, 5 (September–October 1968), pp. 953–70.

'The role of transportation in the economic development of North America,' *Les Grandes Voies Maritimes Dans Le Monde, XVe–XIXe Siècles*. Paris: SEVPEN, 1965, pp. 209–46.

'The United States balance of payments, 1790–1860,' *Trends in the American Economy in the Nineteenth Century*, Studies in Income and Wealth, Vol. 24, N.B.E.R. Princeton, New Jersey: Princeton University Press, 1960.

and Alan Heston. 'The Estimation of shipping earnings in historical studies of the balance of payments,' *Canadian Journal of Economics and Political Science*, XXVI, 2 (May 1960), pp. 265–76.

Potter, J. 'The growth of population in America, 1700–1860,' *Population in History*, eds. D. V. Glass and D. E. C. Eversley. London: Edward Arnold, 1965.

Price, Jacob M. 'The rise of Glasgow in the Chesapeake tobacco trade, 1707–1775,' *The William and Mary Quarterly*, XI, 2 (April 1954), pp. 179–99.

Shepherd, James F. 'A balance of payments for the thirteen colonies, 1768–1772: a summary,' *Journal of Economic History*, XXV, 4 (December 1965), pp. 691–5.

'Commodity exports from the British North American colonies to overseas areas, 1768–1772: magnitudes and patterns of trade,' *Explorations in Economic History*, VIII, 1 (Fall 1970), pp. 5–76.

and Gary M. Walton. 'Estimates of "invisible" earnings in the balance of payments of the British North American colonies, 1768-1772,' *Journal of Economic History*, XXIX, 2 (June 1969), pp. 230–63.

Sheridan, Richard B. 'The British credit crisis of 1772 and the American colonies,' *Journal of Economic History*, XX, 2 (June 1960), pp. 161–86.

Soltow, J. H. 'Scottish traders in Virginia, 1750–1775,' *Economic History Review*, Second Series, XII, 1 (August 1959), pp. 83–98.

Sperling, J. 'The international payments mechanism in the seventeenth and eighteenth centuries,' *Economic History Review*, Second Series, XIV, 3 (April 1962), pp. 446–68.

Taylor, George Rogers. 'American economic growth before 1840: an exploratory essay,' *Journal of Economic History*, XXIV, 4 (December 1964), pp. 427–44.

Walton, Gary M. 'A quantitative study of American colonial shipping: a summary,' *Journal of Economic History*, XXVI, 4 (December 1966), pp. 595–8.

'Sources of productivity change in American colonial shipping, 1675–1775', *Economic History Review*, Second Series, XX, 1 (April 1967), pp. 67–78.

'Colonial tonnage measurement: a comment,' *Journal of Economic History*, xxvii, 3 (September 1967), pp. 392–7.

'Trade routes, ownership proportions, and American colonial shipping characteristics,' *Las Rutas Del Atlantico*. Trabajos Del Noveno Coloquio. Internacional de Historia Marítima, pp. 471–502.

'A measure of productivity change in American colonial shipping,' *Economic History Review*, Second Series, xxi, 2 (August 1968), pp. 268–82.

'New evidence on colonial commerce,' *Journal of Economic History*, xxviii, 3 (September 1968), pp. 363–89.

'Obstacles to technical diffusion in colonial shipping, 1675–1775,' *Explorations in Economic History*, viii, 2 (Winter 1970–1), pp. 123–40.

Watkins, Melville H. 'A staple theory of economic growth,' *Canadian Journal of Economics and Political Science*, xxix, 2 (May 1963), pp. 141–58.

DISSERTATIONS AND THESES

Berner, Richard C. 'The Means of Paying for Colonial New England's Imports.' Unpublished M.A. thesis, Department of History, University of California, Berkeley, 1950.

Ostrander, Gilman M. 'The Molasses Trade of the Thirteen Colonies.' Unpublished M.A. thesis, Department of History, University of California, Berkeley, 1948.

Shepherd, James F. 'A Balance of Payments for the Thirteen Colonies, 1768–1772.' Unpublished Ph.D. dissertation, University of Washington, 1966.

Walton, Gary M. 'A Quantitative Study of American Colonial Shipping.' Unpublished Ph.D dissertation, University of Washington, 1966.

GOVERNMENT PUBLICATIONS

Great Britain. *Parliamentary Papers (Reports from Committees from the House of Commons*, iii), March 25, 1773, 'Report from the Committee Appointed to Enquire into the State of the Linen Trade in Great Britain and Ireland.'

U.S. Bureau of the Census, *Historical Statistics of the United States, Colonial Times to 1957*. Washington, D.C.: U.S. Government Printing Office, 1960. Chapter Z, 'Colonial Statistics.'

DOCUMENTS AND MANUSCRIPT SOURCES

Baker Library, Boston, Mass.
  Bourne Papers, Vol. 9–10.
  Hancock Papers, Vol. 3–6, 8, 13, 15, 23, 25 and 28.
Boston Athenaeum, Boston, Mass.
  Ezekiel Price Policy Books.
British Museum, London, England.
  Additional Manuscript 15485.

Connecticut Historical Society, Hartford, Conn.
  Stone Papers.
Essex Institute, Salem, Mass.
  Cabot Family Papers (1742–1833), Vols 1–3.
  Curwin Papers, Vols 2 and 12.
  Goodhere Papers, Vol. 5.
  Hathorne Family Papers, Vols 1–2.
  Timothy Orne Papers, Vols 1–5.
Historical Society of Pennsylvania, Philadelphia, Penn.
  Meredith Papers ('ships').
John Carter Brown Library, Providence, R.I.
  Brown Papers.
Library of Congress, Washington, D.C.
  Jones Family Collection, Vols 1–13.
London Assurance Company, London, England.
  Rough Journals.
Maryland Historical Society, Baltimore, Maryland.
  Aquilla Hall Papers, 32 items.
  Hill Papers, shipping accounts, 1737–74.
Massachusetts Historical Society, Boston, Mass.
  Cushing-Orne Papers, Folder 1730–79 and Box 1730–1922.
  Dolbeare Papers, 1718/19–40.
  Norcross Papers, 1750–96.
  Wetmore Papers, 1706–54.
Mr John Fleming, Antiquities Dealer, New York, N.Y.
  Jacobus VanCortlandt Shipping Book, 1702–5.
Newport Historical Society, Newport, R.I.
  Walter Newbury Shipping Book, 1673–85.
New York Chamber of Commerce Library, New York, N.Y.
  William Walton Book of Assurance, 1773–89.
New-York Historical Society, New York, N.Y.
  DePeyster Papers, Box 11 and 13.
  J. Lathan Papers.
  Jacobus VanCortlandt Shipping Book, 1699–1702.
  John VanCortlandt Shipping Book, 1770–3.
  Samuel Gilford Papers.
New York Public Library, New York, N.Y.
  Hudson Collection, Vols 1–2.
  Mercantile Papers and Shipping, Misc. A–Z.
  William Alexander Papers, Box 11.
Public Record Office, London, England.
  American Inspector-General's Ledgers (Customs 16/1).
  Chancery Masters' Exhibits, C103–114 (adequate index available).
  Colonial Naval Office Lists:
    South Carolina, C.O. 5–508–11, (1716–19, 1721–35, 1736–64, 1746–65).
    East Florida, C.O. 5–573, (1765–9).
    West Florida, C.O. 5–709–10, (1752–64, 1764–7).
    Maryland, C.O. 5–749–50, (1689–1702, 1754–1765).

Boston, C.O. 5–848–51, (1686–1719, 1752–6, 1752–65, 1756–62).

New Hampshire, C.O. 5–967–69, (1723–60, 1734–51, 1761–9).

New York, C.O. 5–1222–28, (1713–22, 1722–5, 1725–30, 1731–8, 1735–52, 1739–54, 1755–65).

Virginia, C.O. 5–1441–50, (1699–1706, 1715–27, 1726–35, 1735–53, 1735–56, 1736–53, 1754–9, 1759–62, 1762–6, 1766–70).

Antigua, C.O. 10–1, (1704–20).

Bahamas, C.O. 27–12 and 13, (1721–51, 1753–7).

Barbados, C.O. 33–13–17, (1678–1704, 1679–1709, 1708–26, 1728–53, 1730–64),

Bermuda, C.O. 41–6 and 7, (1715–37, 1738–51).

Grenada, C.O. 106–1, (1764–7).

Jamaica, C.O. 142–13–20, (1680–1705, 1709–22, 1727–53, 1752–62, 1766–9, 1762–5, 1764–84, 1781–8).

Leeward Islands, C.O. 157–1, (1683–1787).

Newfoundland, C.O. 199–17, (1772–3).

Nova Scotia, C.O. 221–28–31, (1730–53, 1753–7, 1758–61, 1762–5).

St Vincent, C.O. 265–1, (1763–92).

English Inspector-General's Ledgers (Customs 3).

High Court of Admiralty, Instance Papers, H.C.A.-15, Box 223–26, 228–30, and 233, Bundles 5–58.

Scottish Inspector-General's Ledgers (Customs 14).

Rhode Island Historical Society, Providence, R.I.

Rhode Island Historical Society Manuscripts, Vols 1, 11 and 18.

INDEX